VERONICA:

EYE WITNESS

TO THE MINISTRY OF JESUS

by

JACELYN ECKMAN

Published June 2010

Visit the author at
www.JacelynEckman.com

Copyright 2010 Jacelyn Eckman

All rights reserved.

No part of this book may be reproduced, stored in a retrieval system, or transmitted by any means, electronic, mechanical, photocopying, recording, or otherwise, except for brief passages in connection with a review, without written permission from the author.

ISBN: 9781453608371

Printed in the USA

This is the second book in the series on the life of Jesus, as seen through the eyes of his cousin, Veronica. It begins with his baptism in the River Jordan, and continues through the three years of his public ministry, his arrest, crucifixion and resurrection, ending at Pentecost. While paralleling the four Gospels of the New Testament, it offers a deeply intimate view into the life of this man who so profoundly impacted the world, from his time to ours. It also reveals the indispensable role of the women in his life, especially during the crucifixion itself.

CONTENTS

Page

Gratitude		*viii*
Prologue		*x*
Preface		*xviii*

PART ONE

Chapter 1	Alone With the Shadow	1
Chapter 2	A Tranquil Retreat to Ein Karem	9
Chapter 3	The Return of the Son	15
Chapter 4	A Quiet Welcome to Capernaum	23
Chapter 5	The Watchers	29
Chapter 6	A Shared Vision	41
Chapter 7	Passing the Torch	57
Chapter 8	The Women Gather Power	67
Chapter 9	A Light in the Darkness	73
Chapter 10	Awakening to a Higher Love	81

PART TWO

Chapter 11	Transcendence	93
Chapter 12	Behold My Beloved Son	103
Chapter 13	The Shining Ones	117

Page

Chapter 14	A Deeper Wound	129
Chapter 15	The Perils of Despair	141
Chapter 16	Miracles	149
Chapter 17	A Meeting With the Brothers	159
Chapter 18	Stars to Light the Way	169
Chapter 19	No One Left Unscathed	181
Chapter 20	Standing Together	187

PART THREE

Chapter 21	The Final Journey	197
Chapter 22	Holding Steadfast	205
Chapter 23	The Upper Room	215
Chapter 24	In the Garden	225
Chapter 25	The Trial	235
Chapter 26	King of the Jews	243
Chapter 27	The Silence and the Glory	251
Chapter 28	Three Days	261

Page

PART FOUR

Chapter 29	What is Death?	273
Chapter 30	Life Goes On	281
Chapter 31	Telling Stories	291
Chapter 32	A Brother from Persia	297
Chapter 33	Seeking Direction	305
Chapter 34	Resolution	313
Chapter 35	The Holy Spirit	319
	Afterwords	329

GRATITUDE

The *Veronica* books are such an integral part of my life that those who in any sense have helped lighten my load or shone a light upon my path have also been a part of bringing the books into manifestation. I will forever hold you in my heart.

I offer my gratitude to the following for moral and technical support -- often one and the same: Wayne Wilson, Steve Doolittle, Wally Benson, Sharon Richards, Vicki Eckman, Aleah Fitzgerald, Jan Connell, and the untold others of my soul family, known and yet unknown.

To the great spiritual Brotherhood -- comprised of women and men throughout time -- without you I do not know how I would have found the yellow brick road, which brings us all Home.

* * *

This book is dedicated to all who seek to live their lives by the Law of One. Together we carry on the tradition of the Great Ones, helping others to remember we all came from and are returning to the same Source, called by many Names.

PROLOGUE

This is a true story, drawn from my memories as Veronica, a cousin of Jesus 2000 years ago. I know such a thing may seem hard or even impossible for some of you to believe ... but in many ways my memories of that lifetime are as vivid and real as those of my own childhood in this one. I would ask that you take a step back from your beliefs of what can or cannot be, and approach this story with an open mind and heart.

Ultimately, it isn't important whether you believe this to be a true story or a work of fiction. It embodies my profound love and respect for the one we know as Jesus, and all those who pursue the path he offered, whether Christian, Jewish, with or without spiritual or religious affiliation. During his life he studied with the masters of his time, from India and Tibet, to Persia and Egypt, incorporating the wisdom of all ages and lands into a singular teaching of love, forgiveness, and recognition of our oneness. The story speaks for itself, challenging each of us to ascend the heights of our personal potential, as we seek to live the principles he offered us.

*

I have been a student of comparative religions and various esoteric traditions for 35 years. I don't recall when I first heard of reincarnation, probably because it seemed so right to me that I naturally integrated it into my mindset. It explained why I often knew certain things with no basis of study or personal experience. A life-long global traveler, I frequently anticipated what I would find around the next corner in a place I'd never been before, or had fragments or full memories of having lived somewhere I'd not yet visited.

My first unequivocal past-life memory was of an awful death in my most recent incarnation. I wasn't eager to learn more about other lives and deaths after that. But eventually memory of that lifetime came back in great detail, as have others since then. I have never sought out these memories; they simply come to me. I believe that is the way our souls work. When we are ready to know, when we are ready to learn the lessons offered to us through such memories, our souls will bring them to us (directly or through the assistance of regressionists, or others). Such things are not for entertainment or vain thoughts of I was *so and so* (whether we might be proud or ashamed of the association). Our memories have the potential to help us understand current challenges, providing us the opportunity to heal the past so we might live more fully in the present.

*

Memory of the Veronica lifetime came to me in a roundabout way. Early in 2003 I began to feel a strong pull to visit the small Bosnian town of Medjugorje. In researching the place I learned that in 1981 "the Blessed Virgin Mary" began appearing to six young Croat children who lived there. Since then it has become a pilgrimage site for millions of Catholics who are devoted to Mary. Though I love travel I initially resisted the impulse to go there because, frankly, there were *many* more places I'd rather have gone, especially as I had no sense of connection then to Mary or anything church-related.

But as with anything that is integral to my soul purpose, it was pointless to resist. Next thing I knew I had a ticket to Budapest, Hungary – a place I *did* want to go. From there I would take a train to Rome, and ultimately cross the Adriatic by ferry to Bosnia.

Along the way I spent several days exploring the ancient sites of Rome, and set a day aside for Vatican City. While walking around the narrow gallery inside the cupola of the dome of St. Peter's Basilica I fell into a meditative reverie. Suddenly, without any warning, I felt something like a bolt of lightning hit the top of my head. It literally felt as if my body had been split in two, leaving me inflamed and trembling. I was unable to comprehend what had happened, and when I started coming back to myself – still barely able to keep to my feet – I realized I was crying. And when my surroundings started coming into focus the first thing my eyes lit upon was a small bronze plaque that had the name *St. Veronica* engraved on it.

I had no idea who Veronica was, but something inside me said I was she – that is, I understood that my soul had incarnated as this person called St. Veronica. I saw myself, *felt* myself as this person who I would learn was a contemporary of Jesus 2000 years ago. I knew it without any doubt, though for some time I rebelled at the idea that I had been *saint anybody*. I was raised a Lutheran and we just didn't go in for saints. In fact I had left the church in my teens, and felt no affinity with anything resembling the tradition I'd been born into. I loved the cathedrals in Europe and sometimes attended masses simply to sit in all that grandeur and beauty. But that was pretty much it.

My awakening sense of spirituality began at age 25, focusing first on the Hindu tradition, eventually becoming a teacher of yoga. At 30 I made my first trip to India and spent nearly a year traveling and studying both Hinduism and Buddhism (including several months with the Dalai Lama's teachers in Dharamsala, northern India). My spiritual studies and practice broadened over the years to include Native American/ shamanic practices and finally the Ancient Wisdom teachings reinterpreted in the Theosophical tradition. I honored Jesus as one of many master teachers who have lived and taught in our world, but would not have called myself a Christian.

But all the while there were other forces at work. In 1978 I stayed in a Monastery on the Island of Cyprus, spending many delightful hours talking with the Abbot about God. When I left he gave me a letter of introduction to the Patriarch of the Greek Orthodox Church in Jerusalem. (The Patriarch is the equivalent of a Roman Catholic Archbishop.) Maybe it was because of this that I began to feel a powerful draw to travel to Jerusalem for Easter week, instead of going on to Egypt, for which I was already ticketed. But all flights and commercial ships from the island to Israel were booked until well after Easter. So I went to the port in hopes of finding a cargo ship that could get me there.

A British merchant marine captain cabled his home office seeking permission to take me on board, but the request was denied for insurance purposes. That had been my last hope. As I left the ship, two crewmen approached suggesting I return that night just before they sailed and they would hide me in the ship owner's cabin (who was not on aboard at the time). They would wait until the ship was far enough out to sea that it would be uneconomical to return to port once their stowaway was "discovered."

The whole thing seemed quite insane, even for a free-wheeling traveler like me. There were only a few hours remaining to make a decision, and I went off by myself to pray and meditate. I had two choices: to give up my plans to be in Israel for Easter, or to stow away. And so I took my chances. It was nearing midnight when I threw my pack on board and scrambled up the gangplank. I'm sure you can imagine the thoughts that went through my mind over the next couple hours, as I felt the thrust of the engines and the feel of the sea under us.

The crew woke the captain a couple hours later, as planned. His curses could be heard down the hall, but when I was brought to him he burst out laughing. "Oh, it's *you*. I guess you really *did* want to get to Israel!" Despite the trouble I caused him (with many cables back and forth to the UK) he treated me wonderfully and ordered his crew to do the same. To solve the immigration issue in Israel he signed me on as a member of the ship's crew, librarian to a grand collection of fourteen books – mostly spy novels.

Jerusalem was packed with pilgrims, but I miraculously secured a bed in a convent right on the *Via Dolorosa*, the path Jesus took as he carried his cross to Golgotha. It was a powerful experience being in the middle of tens of thousands of people singing songs of praise as they reenacted the Passion. The following day I took my letter of introduction to the Greek Orthodox Patriarch who invited me to join him Easter Morning at the Church of the Holy Sepulcher for their celebration of the resurrection. It's almost impossible to get anywhere near the church with the massive crowds, yet there I was standing next to the Patriarch just feet away from where many believe Jesus had been entombed after the crucifixion. Any misgivings I had about the religiosity of the event were transcended in the joy of the moment.

I spent three months in Israel, visiting many of the ancient sites,

Christian and Jewish. I also met and traveled with a group of Old Testament Biblical scholars (all Catholic monks and priests) into the Sinai Peninsula. Among other things, we climbed up the mountain known as Jebel Musa (Mt. Sinai) in the middle of the night to be at the top for sunrise. Many believe this was the spot where Moses received the Ten Commandments. I later stayed at their Monastery in Ein Karem -- the town just outside Jerusalem where John the Baptist had lived -- joining them each morning as they gathered to sing the Psalms.

The Greek Patriarch in turn gave me a letter of introduction to the newly installed Pope, John Paul II. Eventually I made it back to Rome. This letter secured for me an audience with him (along with a dozen other people whom I did not know). When he entered the room he walked right up to me, and taking both my hands in his spoke to me in English for some time about my spiritual path. There was never a flicker of judgment in his eyes or a shift in his behavior as it became apparent I was not Catholic or in the least mainstream in my beliefs.

There have been many other events that put me in the middle of the Christian (and usually Catholic) world, in the United States and in other countries. Yet the event in St. Peter's in 2003 was the starting point for my memories of having been incarnated as Veronica: cousin, childhood friend and finally, a disciple of Jesus.

Some time after the shock had worn off from the Vatican experience, and the actual memories of that lifetime began slowly to intrude upon my consciousness, Jesus came to me one day during a meditation. He asked me to write a book, saying that the writing would draw out many memories which had been hidden away deep in my subconscious. (It is said, and I believe, that we have stored within us memories of everything we have ever known, awareness of every incarnation we have lived, and that nothing is ever lost.) I had been writing books since leaving the Foreign Service in 1996, so the idea of writing was not foreign to me. But the idea of writing about *Jesus* was something I would have to get used to, since I had not yet reconciled my lack of affinity with the historical Jesus and my new and growing *experience* of him.

In the meantime I tried to learn what I could about Veronica. Research turned up little, and nothing substantive. There is the tradition of Veronica wiping the face of Jesus with her veil as he carried the cross to his own crucifixion. This event is enshrined in the Catholic *Sixth Station of the Cross*. (Remember, this event played out on the road where I stayed during Easter week in Israel.) It is said his image was permanently fixed on the cloth, which became one of the Church's most sacred relics.

(The Church hierarchy is by no means in accord as to whether the cloth within St. Peter's is the authentic one, or whether it or even Veronica ever really existed.)

I realized that if I decided to write the book, it would have to be based exclusively on my personal memories, since there was no historical record. But would anyone believe me? I had no proof of anything, and did not enjoy the thought of being the target of ridicule. Jesus was always there when I came to express my concerns, but he never pushed or pressured me, waiting till I came to my own decision. It was maybe two years later when I took up the project.

After about a hundred pages he said, "Well, that's all very good. But I want you to write *your* story, the story of Veronica and the other women in my life. Without you [the women] there would be no story to tell. Without you, I could never have done what I did. Your story has been lost, and the world has suffered for it. And *my* story is incomplete without that part. Go back, and start again."

I groaned ... a lot. My first thought was no one would want to read my (Veronica's) story. *It was all about him*. But the more I thought about it, I realized he was right. It certainly wasn't about me personally, about Jacelyn, or even about Veronica. It was, in large part, about the women who comprised the other half of the story.

And so there are two narratives in these books that have been woven together in a single tapestry. It is the story of the women *and* the story of Jesus, the man, the teacher, the great one who came to show us the way – all told through the eyes of Jesus' cousin, Veronica. It is the story of Miriam* (known to us as Mary Magdalene), of

Veronica's mother Salome and her sister Mary, mother of Jesus, and the story of our friends and families, of Jewish religion and culture, the Roman occupation and its terrible consequences in our lives at that time.

The first book (*Veronica: The Lost Years of Jesus*) details the extensive journeys undertaken by Jesus, and speaks of a great and ancient Brotherhood that existed throughout the known world (of which the Essenes were a part). His teachings were a reflection of all those influences It also illuminates the lives of the women, their esoteric and spiritual training and growing role alongside Jesus in preparation of the fulfillment of ancient prophecies. This, the second book in the series, parallels the Gospels of the New Testament, bringing through a distinctly unique viewpoint of those three years of Jesus' life, and the lives of his friends, family … and enemies. His life and teachings have left their mark on the world we live in today, influencing our world view, from religion to politics to economics, to the way we care for the planet – even if we do not think of ourselves as Jewish, Christian or Muslim.

This book is not channeled. Neither Jesus nor anyone else told me what to say. It is the story of a life remembered: I *feel* Veronica's feelings, see through her eyes and think her thoughts as clearly as my own. I *relive* what I am writing about, and Jesus is with me, coaxing me, guiding me, and on rare occasions pointing out inaccuracies.

Like many of you, my life has taken many strange and unexpected turns: from an ordinary childhood in Minnesota to the nomadic life of a seeker, into the U.S. Diplomatic Corps for a dozen years, and from there – finally – to following the soul impulse to write. Even then, when I left the government to begin this latest task, I would never have dreamed that one day I would be writing a trilogy** that revolves around the life of Jesus the Nazarene.

Jacelyn Rae Eckman

January 2010, Pacific Palisades, California

* Miriam of Magdala, Veronica's closest friend, is generally known today as Mary Magdalene. Though Mary had been her given name, she said she preferred Miriam because 'there are just too many Marys around.' And so I have honored her preference in these books.

** The third book in the series begins when the followers of Jesus begin to leave their homeland following the Pentecost. Roman persecution of the Jews is increasing and they must leave if they are to survive. The temple is destroyed and Jerusalem falls in 70 CE. By that time the *diaspora* is in full force. This story follows a number of disciples (Veronica, Paul, Thomas among them), as they carry Jesus' teachings into the world.

PREFACE

The silent crowd parted to let him pass. John watched as Jesus came to the water's edge, where he paused to look at his cousin. John lifted his arm and pointed toward him, crying out, "Behold the lamb of God who sees us blameless, restoring us to ourselves."

His booming voice echoed up the steep hillside where the growing multitudes had gathered to hear his daily homily. Some waited their turn to be baptized; others stood apart, not yet persuaded by his exhortations, or perhaps fearful of being labeled his supporter.

Jesus hesitated only a moment before entering the chill water. Grabbing John's arm to steady himself in the strong current, he dropped down on one knee. "Baptize me," he said.

I had been watching John for days, his face alight with an inner fire as scores of people came to be baptized. But suddenly his features contorted at the man kneeling before him. "No, stand!" John said through clenched teeth, as he tried to pull Jesus to his feet. "It is I who must kneel before you!"

Only those of us who stood close by could hear the anguish in his voice.

"It is my right to ask this of you," Jesus answered softly. "If you do not fulfill your role, I cannot discharge mine.

"Baptize me," he repeated, with authority.

John turned his eyes to heaven, lips moving in silent prayer. At last he nodded and Jesus dropped back down onto his knee, the waters rising up around his chest.

John's eyes glistened as he spoke the words of blessing. "In the name of the Father, I baptize you, His true Son, in the One Spirit."

And thus began the *great awakening*.

*

"Let me go!" I screamed, trying to pull away.

But his nails only dug deeper into my arm. "No, Veronica, he said gently. "It is not yet our time."

A flush of anger blazed through me and James dropped my arm, as if singed by fire. But instead of running I slumped to the ground, suddenly drained of the furies. "I am ... sorry, so sorry. I .... "

"Shhhh," he said, drawing me to him.

Sheets of lightning exploded from the two men in the water, and rolled up the hillsides bathing everyone in the eerie light. A stunned silence had followed the baptism, but my outburst broke the spell. People began to shout, running down the hill and spilling into the river that they too might be cleansed in the waters of spirit.

Several of John's followers, burly men as strong as he, rushed in to shield the two men. But their efforts proved unnecessary; the crowds were repelled as if colliding with an unseen wall. Some ran away in fear, making the sign of protection. But the others fell back to form new lines, and the rest of the people settled in to see what would happen next.

I do not recall much else from that day. That evening we could hear muffled shouts and laughter some distance away from the hilltop where we gathered. I do not know where the Baptist went. We never did. He simply disappeared into the night. Jesus sat among us, saying little; his silence at turns comforted and unnerved me. And then he too went off into the darkness.

Later, as my husband and I lay together I started to apologize again for my outburst, but James would not hear of it. "I also felt an overwhelming urge to run into the waters," he said. "I would not have been able to restrain myself, except that an unseen hand rooted me where I stood. It passed to me the authority and strength to hold you back.

"In the days to come, we must not think of ourselves, or even of him. Despite a lifetime of preparation, I still understand little of what is to come. You saw the light go out from John and into him as he knelt at John's feet. Not even the rushing waters could dislodge him from his destiny."

"What do you mean ... not think of him? He will need our protection," I insisted. "He seems hardly to eat these days, unless someone reminds him. And his enemies are gathering."

"Veronica, think. Would God abandon him now? Abandon the Brotherhood, and all they – we – have worked for, for ages? Is it possible *he* does not know exactly what he is doing?"

"No, of course not," I whispered. But still, I was troubled. I had no doubt that things were unfolding rightly. Yet I shivered with foreboding. "I wish I knew what will happen" – and added under my breath – "though perhaps it is better I do not."

James pulled me into his warmth, and at last I slept. A fog settled down upon us during the night and with it an increasing sense of unreality.

The next morning Jesus was noticeably absent. He often slipped away from us -- sometimes with Miriam, more often on his own. But this day was different. Somehow I knew the baptism had changed everything. As we turned to the sunrise for our morning rituals, even the air shimmered with expectation. Yet I felt wary, as if a wild animal stalked us. James and I did not speak of it, though I could tell by the tension in his face he felt it too.

Our small group was unusually quiet as we broke our fast. Not knowing what else to do, we returned to the river and there found John again urging the crowds to surrender the burden of their sins by confessing their wrongs and entering into the waters of life. He was thronged by people, the crowds even greater and more unruly than before.

But Jesus was nowhere to be seen.

A shadow fell across us and I turned to find Thomas standing there. "Come, let us leave these crowds and return to the lake," he said. "At least we will find shade there."

From that point on we often felt we were being moved by a powerful yet beneficent hand.

PART ONE

Chapter One

ALONE WITH THE SHADOW

'*Who* stands here on this rock?'

The man spoke aloud, though he was alone. Stretching out his arms in front of him, he gently touched each hand with the other as if seeing them for the first time.

'Whose hands are these? And of what good are they if I fail in my mission?' he asked of no one, despair creeping into his voice. Slumping to the ground he cupped his hands over dry eyes.

Jesus could not have said how long he had been there alone in the desert, or when he last took drink or ate. Nor could he that day explain why he had gone there in the first place. Fears, long buried in the depths of his being, marched across his mind like a phantom army. Most days he could not distinguish reality from hallucination, and couldn't be bothered to know the difference.

A serpent coiled around his arm and poked at his ribs. "Fool!" it hissed into the charged air, yellow eyes mocking him. "You are wasting away. Some king you'll make. Who would take *you* seriously?"

Jesus turned away from the thing, and it disappeared.

Eyes turned inward, he walked down a gentle rocky incline and slipped into a small niche out of the relentless wind. There were no trees, no water. Food he had long ceased to desire, but the craving for water clawed at his throat. He muttered something under his breath, triggering spasms of a dry cough.

The Overseer of his soul prodded him to move on. Wrapping his over-cloak about his head he shuffled along under the scorching sun. A thought drifted across his awareness, memories of a wild dog long ago. He smiled and the taste of blood from his cracked lips brought the sudden realization that he must find water, or die.

Shocked, he looked around and for the first time in days took note of his surroundings. Yes, of course, he was in the desert. He had gone there seeking clarity of purpose and direction after the baptism. During his more lucid moments he recalled the place within himself where he and God dwell as one.

But there had been little comfort for the man. The flesh and blood man had become acquainted with fear and weakness. Not the weakness of the body – though that laid claim to him as well -- but weakness of the self who wanted nothing more than to live an ordinary life, with the same concerns that confront all men.

"Why can't you leave me alone?" he cried out to the wind … to God. "Let me go!" he shouted, shaking his fist in the air. In that moment, death would have been welcomed as a friend.

But he knew he could not escape his self-chosen fate. Not even if he were to ignore the call of the body for water, and perish that very day. No, peace would not come from denial.

He began to cough again, and sat down to compose himself, endeavoring to focus upon the quest for water. Too much depended upon him. If he shirked his destiny, the whole cycle would have to begin again; an entire age would be wasted. He knew he was only an instrument, and in the beginning he had asked in all humility to serve as such.

Or had it been pride?

Who did he think he was? Surely it had been arrogance that goaded him into thinking he might be strong enough to sacrifice himself for a greater good? He was just a man. No more. *A man.*

And now that man was desperate for water.

'If I cannot bear even the lack of water, how then can I endure the sacrifices that may come?' he chided himself.

"You have lain in the tomb once, and arisen of your own power," came a voice. "Death has no claim on you."

Yes, I remember ... he thought. Egypt. The great pyramid. The lid of the sarcophagus weighed down upon the mortal man, that he might come to know himself as immortal.

I am That.

He stood, squared his shoulders and silenced the inner dialogue, so he might concentrate on the quest for water. While the body is inferior to spirit, spirit finds its way into our world through that very body, giving it meaning and sacred purpose. If he quit it during that moment of crisis, his work would go unfinished.

'That cannot happen,' he shouted into the howling wind, and it subsided. A gentle, cooling breeze took its place, and he saw directly ahead of him a small thicket of green within an ocean of drifting sand.

For some moments he stood still, transfixed at the sight. There was a hint of dampness in the breeze and he gratefully drew it into his lungs. The color alone of the growing things soothed his heart, reminding him he *was* capable of walking into the arms of death again, should he be called.

The wild dog from his youth returned to mind. That was the first time he had gone into the desert alone. It marked the beginning of his journey, and this, now, the end of the cycle. How far he had come!

A small pool lay hidden in the thicket. He lay down on his stomach and dipped his fingers into the pool, letting fall a few drops upon his tongue, savoring the sensation of wetness. Once again he dipped into the pool and traced the cool water across his eyelids, in place of the tears that had abandoned him. And then he sipped, gratefully.

Having slaked his thirst, he sat next to the heavily silted pool, wandering through memories of his many travels. Especially he thought of the people he had known and loved, Hebeny, Krishna and Pursa, Jingu and Norbu, Sita............

Sita. 'What if ....?' he asked himself. Surely he had loved her. Knowing her had seared, and then cauterized his soul, as first loves often do. It had been long since she'd come to mind, and he hoped with all his heart that she was happy. 'She probably has many children by now,' he laughed to himself.

And in that single thought the weight upon his heart fell away and he recalled his strength of purpose. He slept through the night for the first time since he had come to the desert. He awoke to find a set of tiny prints that passed less than an arm's length from where he lay, leading to and from the spring. His heart opened to the creatures living in that desolate landscape, and to the many men who live similarly desperate lives everywhere.

The day dawned bright in the love of the One who shines upon us all. Since his encounter with John in the river there had been days when his path seemed clear, and his strength adequate to the task ... but there were others when he sank into the shadows of doubt. He knew he had to resolve those extremes before returning to the world of men.

On their journey to Juggernaut when they were young men, Krishna told him the story of Prince Siddhartha who extolled the virtues of the middle path. And the old Tibetan priest in the high mountains taught that the way to happiness lay between pain and pleasure. Jesus spent the day pondering these things, and there under the darkening sky he rediscovered the peace he had known in the carefree days of his youth.

One full moon night – when sleep would not come – he climbed up the rocky cliffs and like a mountain goat sat out on the edge of a precipice. This is like my life, he thought. I have come far and now find myself alone out on a high place. Will I fail? he asked himself for the hundredth time -- and shuddered at the thought.

So much depended upon him. *Too much.*

In his travels he studied with the wisest of teachers, learning to speak with the departed spirits of saints, to walk with angels, bring forth life in consort with the Mother, and to commune with the Father of all. But out there in the vast desert, he walked alone.

Sooner or later each of us must enter the dark night of the soul. An initiate into the mysteries must find the source of strength and wisdom within him, relying upon that alone. Jesus knew that, but it was hard all the same.

That night he thought about his mother, Mary, wondering about the hardships she had faced. She must have been pushed to the limits of what a mother could bear, having to set aside her maternal instincts and surrender her son to play his part in a plan that had been set in motion long ages before either of them was born.

Though he did not know it, his mother – the holy mother – sat in spirit watching over him. She prayed for her son, but also that she might be equal to her own commitments.

The following day he came upon a tiny spring drizzling down a rock face. It was the dark color against the lighter rock that had drawn his attention to it. The water had a strong mineral taste. Drop by drop it fell into the sand below, disappearing into the earth. He cupped his hands, hoping to collect some to sip, but was forced to gather it on his tongue.

There was not enough water to wash his face or hands; it did little more than trace muddy stripes across dusty skin. But he was grateful all the same. Leaning against the damp rock he said aloud, "Father … Mother, give me strength to do my part in the trials to come."

And again he asked: "Help me to find the strength within myself, to do what needs be done."

A spirit clothed in form approached and sat down across from him. He smiled, and Jesus felt his heart open. He had been so alone. After a time of silence, they began to speak as friends do, about little things, ordinary human things. They spoke of the rigors of the desert, and the way hunger disappears after a time. The man said, "Beware if your thirst slacks off. It is a sign your judgment has been clouded. If it is available to you, drink, drink deeply."

After a silence the stranger continued, "You don't have to go forward, you know."

A chill ran up Jesus' spine.

"Nothing is asked of you, except that which you willingly give."

Though much had been hinted at over the years, there were few details about what lay ahead. Judy had been his first teacher, both in Nazareth and in Carmel, until one day she said she had nothing more to teach him. It was time to leave his home and family, to begin his journey of self-discovery. Jesus was barely thirteen at the time, but managed to make his own way across the desert to Alexandria. There Zar – who headed the school – told him, 'no one knows for certain what will happen. The ancient prophecies are interpreted differently by different people, and besides, it is for you to decide what you will do."

All that seemed so very long ago!

The world changes, and even those things prophesied by the Patriarchs must change accordingly. All he knew, even then, was that some believed him to be the Messiah, come to free the Jews from their oppressors. There was little love for Romans in the land. His people suffered under them and their puppets among the Sadducees. Some championed war; others expected a miraculous liberation – perhaps, some hoped, God would simply strike their enemies dead.

How senseless, he thought. The time of killing in God's name was surely over. His was a God of love. Jesus promised himself he would stand only under a banner of forgiveness and righteousness.

By the time he returned from the desert he knew that such a message would not be well received by many, and he himself would then become the target. A few of his own students had already turned their backs on him to join the Zealots, and worse.

"Father, guide me in wisdom. Mother, guide me in love," he prayed fervently. "Oh Spirit of love and wisdom, help me find the courage to fulfill my purpose, an example to Jew and Gentile alike."

He could not love one and not the other, champion one side over the other.

*

One morning not long after that he rose with the sun and began the long walk to home and family, radiating light as one who has conquered the fear of life and death.

Chapter Two

SANCTUARY ON THE ROAD TO EIN KAREM

"Ah, thank you. But what is the purpose of this celebration? It is not even the Sabbath, and yet you have mixed lamb with the lentils, and brought out the best wine. And the honey cakes ….." Joseph trailed off, licking his fingers.

Mary just smiled. She knew in her heart her son was on his way back to them, and rejoiced. It was indeed a celebration, and a rare peaceful interlude with old friends.

Nicodemus pushed his chair back and sighed. "It is good to be away from Jerusalem. I do not care for the infighting that has been going on in the Sanhedrin. They seem to have forgotten we are there to uphold the law and protect the rights of the people, thinking only how best to use their position to increase their own power and wealth. It sickens me."

"Neglecting Jewish law, they strike a devil's pact with Pontius Pilate and his Roman overlords. Caiaphas is the worst," Joseph said, under his breath.

Both men were respected members of the Sanhedrin, and rarely spoke of the assembly, let alone with such scorn. Their words shocked us.

Matthias glanced over his shoulder. "I think it best we continue inside."

Nicodemus and Joseph had spoken quietly, but he was right. Most of Joseph's servants had been with him their entire lives and could be trusted. But Judea was becoming increasingly unstable and it was prudent to be cautious. The men went into the house.

A hand rested on mine as I stacked bowls for washing. It was Sarah, sister to Barnabas. "I am afraid," she whispered, her face flushed. "This morning as I stood waiting for the vendor to wrap my purchase, a fight broke out behind me. The dye-maker grabbed my arm and pulled me safely behind his stall.

"I could not see the fight, but heard their argument. One man accused another of treachery, saying he had handed his son over to Roman soldiers. The other shouted that the son deserved to be shackled: his plans to burn the Procurator's home would bring the wrath of Rome down upon them all. 'They do not know one from the other of us, and would destroy all our homes, kill us all in retribution,' he screamed. A large crowd was gathering, and I grabbed my purchase and ran down a back alley. I do not know what happened after that.

"Salome, you told a similar story yesterday," Sarah said, looking over my shoulder at mother. "Maybe we should return to Galilee."

Mary and Rachel joined us in the cool shade behind the kitchen. Mother picked up a bowl to wash. "No," she answered, "we must stay for now. You do not see it, but we are protected here as nowhere else. Joseph has many friends, even to Rome."

"But what of Antipas?" Sarah persisted. "He calls himself a Jew, but I fear him more than the Roman soldiers."

Mary covered the leftover stew and set it in a cool niche. "At the moment Herod is distracted by the Nabatean king who would see him destroyed. His brother Archelaus is even weaker."

"Herod was a fool," muttered Rachel, "humiliating the king's daughter by publicly divorcing her and then marrying Herodias the very same day!"

The women fell silent, knowing the scandal bought us scant time. Herod had already lost an army and was now trying desperately to mollify the king. It was inevitable he'd soon turn his attention back to problems closer to home. He had no choice. We heard rumors a delegation had arrived from Tiberius' court with a message from the Emperor himself to quell the disturbances, before they turned into an uprising.

Herod had a vile temper and whenever he felt pressure from Rome, he took it out on whoever was in front of him. And so everyone tried to remain out of the way as much as possible.

When we entered the house, the men fell silent and we knew they had been talking about the same things. Zacharias cleared his throat. He was older even than Joseph or Nicodemus and had often served as a confidant to the other Herod, Antipas' father.

"Events have moved beyond our control," he began in his gravely voice. "And it is good they have, else fear of the unknown might tempt us to try to put a stop to them."

He labored for breath, and we waited for him to continue. The dry winds sometimes took his voice away altogether. Rebecca, Joseph's serving girl, handed him a cup of water, and returned a few moments later with a tray laden with cups for the rest of us. Joseph himself stood near the doorway, declining the chair offered him.

"It is for this we have waited. It is what we have lived for, prayed for and will now die for," he said.

"Well," said Zebedee, "I would prefer to think about living rather than dying just now."

I think he meant to make a joke, but no one laughed.

Zebedee went on. "We stand at the gate of a city never before seen. The one who was sent to lead us through the gates has been called aside for a purpose of his own, and we await his return."

He spoke of my cousin, Jesus.

Zebedee looked at each of us in turn, and I felt the thrill of fear mixed with anticipation as his eyes met mine.

"Zacharias is right," he said, eyes now staring off into the gathering shadows. "The angels are gathering round. The darker seems the way, the brighter shines their light upon our path."

"When will he return?" someone asked. Faces were retreating into the darkness.

"Soon. Very soon." It was Mary's voice.

"And then? What will we do then?" asked my sister Elizabeth, youngest among us. She was Zacharias' favorite and sat close to him. Mother had tried to protect her from the gathering storm, but she would not be dissuaded from joining us. The younger children were in Nazareth with relatives.

Thaddeus, also called Judas, sat to her other side. When no one else answered her, he spoke up: "We will stand with him, no matter what comes. He will guide us."

He spoke with such certainty, for a moment my concerns subsided. Of course ... he will guide us, I thought.

A soft cocoon wrapped itself around our little gathering, and I imagined myself safe, like a babe in swaddling clothes.

Loud voices in the courtyard interrupted my thoughts. Joseph and someone else slipped out the door while we waited. My heart beat against my chest, and only when I felt James' hand on my shoulder did my breath come back to me.

"Ruth, light the lamps," said Joseph when he returned.

Shadows sprang up across the faces in the room as they were lit. James, son of Zebedee and father to Judas, entered with Joseph. Zebedee was right behind them. Joseph nodded to James to speak.

"There has been fighting in the city," he began, meaning Jerusalem. "Two of the gates were closed, and the others are under heavy guard. I barely made it through to come here."

No one asked if he had been followed, though worried looks spoke the question. James was hot-headed and seemed often to draw trouble to himself, though conflict needed no excuse in those times.

"I was not involved," he said defensively, "but I heard there was a deadly skirmish between some Zealots and Roman sentries. Two men were killed."

"Who?" whispered Rachel. I would learn later one of the Roman guards had sympathetic ties with the Zealots, and sometimes passed information to them through Rachel's son Simon, even though Simon did not take part in any of the fighting himself.

"I do not know even if the dead were Jew or Roman. I had been at a nearby tavern with some friends and we scattered before we could be drawn into the conflict. I thought you should know."

Joseph's compound, though large, was only lightly fortified. It sat along the road on the way to Ein Karem, not far from Jerusalem. Our sense of safe haven came from the goodwill he had built through his long life, working with men of all nations and religions. I knew of no one as universally respected as he.

"You will all stay here tonight," he said, "and we can talk about this in the morning. Rebecca, go get Martha and Jonah, light lamps and show my guests to their rooms." She ran out the door and returned a moment later with the older couple. They must have been listening just outside the door.

*

"I wish James had not come here. He might have drawn trouble to this house."

My husband James and I lay in bed whispering together. There weren't enough rooms to go around, and Elizabeth slept in the bed next to us. He had never said so, but I sensed he did not entirely trust the younger man. 'A man who is not the master of his own temper is but a slave,' I heard him say more than once.

"But we need to know what is happening," I countered. "Otherwise, we would have followed our plans to go into Jerusalem tomorrow."

"I wonder why mother wants us to remain here another day. I would prefer leaving at first light," he persisted, somewhat peevishly.

"We will find out soon enough," I replied as calmly as I could. I whispered so as not to wake Elizabeth. "We should talk about where to go from here. Joseph will leave for his apartment in the city, as the Sanhedrin is sure to meet after today's events." He and Nicodemus formed our lifeline to the inner councils of Judea. Somehow he had even managed to retain Herod's trusT.

"Well," he sighed, "I think we should return to Nazareth for awhile, until things calm down."

"My dear James, we both know it may be a good long while before peace returns. As Zacharias said tonight, events have moved beyond the control of any of us. I know in my heart he is right in saying this is a good thing, though I am fearful for Jesus' sake … and our own."

Chapter Three

THE RETURN OF THE SON

My eyes opened into darkness. Something had awakened me.

Veronica. My name came in on the wind.

"Veronica, wake up." Mary stood just outside in the shadows, shawl pulled tightly around her shoulders against the chill.

"What is it?" I whispered through the window.

"Come," she said over her shoulder, retreating into the night.

I slipped my sandals on, grabbed a wrap and ran out the door. James had not stirred.

The previous night's conversation left us wound tight as thread on a spindle. How much more we could take before snapping, I wondered?

"Aunt, what is it?" I asked when I caught up to her. She kept walking.

Joseph had originally tried to convince us to stay in his home near

Caiaphas' house in Jerusalem. But we all agreed we would be safer at his house in the country. And that was before the recent troubles in the city had started.

"Besides, he will need to rest when he returns," Mary said to James and me, speaking of Jesus. "At least here he can slip in unnoticed."

There was a small cluster of guest houses on the other side of the compound from the stables and the building where unmarried workers lived. Joseph had never kept slaves, and would not even refer to his workers as servants. "We are all servants of God," he would say, "and of no man."

A slit of light unfurled across the horizon. Mary stopped not far outside the gate and peered into the eastern shadows. I stilled my breath and with a thrill, understood that we were waiting for Jesus. I sensed his thoughts going ahead of him as surely as if he were already standing in front of us. She silently took my hand as the day's first breath set dust whirling around us.

The sun burst over the landscape just as he came into view, bathing him in flames of gold and red. Mary was unaware her nails dug into my hand. I was glad she held me though; else I might have broken into a run like a small child.

It seemed a long while before he came to a stop in front of us. Mary embraced her son, and I noticed her flinch. I understood soon enough. My cousin had always been muscular, but I could feel his bones through the robes.

"Come, you need food and rest. But first drink," she said, handing him a skin of water." Her eyes betrayed her concern.

After he had drunk, she held out a scarf in which were tied a bunch of dates. But he waved them away. "Later," he said with a weak smile.

I dropped behind mother and son, putting my attention on my heart, and then at a point just below my navel – as I had been trained to do in Alexandria. Gathering the life force I sent it spiraling from this point into an area between his shoulder blades. I was careful to send a slow, steady stream of energy so as not to draw attention to my action. Besides, he would be restored soon enough through the loving care of his mother.

I do not think any of us said a word on the walk back. Mary prepared his bath herself, and then set the fire to warm last night's stew.

"Oh, thank you Father-Mother, for watching over him," I prayed earnestly, "and returning him to us unharmed."

"What is it? What's wrong? Why are you weeping?" exclaimed James when I walked through the door. "I worried to find you gone!"

"He's back." I whispered.

James blinked hard; his eyes filling with tears. More than a few nights I had awakened to see him pacing the floor during his brother's absence. I went to him, sharing his joy and relief at Jesus' return.

Since his return from the years of travel I had devoted myself to helping my cousin in any way I could. We were a close group, forming what we hoped was an impenetrable circle of protection around him. But people often distorted his words, either through ignorance or self-interest. Sadly, this often led to mistrust and the creation of opposing camps, which threatened everyone. His lasting hope was to bring people together, to help them learn to recognize each other as brothers and sisters instead of Jew or Gentile, well-born or lowly-bred, those who loved him and … those who did not.

*

We did not announce his return beyond our group. Mary sequestered him for a few days, so he might regain his strength. While I waited to hear what would come next for us, my thoughts ranged over our travels, our studies and teaching in recent years. I thought too of the events at the river with our cousin John, before Jesus went into the desert.

Following the ritual anointing in the river, a throng of men and women had begun following Jesus' every move, making extreme demands upon him. They wanted him to feed them, to heal their ailments, to rid the land of the Romans and the cursed taxes that increased with every year. Few of them were interested in what he had to say, talking loudly among themselves or turning away whenever he laid responsibility for their lives at their own feet.

"I must get away," he had said one evening, "or I will go mad."

I had never seen him so frustrated. It was easy to forget sometimes that he was not so different from us.

"I must get away," he repeated, more quietly.

"I will go with you," offered John, Zebedee's second son.

His hands covered his eyes, and I am not sure Jesus even heard the offer. So we waited in silence with him. At last he looked up, breathed a deep sigh and said, "I leave tonight. I will go alone to commune with our Father."

There were protests, but he waived us away. In the end he allowed John and James to accompany him as far as Jericho, and there he took their leave. James told me it had been one of the hardest things he'd ever done, watching his brother walk off into the wilderness alone, unprotected, with nothing to sustain him.

Before leaving, Jesus sent most of his followers home, to await his summons. "Use this time well," he told them, "searching your soul for its strength and wisdom."

This puzzled some of the younger ones. He knew their thoughts, and said, "You think these virtues come from me. You believe I alone own the truth. But you are wrong. I have come only to guide you to your Self, where all strength, power, beauty and truth reside."

Some walked away muttering to themselves, a few for good, while the others went to await his return. Most found his words hard to believe, preferring to think he held all power within himself, and that all they had to do was follow him.

I understood that. I would have given anything to believe he would always be there for us, with the right answer, telling us what to do. But I had seen him in those rare moments of self-doubt, exhaustion, and maybe even fear. They were few and brief, but they gave weight to his words that any and everything he did, each of us was capable of doing as well. If he could overcome his human weaknesses, so could we.

*

He had been gone more than a full lunar cycle. I could see the strain on his face, the weariness in his eyes, and knew he had confronted the shadows that clung to his soul. But there was something else: by the time he had gone into the desert his shoulders had begun to sag as if he carried the weight of all nations upon him. But now he stood, shoulders squared, in acceptance of that burden.

Seeing the change in him helped me find my own courage. Now he was back, I could not imagine going away from him – and was glad when he asked James and me to stay.

He rested there for seven days, during which he spoke little, and did not go out beyond the gate. John and Philip came to sit with him, honoring the reserve he had brought back from the desert.

I hoped he would eventually tell us of his days of isolation, and more so that he would quickly resume the stories and homilies for which we all hungered. I had missed those -- but mostly, I had missed my cousin and friend.

The new moon came, and all of us felt the turning of the tide. I could see it in their eyes; a new sense of expectancy, of urgency. No one spoke of it, but we knew it was soon time to leave the sanctuary that had been provided us.

Uncle Joseph came to me one evening before the evening meal. "My daughter," he said, taking both my hands in his, "I have prepared for your departure tomorrow.

"No, don't worry," he laughed, seeing I was about to protest. "We will all leave together."

For a moment, I *had* felt the lightning bolt of fear … that I would be sent away on my own.

"I must go to Jerusalem now, but will join you soon. You will travel to Galilee. Jesus … all of you need to be there now, for this is the moment foretold from the time of Abraham, and for which the

Brotherhood has long prepared.

"It is *his time.*"

Prickles rose up my back, a blend of anticipation and dread. A door was closing behind us.

*

We were a merry bunch when we left the next morning, even though Joseph had at the last minute prevailed upon James and Matthias to go with him to Jerusalem. "A smaller group will attract less attention. It will be safer. Besides," he said to James and Matthias, "I need you to help me decide whether to divest some of my foreign investments in the north, or expand them. With the political situation around Marseilles ...."

The three men walked away and I did not hear the rest of their conversation. No one really knew the extent of Joseph's businesses, but I had seen some of them firsthand years before when Miriam and I traveled with him to Britannia and the Holy Isle. It seemed he was known no matter where we went. And the deference offered was obviously borne of respect and not fear. He was one of the wealthiest men in the Sanhedrin, and one of the most generous and kind spirited souls I have ever known.

I wondered whether he really needed James and Matthias to help with business, or did he have other, unspoken motives for spiriting them away from us? One did not ask my uncle such questions. But in their place he sent three strong men from his warehouse, who would intimidate anyone thinking to bother us on our journey. Marcus, Julius and Arturus were Roman citizens, though Arturus had been born near Penzance (close by the Holy Isle) far to the north. They turned out to be good companions, and I soon learned to trust and rely upon them.

*

"No doubt Matthias and James have joined the *other side* by now," Jesus said with a grin, "living in comfort while we sleep on the ground." It was our first morning out. He had lost the reticence he'd brought back from his desert sojourn, reverting to the mischievous ways of our youth. When still a child I was sensitive to his occasional taunts, but now I treasured them, as they brought to mind simpler times.

"Yes, and I might be next if you expect us to eat wheat berries out of some farmer's field tonight. Last time I did that I nearly choked to death," I teased back.

"There will be an insurrection, unless I have at least one cup of wine to wash down whatever we eat," laughed Philip. But there would be no deprivation on this journey. Ruth and Martha had packed more than enough food – and wine – to last us to Nazareth, our first destination.

We probably appeared more like the traveling minstrels Miriam and I had seen in Britannia than what we actually were: a gathering of disciples drawn forward by invisible forces toward a destiny we barely understood. But Jesus often told us we must honor our humanity as well as our divinity, and joy and laughter brought the two together.

In those days most Jews traveling between Judea and Galilee took enormous pains to avoid Samaria, crossing the Jordan to go north through Perea, cutting across a corner of Decapolis before turning back over the Jordan. There existed an ancient enmity between Jews and Samaritans. No one really remembered how it came about, but both sides resolutely kept the feud alive. I was pleased that my cousin, despite misgivings by Joseph's men, insisted on traveling to Nazareth by the quickest route possible, directly through Samaria. The Romans were to learn that if Jesus wished to explain his decisions on any matter, an explanation was offered without the asking. If not, no amount of questioning would entice him to speak, nor would anything bring him to change his mind.

Our group arrived exhausted, after only four nights on the road. We had walked from dawn to dusk each day. And while it would have been far easier to travel with an ox cart, it would have slowed us considerably.

We found mother waiting for us. "I could hear you while you were yet beyond the city gate!" she laughed, throwing her arms around me. "Come in daughter. Come in, all of you. Rebecca," she called out to her serving girl, run to the school and ask the headmaster if the children might come home early today." Mary had clearly been disappointed not to find her children at home.

In short order Andrew and Elizabeth, the two youngest, flew through the door and into their mother's arms. And while my little brother John had not been deprived of his parents, he ran through the door behind them and threw himself at me with the same enthusiasm. The rest of the children had been away to school in Carmel for the past year, and were expected back soon.

We did not wait to see them, staying just long enough to recover our strength and have a little time with our loved ones. On the third day we set off for Capernaum, on the northern shore of the great lake. This time Mary stayed behind with her sister Salome. "I will not have my children come home after all this time to find me gone. Besides, Anna and Sofia need a break from their duties here, to visit their own families."

Mother walked with us to the edge of town, to see us off. "I promise we will join you soon." she said.

We were surprised that Julius and Marcus stayed behind. Marcus said Joseph had charged them with the women's well-being. Of the Romans, only Arturus left with us.

Those were strange times. Few of us had children of our own, a major reason for the deep mistrust many of our Jewish brethren had of our group. To them childlessness was a sacrilege, and a sure sign of God's displeasure. Thinking of Mary's large brood I recalled my sister Elizabeth's comments to me just before her first woman's ceremony years before. She had asked what would become of us if we did not conform to sacred tradition, especially in this matter. I too felt troubled by it at times, not because of Jewish law, but because it did seem most *unnatural*. But now, as the storm approached, I considered it a blessing.

Chapter Four

A QUIET WELCOME TO CAPERNAUM

The first glimpse of Galilee always brought tears to my eyes, no matter how many times I had seen it on the horizon. The lake is beautiful, to be sure, and from the high distance it projects a sense of deep peace. But it is more than that. I was born in Nazareth, but my heart feels at home at the lake. Galilee would be the setting for my happiest days.

We had planned to stay at one of Capernaum's inns, but came upon Miriam sitting on a rock alongside the road just outside the city gate. None of us had seen or heard from her since a few days after Jesus' baptism in the River Jordan. She disappeared without a word the same day he went into the desert. I had asked my cousin after his return if he knew where she was. He nodded, and by that I knew I needn't be concerned about my friend.

She sat watching our approach, the wind rustling through her long dark hair. Biting her lip, she did not move. I glanced at Jesus to see his expression. They had such an obvious, powerful bond, I wondered why they had not married. If nothing else, the Rabbis might have been more accepting of our band of travelers. But I did not pry, knowing how hard it is to answer to such questions myself.

Philip called out, "Miriam, I had hoped to find you here. Well, not *here* exactly, sitting on a rock, but ... here, at the lake." She laughed.

"And you," she said, throwing her arms around me. "I've missed our talks! Where is James?"

"He is with Joseph and will join us soon. How did you know we would arrive today?" She laughed without answering, and turned to Arturus, the only one among us she did not already know.

"This is Arturus," I said, "an old friend of Joseph's. He has been our good companion along the way, and become a friend to us all."

Arturus gave Miriam a slight bow, which sent us all into giggles as we had not seen him do such a thing before. She was, after all, a fine-looking woman, with no apparent husband. Our reaction brought a flush to his cheeks, and I was immediately sorry for having embarrassed him.

"Do you know our beautiful lake, Arturus?" asked Miriam, graciously. "I was born not far south of here."

"Yes, though I would know more of it."

Try as she might, my friend could not keep her eyes from straying back to where Jesus stood, where he watched her with obvious amusement.

Elizabeth could no longer contain herself, and broke through the group to throw herself at Miriam, dispelling the awkwardness.

"You have grown up!" Miriam exclaimed as if surprised, though my sister had long since passed into womanhood.

At last Jesus approached and brushed Miriam's cheek with his lips, then took her hand without a word. Poor Arturus.

"Samuel said you all must stay with him," she called back as our dust-covered troop entered through the gate.

"Samuel -- does he no longer live in Magdala then?" asked Philip. "We stopped on the way through there to ask after you and your brothers, and were told only that you had left."

"Well, he is here now," she replied. "And he bought a new house that could use some laughter. Your timing is perfect."

"How *did* you know to meet us today?" prodded Elizabeth. "We had not sent word ahead of our arrival."

"Oh, but you had."

Thaddeus blurted out. "Who had? Who sent word?"

"Sometimes words come on wings," she laughed again, clearly enjoying herself.

"You are Roman, Arturus, but it is your name that gives you away rather than your dress. How do you know Joseph?" she asked, as we neared Simon's house.

"My father was a foreman at one of his mines near Penzance. I met him when I was still a boy, and from the first he treated me with kindness. How many men of noble birth will listen to a young boy prattle on about childish things?" he asked of no one in particular. "I think I was just fifteen when I asked if I might return with him as his servant. My father was shocked, and angry at my impertinence. But Joseph only laughed, and said of course, if my father allowed it.

"It took some doing, but I left with him on his next visit. And I have been with him ever since, though I only recently come to live in Judea." His voice belied his love for the older man.

"Have you seen your father since then?" asked Thaddeus, having gotten over his confusion.

"Oh yes, I returned with Joseph several times. Father and I made peace over what he considered my betrayal in leaving him. But I do not think I will see him again. He was not well when we left last year, and we said our farewells."

"I am sorry," said Thaddeus, "though perhaps you are wrong and he has recovered."

Arturus shrugged his shoulders. "Joseph wanted to cheer me up on the long journey back to Judea, and told me about the time you two went with him to our land," he said, pointing to Miriam and me.

"Ohhhhh yes, that *was* an amazing experience," I said. "I would love to return there one day." Unexpected memories of the first surge of youthful passion with a young boatman there brought a flush to my face. But no one seemed to notice.

Our group chattered away until we reached the gate of a modest size compound a short walk up from the lakeshore. "Samuel," Miriam called out. "Samuel." Not getting a response, she reached over and unlatched the gate and walked through, the rest of us following close behind.

The moment Arturus closed the gate behind us, a man rounded the corner from behind the house. "Jesus," he said, a huge grin on his face, "and Thaddeus." One by one he embraced us, and when Arturus put his hand out to the stranger, Samuel grabbed him as an old friend and pulled him into a warm embrace, though he had never seen him before.

That evening over dinner Samuel told us his reason for moving away from Magdala.

"I never thought I would leave our home. Miriam is the adventurer in the family.

After our parents' death, I took over father's business. We had loyal customers not just from Galilee, but Romans and others stopped at our stall in town to buy salted fish to bring back on their long journeys home. I had heard that even *Tiberius* asked for our fish!" he said, with obvious pride.

"Eli never showed an interest in the family business, and seemed content to spend his days in the synagogue discussing scripture. Nevertheless, I have done what I could, giving Eli his share of the profits. He never said thank you or anything else. He would just take the money and walk out.

"I don't know what else I could have done," he said, somewhat flustered. Miriam glanced up at her brother, and then away. "One day

Eli threw the money back into my face and began cursing me, saying our sister and I would bring disgrace on our parents' memory, and evil into our home."

The burly man covered his face, shoulders heaving soundlessly. Miriam pulled her chair up next to him and we all joined in silent witness to his pain. Elizabeth rose and went out to put a pot of water on the fire for tea.

After a time, he went on. "There is a faction in our synagogue that fears the Romans more than they do God. They are afraid that you will bring the wrath of Rome down upon us," he said, nodding toward no one in particular.

"Herod has inherited his father's hatred of anything or anyone he deems critical of his rule, vowing to destroy it before it destroys him. He broods upon the rumors that have come to him of a new king of Israel, a new king of the Jews, expanding upon and passing these rumors through Tiberius' emissaries back to the Emperor. And now he has gotten what he wanted all along: Rome's endorsement to carry out his vendettas.

I looked up to see Elizabeth standing in the doorway with the pot of tea in her hand, weeping silently. The fragrance from the tea came in on the night breeze, filling the air, calming me despite Samuel's fearful tale.

"I didn't know what else to do, but to put the business in the hands of the two men I trust most. They have been faithful servants to our family for a generation. And then I left.

"Eli threatened me," he whispered. "And he threatened Miriam."

My friend sat looking down at her hands.

"Though I do not agree with Eli, I did not want to endanger him, should trouble come. And I thought my sister and I would be safer here, for now at least. Besides," he said, brightening, "it gives me an opportunity to offer you hospitality."

He sat up straight and cleared his throat. "Come, let us talk of brighter things. Tell me of your journey. And you, my dear brother," he said, nodding at Jesus, "I wish to hear of your desert retreat, and your plans for the future."

"Yes, added Miriam, I too would hear of these things. I have missed you all," she said, looking only at my cousin.

*

We spent the next several days getting caught up on each other's lives. It was apparent there were pockets of resistance to our group among the Jews, and especially to Jesus' ministry. It was impossible to know how strong or organized or widespread the opposition was.

And it wasn't only directed at us. Samuel said cousin John had been receiving death threats. John is so single-minded he probably wasn't even aware of such things, though it would not have deterred him in any case.

Nor, I knew, would threats of any kind dissuade Jesus from his work. That which had been leveled at Samuel was obviously intended for him. As of yet, no one dared approach him directly, as he had too many supporters. And those would soon increase a thousand-fold.

Chapter Five

THE WATCHERS

"It was awful," said Miriam. "It looked like they would come to blows. I had never seen my brothers so angry, especially Eli. I knew he judged me my life. And to be fair, he must have to put up with a lot in the Sanhedrin, always explaining our unconventional behavior. But ... he was vicious!"

I took my friend's hand as we walked the narrow streets to the market. Despite the crowds and noisy hawkers, I loved Capernaum's bazaar. Stalls ran right down to the water's edge. The fresh air off the lake dispersed the smell of freshly killed animals and rotting fish, yet somehow left undisturbed the fragrance of flowers and spices on nearby tables.

"You are here now, and safe," I told her.

"But everyone knows us here, and knows we've had a falling out. I cannot hide unseen among the crowds."

"And well you should not. You have nothing to hide, nothing to be ashamed of."

"But from *their* viewpoint, I do."

That was so, but there were things to buy and chores to do, so I changed the subject. Galilee tended not to be as conservative as Judea, but ever since her parents died the two men felt increasingly pressured to get their sister married.

Worst of all, the Torah insinuated it was a sin if men and women did not assume the responsibility of marrying and producing children. Few among our group were married and except for the occasional visit of Nicodemus and his wife Judith, most of the men who were married had left their families at home to come with us. No one, least of all Jesus, had asked them to do this. But they said it was easier and probably safer for their wives and children not to be on the road with them. None to my knowledge had left their families behind uncared for. Most often a brother or uncle, sympathetic to the teachings of Jesus, had volunteered to watch over them.

But for the old priests it was just another abomination on a growing list. Never mind many of *them* had fallen short in their husbandly duties, preferring to argue doctrine with each other to spending time with their own wives and children.

Our shopping done, a young boy offered to deliver our purchases to the house for a coin. This gave us leave to walk along the shore before returning home. There we came upon my cousin and the brothers Simon and Andrew, Rachel's sons. I had not met them before, though they knew Miriam, greeting her as a sister.

I liked them immediately. They seemed opposite in every way: Simon, dark and stocky with a fiery look in his eyes, and Andrew, fair haired and slim of build. Simon commanded eye contact when he spoke, which at first made me a little uneasy. Men did not usually act so bold with women outside their family. On the other hand, Andrew was so shy I could not tell the color of his eyes, even after a long conversation with him.

"Simon and Andrew have asked us to their home tonight, to share their catch of the day," said Jesus. "There are others whom they wish us to meet."

"We have told them of you, of your group, and the things you say about all men being brothers, and how women are to stand alongside men as equals!" Andrew blurted out. He blushed, surprising even himself with his bold statement. "Mother has always taught us thus," he added, looking down at the nets in his hands.

That evening just before we were to leave the house we heard a shout in the courtyard. A flash of fear crossed Miriam's eyes as she turned toward the door. I followed her out and saw my dear husband standing there, with a grin as wide as the Jordan.

"Beloved, are you weeping?" He stood back, eyeing me with concern.

"Am I?" I had not even realized I'd been anxious about James until I saw him standing before me. I brushed away my tears. "It's nothing: I am just happy to see you."

"But it can't have been more than seven or eight days since we parted," he said with a laugh. "And you, my brother, how are you?" he said, turning to Jesus. They held each other at arms length, as if gauging the changes in the world about them in each others' eyes.

As James turned to greet Simon, I gave Matthias a hug. "I am surprised to see you here. Have you been to Nazareth yet?" Love him as I did, I had always thought of him as mother's husband, rather than my father -- probably because I was a woman already by the time they married.

"No, not yet. Marcus sent word that everyone there is in good health. I will go soon."

"Come," said Miriam," thrusting bowls of food into our hands to take with us. She would not be turned aside from the object of her attention. "We were just about to leave; had you lingered you would have arrived at an empty house. We can talk on the way." Jesus gave me a wink and hurried after her retreating figure.

Miriam's brother called out from the gate to let our hosts know we had arrived, and the five of us entered without waiting for a response.

"Welcome" shouted the other Simon, pulling each of us in turn into a strong embrace. Andrew and his mother stood smiling from across the courtyard.

"Well, you are strong indeed to have survived one of Simon's hugs!" laughed Rachel, coming towards us. "Welcome to our home. And how wonderful to see you two! When did you return? And what news have you brought? No," she added, waving her hand into the air when Matthias opened his mouth to speak. "Time for that later. Andrew, will you help take these to the table?"

He stepped up to take the dish from my hands and gave me a quick kiss on the cheek. As I got to know him I learned that Andrew's feelings ran deep, surprisingly given to expressions of affection. In times to come this gentle soul would demonstrate an even deeper core of strength than other, more combative men lacked.

It was quite a gathering. Most of those who had been with us at Joseph's house were there. We had seen Arturus that afternoon and asked him to join us. Only later did I understand why he declined. It would take awhile for some of the men to come around to accepting a Roman into our midst. I'd assumed that people who themselves had suffered discrimination would be more charitable toward others. But in that I was wrong. Some of them proved to be the most intolerant of difference.

We met many new people that night, gathered from around the lake, each curious to meet this teacher before whom John had knelt. Some of them had counted among John's followers. But even those who became disciples of Jesus remained loyal defenders of the Baptist until the end.

It was good we brought the extra food, for we were a large group. There wasn't enough left over even to feed the wild dogs that night.

"Why did Joseph call you to Jerusalem?" Philip asked James. I would learn that Philip hated being excluded from anything.

James glanced at Matthias. "For several days we did not know the reason," he began. James was sitting directly across the table from me, but he avoided my eyes as he spoke. He was holding something back.

"Joseph disappeared in the morning and returned at night, leaving us to wander the city on our own. I love Jerusalem so did not mind this time to relax and simply enjoy myself. But on the third day Matthias and I confronted him. He insisted he had to go out alone again, but would talk with us that evening if we wished to wait up for him.

"He came in late and it seemed to me he had drunk more wine than usual that night." Matthias nodded agreement. "Everyone else had gone to bed and the three of us sat down next to the fountain in the central courtyard, far from any wall. No one would have been able to hear our conversation. He chattered on about this and that, and then right in the middle of something about taxes, he stopped. In that silence I thought I saw fear in his eyes – which shocked me. I had always thought him the most intrepid of men"

James' eyes were far away, and in the stillness we heard a dog bark, and a chorus of frogs down by the lake.

Matthias picked up the thread. "He told us the Sanhedrin had been discussing whether John … the Baptist posed a threat to them."

Matthias paused for Rachel to light the lamps, setting them at intervals along the table.

"Discussion was heated. Joseph wondered if talk of John might have been a cover to avoid speaking of Jesus, since they all knew how close he is to his nephew."

Jesus stared into the flickering light in front of him. My heart beat hard, and I felt the knot of dread rise into my throat. James' eyes were downcast as well, and I could read nothing of the two men's emotions.

"There are those in the Sanhedrin who will do anything they can to curry favor with Rome," continued Matthias after draining his cup. "Herod already hates John, and they know he will not stand in their way. And Rome, well, Rome can be swayed in any direction with promises to prolong the peace awhile longer."

Even at that table, opinions of John differed greatly. Of course, there were his devotees. But a few spoke up, calling him a trouble-maker who drew unwanted attention to all of us. Someone called him a lesser rival to Jesus.

"Not so," Jesus said in a voice so low those at the end of the table had to strain to hear him. "Without John I would not know my name."

"What do you mean?" asked Thaddeus, but James, his father interrupted, changing the subject. "Matthias, I had hoped Joseph would return with you. Did he tell you his plans?"

"He will remain awhile in Jerusalem, sending messengers now and then with what information he can glean."

Matthias looked directly at Jesus then, whose eyes rose instinctively to meet his. "We are to remain vigilant to our surroundings, while not succumbing to the ill winds of gossip, either in the giving or receiving of it. He said to be fearless, yet not foolish. Stand together, and stand *for* one another."

He then looked around the table, to make sure we were all paying attention. "We are to follow Jesus' lead. He is our elder brother, yet walks with us shoulder to shoulder."

Zebedee opened his mouth to speak, then closed it with a grunt. As the eldest among us, it must have seemed peculiar to think of the young man as his elder brother.

That night John, Zebedee's second son, along with Nathaniel and Matthew threw their lot in with our little band. Thomas had come in near the end of the evening with apologies for being late. He picked over the empty plates, obviously sorry to have missed dinner. He too would soon join the group.

Martha and Ruth, wife of Barnabas, also joined us that night. I had met Ruth before, but Martha, a friend of Rachel's, was unknown to me. Everyone, except for Matthew, lived along the northernmost part of the lake and all were in some way related to the fishing industry.

Matthew was there at Simon's invitation. James and I met with Matthew several days later in town. He was a tax collector in

Capernaum, and generally reviled among his own people (as was usual for that profession).

"Just the other day I was walking down an alleyway when an old woman stepped into my path, stopping my progress. She looked me right in the eye and slapped my face. I didn't even know who she was," he said, throwing his hands into the air. "Within moments, I was being pelted by stones. I fell to my knees and covered my face, fearing I would be stoned to death.

"But suddenly the shouts stopped and with them, the stones. I looked up to see a man standing over me, his hand reaching out to take mine. He pulled me to my feet, which was no easy task as my legs were shaking so hard they barely supported me."

"'They take their anger out on you, but it is poverty and oppression they hate,' said the stranger. That man is your Jesus. I had never seen him before, nor, I confess, even heard his name. Though I *had* heard stories of the one you call the Baptist.

"His were the kindest eyes I had ever seen. I do not know what he did or said to those people to stop them in their fury. But I shall be ever grateful. When I asked what I could do to repay him, he shook his head and said he needed nothing, that he had treasures more than enough already. I assumed that meant he was a wealthy man, but his robes told me otherwise. And so I followed him, sure there must be something I could buy him or his family. Later I discovered my friend Simon knew him, and he invited me to dinner the other night.

"Who *are* you people? What manner of man is he?" he asked, with all sincerity.

Here stood a man whose heart had somehow not been hardened by his terrible experiences. "Stay with us awhile," I answered. "You will discover for yourself. In him you will find the answer to all your questions, as well as a healing for your headaches."

"How do you know of my headaches?" he shot back, with a startled look.

I had spoken without thinking. "I don't know how I know such things," I answered honestly. "Sometimes thoughts steal in on me unawares. I believe it is for good though, as it often leads to healing of one kind or another."

*

Palestine stood at a crossroads of trade and culture. The Romans were great road builders, a necessity for transporting men and materials in their insatiable zeal for conquest. The major road from Damascus to the coast and on to Egypt passed right through Capernaum. Even the cities of Jericho and Jerusalem were reached by a spur off this highway.

And so we were accustomed to seeing all manner of people in town, whether Galilee was their destination or simply a rest stop along the way. People of every skin tone speaking an array of dialects filled the inns. Romans, Persians, Egyptians, Greeks and Jews sat at tables next to each other, though seldom mixed.

It was uncommon to see women in such establishments after dark. There were no laws prohibiting their entry, yet such places remained the domain of men who ate and drank and argued, often until dawn.

Barnabas' brother Peter owned one such place which sat just off the lake. He had bragged the other night about the good food served there. In hopes of buying some quiet time for Jesus, away from the public eye, James, Miriam, and I brought him there to eat.

A burly man with a great full beard met us at the door and stood there, blocking the way, eyeing each of us in turn. His gaze settled on James and after a moment he slapped him good naturedly on the shoulder and boomed, "Ah, you're Justus' friends, aren't you? Come in!"

James responded, "You must have confused us; we do not know anyone named Justus."

The man's brow furrowed, "but surely you do. I have seen you at the lake, and in the synagogue. And you are called Jesus.

"Justus, my brother…" he persisted, "or maybe you know him as Barnabas."

"Of course, you're Peter," said James. "Though you look nothing alike, you have the same voice."

He seated us at a table near a window covered with a fine cloth to keep out the dust and provide us some privacy from passersby. But instead of leaving us to our meal, Peter pulled up another chair to join us. We had been looking forward to some quiet conversation, but he seemed such a genial man we could not refuse him. Now and then throughout the evening he would jump up and go into the kitchen to make special requests of his cooks.

I sat with my back to the window, looking into the room. No one else at our table seemed to notice but across from us sat a group of four men, dressed in colorful robes. That alone would have them stand out, but one of them wore a turban wrapped around his head and a long curved sheath at his girdle that reflected light from the overhead lamps when he moved in a certain way. Curled wisps of hair fell down at each ear. His almond-like eyes watched us impassively.

"What are you looking at?" whispered Miriam, when Peter left our table to check on his other customers.

"Do not turn around all at once, but there is a man, perhaps a Persian or, I don't know, a Parthian who has been watching us the entire time we've been here."

The stranger must have sensed I was talking about him, as he looked away to speak to the man seated next to him. Then before I could describe him, he rose and came directly over to us.

"Forgive me for being rude. I could not help but stare, and hope I did not make you uncomfortable," the tall man said to me with a graceful bow and sweep of his hand in my direction.

I found myself unable to respond.

"Will you sit with us?" asked Jesus, pointing to the now-empty chair.

He nodded and sat in a single fluid movement, the sword sliding over to one side without his having to move it out of the way. It seemed almost a part of him.

"You are kind. Thank you."

I noticed his table companions had stopped talking and were now watching us, as were all the remaining guests. It was late evening and the lamps hung outside the building pierced the window covering, throwing light and shadows onto the stranger's face. He was darkly handsome.

"Do I know you?" I thought I asked the question aloud, but he didn't answer me, looking instead at my cousin. Jesus narrowed his eyes, then jumped up, knocking his chair onto the floor.

"Pursa! Pursa, my old friend!" Tears sprang to his eyes as he embraced the friend of his youth.

"No wonder," I said, standing up. I had only seen him that one night so many years before. Pursa had accompanied Jesus back to Palestine from their journey to Persia when Joseph, father of Jesus and James, had left his earthly body. Despite the years I could vision his face clearly, as he had looked then.

Neither James nor Miriam remembered meeting him, recalling only that Jesus had come to us with a friend from the East.

"Call your friends over," suggested Jesus.

"Yes, do," echoed Miriam, "we would like to meet them."

Their names were Mahmoud, Ravi and Safa. The four men returned with us to Simon and Miriam's house. We gathered around a table in the garden. It was by then quite dark and Miriam and I lit the lamps. I wanted to see the men's faces as they spoke.

A serving girl set out wine and cups. Pursa spoke first: "we four have come at the behest of the Brotherhood, representing four lands to the East. Pursa smiled and nodded at the one called Ravi. The younger man broke into a grin and stretched his hand across the table to Jesus, handing him a small parcel wrapped in a piece of yellow silk.

"What is this?" he wondered aloud.

"Your family has not forgotten you," replied Ravi.

"My family? Oh! My family!" With trembling hands Jesus pulled the fabric back to reveal a leather cord strung with a single faceted bead.

Eyes sparkling, he held it to the light and saw the elegant letters from the ancient Sanskrit carved on each facet.

Ravi stood and took the cord from him and tied it about my cousin's neck.

"It is from Krishna. He wanted to come himself, but ... could not," he said, his own eyes welling up. "I have letters too," and he pulled a packet out of his robe, laying them in front of my cousin. Jesus left them lying there until dawn's light when he would take them back to his room to read alone.

The eight of us talked through the night. It was wonderful hearing the stories of Jesus' and Pursa's travels together and the time spent with the Magi in Persepolis.

"How goes the city?" my cousin asked. "Was it rebuilt after the great quake?"

"The dome has been repaired and most of the temples. Homes were fashioned from the rubble, but it has not fully come back," he said sadly. "Many thousands were lost and others left the city afterwards, their hearts broken.

"It is a sign of our times, really, when there is no firm ground upon which to stand. The foundations of our world are being shaken, whether by Rome or simple fear and avarice," he added.

We learned the Brotherhood had been sending emissaries from all the lands where they resided to take up residence in places of turmoil, no matter the source. Simon and Andrew had by then come out of the house to join us, and offered to help them find a home on the lake.

"I can think of nothing that would bring me greater pleasure, but that is not why we are here. Tomorrow we four will separate and find places to live among the many immigrant communities along the trade routes of Palestine. It is essential we not draw more attention to ourselves – or to you. We had not expected to meet you in such a public place.

"The Brotherhood has existed from the beginning, and will endure as long as time itself. But to remain strong, to accomplish the great work and fulfill our reason for being, we must for now at least, remain behind the scenes." Safa spoke into the quiet night.

"Only rarely does a brother stand alone within the light of day, an example of man's potential for all to see," he continued, looking directly at my cousin. "It is not an enviable position."

Mahmoud, looking at each of us in turn, added: "Take care to be there for him, at all times. We will do what we can."

A cold wind suddenly moved among us, and I shivered.

Chapter Six

A SHARED VISION

Now and then we'd see Pursa or another of the brothers in the crowds that formed around us, but they always disappeared before we could speak. Before long we were so busy I no longer had time to think about them, or the other strangers in our midst.

"Did you see that man standing next to the tree tonight?" Simon asked, of no one in particular.

"We really must replenish our food supply," said Philip, ignoring the question. "Matthew, how much is in our coffers? We have been spending too much lately, and should go out onto the lake," he added, not waiting for his reply. "Who will go with me?"

Simon Peter, Andrew and Thomas went with Philip. Jesus got up and went in the opposite direction. I followed him.

Matthias and Barnabas had gone with Arturus to Nazareth to bring Mary and Salome back to Tiberius. We planned to join them there within a few days. I do not know where everyone else had gone that day.

Jesus started off in a hurry, then stopped so suddenly I nearly ran into him.

"I am sorry, cousin," he said, laughing. "Actually, I do not even know where I was heading, so haste is completely unnecessary. Come, sit with me awhile." He took my hand and led me to a cluster of trees at the edge of town.

It had been long since we'd spent any time together, just the two of us. I wondered if he hadn't gone off to be by himself, but didn't want to spoil the opportunity by asking.

The wind sighed in the trees. It was early spring, cool days alternating with hot. Small brown patches began to appear here and there in the green grass. But there under the trees, it smelled of damp earth and sweet grass. I felt full of hope.

Jesus sat against a rock and patted the grass for me to join him. He put his arm around me and I leaned onto his shoulder and sighed. The innocence of youth returned to us one last time with its silent embrace.

Neither of us spoke for a time. My eyes were closed to gentle visions of days gone by, loved ones passed to the other side or simply gone from human sight. I thought neither of the pressing demands on our time, nor what may lie ahead.

"Veronica," he said after a time, "I must ask you a hard question."

Reluctantly I sat up and moved to meet his eyes. My heart began to pound and a wave of panic swept over me.

"I see many things in my dreaming and my waking. Sometimes ... I do not even know if I am awake or asleep," he mused, almost to himself. "As time goes by I am given to understand more and more of what I see, but there is still much beyond my comprehension."

I forgot sometimes that my cousin, however wise, was not so unlike the rest of us. His sudden confession unnerved me.

"I do know one thing with certainty. We stand on the cusp of a new epoch, one setting darkness against the light, brother against brother. Many will falter, and many fall. Each of us will be tested."

He took my hands in his. I cannot find words for what I saw in his eyes, but I would have given anything to turn away. But he held my eyes with his.

"I am sorry. I wish, more than anything in the world, that I could spare you … that I could spare mother, Miriam, my friends. But I cannot allow you to follow me blindly. You must know somewhat of the future, as far as I can see it."

He tried to explain his visions, to fill in the parts of prophecy which had been left out of my training.

"In time to come I will increasingly rely on you, and the other women. You, more than the men have been trained to stand alongside me as healers and teachers. I used to wonder why it was you who went to Alexandria, you and Miriam and some of the other women. I wondered why my mother and yours had been brought to Carmel in their own youth to be taught the mysteries, awakening their inner sight. Why was it not our fathers? I have prayed, asking for answers to these questions. Why were *you* always there for me at the sunset? And even before, when other children taunted me for my differences, you were there, never judging, never doubting."

I could no longer see his face through my tears. But his voice insisted I hear him out.

"You, the women, are the strongest of us. You know the heart that beats in all that lives as your own heart. I have seen it is you, my sisters, who will stand with me at the end."

"*Stop!*" I tried to protest. Yet he went on, and I knew he had to say these things. And it may be I was the only one who could hear them.

"You – my cousin – are my sister, my friend, my very heart. You, and Miriam."

He was quiet then, but still he held my hands. At last the tears cleared and I could see his eyes again. I did not know how I could bear the tenderness I saw there.

"…at the end," he repeated. "And you will go on, doing the work we all have begun – as will the men closest to me: James, John, Thomas … and some of the others."

His eyes lost their focus, but he held my hands even more tightly. A bird called out and I felt him jump.

"Veronica, you are stronger than you know. Be patient with them. Not all the men who walk with me understand your role. Some of them feel threatened by the women who surround me, feel cheated of my affections." He smiled then. "As if love were limited, as if our heavenly Father or Mother could love one less than another. Love is infinite. This cannot be taught. It can only be experienced. *You* know this, dear cousin."

I tried to protest, but he would not hear it ... how far I fell short of his example.

"You see only the best of me. You think I am without fault," he said, knowing my thoughts. "But I have the same concerns as you. I have sometimes lain awake at night looking for a way out that would not bring shame upon my family."

"I do not believe ..." but he cut me off.

"It does not last. God does not give up on us, despite our weaknesses, always inspiring in me a renewal of my commitment to serve in any way I can. You and I have been given much, and now we must pass it on to others. This is a sacred covenant. We are bound to it, body, mind and spirit.

"Help my mother, my brothers and sisters, our friends to remember this. There will be times when I am distracted, perhaps not noticing their fears and doubts, or unable to attend to them. I have spoken with Miriam about this as well. She has promised me, and I ask your promise also, to put aside your own small self to do this."

He stopped speaking then, but his eyes continued to probe mine. I was sure he would discover only weakness there, and be sorry he had confided in me. I wanted to tell him he was mistaken about me.

But then, from one heartbeat to the next, I felt something inside me crack, and all my resistance was washed away in a flood of divine love.

*

"Mother," he shouted, and ran ahead to greet Mary, sweeping her up into the air like a girl. Ever since our conversation a few days back, my cousin had seemed as lighthearted as I'd ever seen him. His attitude was infectious; laughter came easily those days to our small group.

"And Salome, thank you for taking care of her for me," he said, embracing her.

I had missed Mary and my own mother over those many months. It was a joyful reunion. The two sisters assured us they were well: to me they had never looked better.

We'd been kept busy on the lake, and the time had gone quickly. Jesus was rarely left alone; people came in search of healing, words of comfort and cheer. Though he turned no one away, at the end of a long day he often disappeared into the shadows for rest and time to himself.

When he did so, the crowds pressed in on those of us who remained, especially the women. As he had said, we were well trained in the healing arts and though none of us was as gifted in speech as he, we had learned our lessons well and did what we could to reinforce his teaching. Sometimes, quite unexpectedly one or the other of us would be the instrument for what people called miracles. Though I was humbled and grateful for what God did through us, such events made me uneasy since people began to think *we* were the ones who produced the cures or subdued the elements.

"All you can do, child, is to firmly remind people that it is the One Spirit who lives within all of us who does the work," said Mary.

"But they do not listen when I say this!" I protested.

She laughed. "I will tell you what I have told my son: people are wont to hear and see and believe what they are already disposed to do. And it is true they will mistake you for the Source at times." My aunt's voice took on a serious tone. "Just as often they will place blame upon you for what they do not like in their lives."

She looked over at her sister. "Salome and I have experienced this many times."

"You have been given a gift," mother said. "Bearing responsibility for whatever comes is a part of that gift. It is not yours to give or to withhold. It is simply yours to offer with as much grace as you can find within yourself."

We stayed in Tiberius seven days. One day the crowd pressed so hard against my cousin that Andrew brought a small boat around for him. Jesus got in and pushed off a dozen cubits from the shoreline and continued his talk from there until the late afternoon wind forced him back to shore. Still the crowd would not move back for him to disembark. The waves were becoming perilously large, so Simon and Andrew climbed in with him and rowed round a bend, leaving the crowd behind. And when they pursued him over the hill, all they found was an empty boat.

While they argued among themselves as to what had happened to the three men, Miriam and I slipped away to Samuel's house. As I expected, they were seated out in the courtyard talking as if nothing out of the ordinary had happened. Jesus looked up and grinned conspiratorially, but no one said a thing.

*

We left the next morning for Jerusalem, planning to be there for the Festival of Weeks. I always enjoyed the sites on those longer journeys, and pleasured in the exchange of news and ideas with people we met along the way. That was the good part.

But there were many evenings along the way when we could not find a bath for our rituals and to clean the grime of the day from our bodies. Many people (including some Hebrews) considered our habits related to hygiene and diet peculiar or extreme. Now and then we'd hear an innkeeper or servant girl muttering under their breath about those *Essenes.* All Jews are guided by the Torah about such matters, but few were as resolute as we.

Some Essene communities *were* obsessive, even in our way of thinking, eating nothing more than berries, nuts and water, wearing a single unbleached muslin robe no matter the weather, never cutting their hair, keeping celibate, and so on. Some few refuse clothes altogether, spending their lives in dark caves away from the blessed sun and the gifts of the earth. My grandmother Anna's uncle had been one of those who shunned all things of the world, never speaking another word when he left the family home after his mitzvah.

I thought it especially odd to turn away from one's family, and sad to deny the spiritual gifts of our world. But I have been taught and strive always to remember that there are many roads back to our heavenly home, and none of us knows with certainty if one is better than another.

We arrived in Jerusalem late on the third day. Instead of going straight to Joseph's, which was our habit, Jesus insisted we take rooms at an inn. Though we would have preferred the privacy and comfort of Joseph's estate, we agreed. He had his own reasons for things, and we trusted his instincts.

A little later, when walking through the courtyard I came upon a table where some of our group sat talking. They called me over to join them. Thomas was telling a story that took place the previous Passover. It was a story I had not heard before.

Jesus, the two Simons and Thomas were out walking, when Jesus stopped to watch the crowds just outside the temple. Men were selling animals for sacrifice, and as always the wretched poor were being pushed about by people of wealth and position. Someone bellowed into the crowd to stand aside for a member of the Sanhedrin who wished to pass. When one of the beggars did not move quickly enough to suit him, the official's servant pushed him to the ground and kicked him out of the way.

Jesus, shocked at the inhumanity, positioned himself between them and the beggar. Thomas said he thought Jesus was going to strike them as they cowered in front of him. But he struck with words and not his fists.

"This man whom you have dispatched to the gutter will one day dine at our Father's table," he said through clenched teeth. "You are starving and think food will fill you, blind, believing riches will restore your sight. Our Father does not care if you are rich or poor, of high birth or low; all alike are invited to His feast. Only he who does not see in another his own brother will be turned away."

The priest shrieked at the servants carrying his litter to take him away from the man whom he thought possessed. But the servant who had passed before him clearing the way stood as if rooted to the ground, staring at Jesus until the priest screamed back at him to follow if he valued his life.

Once they were gone from sight Jesus knelt and whispered something into the beggar's ear. Simon Peter said the man's face lit up at what was said to him. And then with the gentleness of a mother, he lifted the man to his feet and set him on his way.

That priest was among those who would scheme against my cousin inside the temple ... while his servant would return, hiding behind others as he listened to Jesus speak. Thomas said Jesus told them that one day that man will step out of their shadows and leave his master to become a seeker of truth.

But the story did not end there. Thomas described how no one could enter the temple without walking past the many money changers, since their tables lined both sides of the passageway. Pious Jews came to Jerusalem from many lands for the holy days in that time. In order to buy animals to make the appropriate sacrifices, they were required to change their currency for the only unit that was accepted in the temple precincts. Of course the money changers kept a healthy portion of the exchange for themselves, sharing some of the profit with the priests.

As they approached the tables, they heard shouting. A single voice rose above the others, calling the money changers thieves who preyed upon men's fears. Suddenly coins were flying through the air, and the many beggars who had been standing outside the temple steps dove in to collect them. Not wanting to get embroiled in yet another dispute they were about to turn away, but something stopped Jesus.

He recognized the voice. It was his youngest brother Andrew creating the disturbance. Jesus pushed his way through the crowd, grabbed Andrew and pulled him away, shouting to his friends to follow them ... NOW. The money changers were so stunned no one pursued them. But one of the priests standing on the temple steps returned with a Roman guard just as they were about to turn a corner.

"Stop!" the guard shouted, blocking their way, a spear pointed at Jesus' throat. He complied without a word.

Andrew cried out, "It was me. It wasn't him. I did it. It's my fault. Let him go!"

The guard looked from the younger to the older brother, and back again. "Well, give him to me then," he said. "I will see that he pays for the disturbance."

But Jesus would not turn his brother over to the Roman, or to the priests who had followed them. "Someone has to pay!" they kept shouting.

Still holding on to Andrew's arm, Jesus ignored the guard and the priests, surveying the crowd.

"You have been told our Father requires blood sacrifice as recompense for your sins. What need do you think God has of burned flesh and spilled blood? He calls you to sacrifice *yourself*, not on the altar of death but of life. He asks for your hearts, that you may serve each other as a mark of your devotion to Him. He has no need of your gold as proof of your worth. He *knows* your worth. You are His blessed sons, with whom He is already pleased. He has opened the gate and invited you to sit with Him at the table. Why do you hesitate? *He* finds you worthy. He enfolds you in His embrace and yet you deny Him!"

He threw up his hands in disgust and walked away from the now silent crowd, shaking his head. Andrew trailed behind sheepishly. The priests did not follow, nor the soldier. But he had ceased thinking of them, worrying instead about his hot-tempered brother.

*

Simon Peter made one last appeal for us to return to Joseph's. "I am not sure we should stay here. This is too public a place and we will have no privacy. It would be more comfortable, would it not, for a group this size to stay at Joseph's compound *outside* the city walls."

He looked around, hoping someone would back him up.

But my cousin only smiled. "It is alright, my friend. Death stalks us from our first breath. It is not our enemy; fear is. We are safe here. Besides ... it is not yet my time." He said the last words almost to himself.

The inn had two large tubs and a huge hearth for heating water. It was not long before we were all refreshed with clean clothes and at prayer giving thanks for our safe and speedy arrival.

I loved Jerusalem, knew its stones as well as the bones of my own body. And Shavuot was an especially colorful festival, enlivening a city that had lately been laboring under rumor and oppression. Each family drew a cart from their own villages laden with the first fruits of the year. The layers were set down according to strict tradition with wheat sheaves at the bottom, then dates and other dried fruit, olives and grapes piled on top. If poor, the men pulled the cart with their own strength. Goats or even donkeys pulled the larger carts of the affluent.

The outer courts were filled with men waiting to offer gifts to the temple for the annual blessing. Here and there people spontaneously burst into songs of thanksgiving. They were commemorating the day Moses sealed his covenant with God, and expressing gratitude for the first harvests of the new year. Beggars lined the roads with hands stretched out, hoping for their share of the abundance. Dancers and musicians played hand-made instruments or beat tambourines and cymbals, hoping to earn a few pennies. No one went hungry during this festival.

"It makes me sick," said Naomi, "this smell of burning flesh."

Our arms entwined, I nodded agreement. There had been abundant rain and perfect temperatures, resulting in an overflow of offerings to the temple. But some wanted to be seen as more generous than others, to win favor with the powerful Sanhedrin. And only the sacrifice of animals could accomplish that.

Naomi and I walked together toward Joseph's city home, where we would convene for dinner. James and the other men had spent the afternoon there, engrossed in some business or other. The other women had gone ahead and the two of us lingered awhile just outside the temple, watching the crowds.

It had been long since I'd seen Naomi. She was like a sister, traveling to Egypt with Miriam and me where we studied the mysteries, and the sacred arts of healing and the dance.

"I've missed you, my friend," I said, squeezing her arm.

"And I, you. Elois insisted she needed me in Carmel. Often I told her my heart was calling me to join the rest of you, but each time she asked me to trust her that my place was there, teaching, preparing the next generation for what is to come. 'But *what* is that; what is to come?' I'd ask her. She would never answer this question.

"And so I stopped asking. Then last week she called me to her room after classes were finished and told me – without any preliminaries – that it was now time to go."

"I am sure Elois and your students will miss you, but it seems right that you are here with us now. Jesus is your cousin too, and from what he says, and even more from what he doesn't say, there will be need of our training in the healing arts. We were initiated in the chamber of death in the great pyramid for a reason. We need you here."

"Your words frighten me, Veronica."

"They are not meant to. It is my hope they will instead rekindle the flame of those days, bringing your learning to mind, and reawakening the instincts needed to offer healing wherever it is needed. You are back among your family now."

"Yes, I know that. Elois treated me like a daughter, but I never really felt at home there. And while I loved teaching, I always felt I was in exile."

"In some ways, it's true. We are all in exile here, away from our true home," I replied.

"You are starting to sound like *him*," she laughed.

She's right, I thought. I suppose it was to be expected that those of us who lived our lives around Jesus would begin to reflect the teachings he had shared with us.

"Shall we start for Joseph's?" I asked. Naomi nodded. "When did you leave Carmel?"

"Two days after that conversation I was on the road to Jerusalem. It was like a dream. I had been at the school so long I'd forgotten what the rest of the world was like. And now I'm here, with you and Miriam, and Jesus and James and ... and everyone!"

I felt the emotion in my friend's voice, as we walked through the colorful crowd. Suddenly, a hand tugged at the bag where I'd put the packets of spices just purchased. I jerked the bag away and found a pair of frightened eyes looking up at me. The woman was dressed in rags, with a baby secured in a shawl tied at her shoulder. I grabbed her arm to keep her from running away.

"Here, sister" I whispered, removing a coin from the scarf at my waist. "Take this."

Eyes that loomed impossibly large above bony cheeks, filled with tears. Her mouth opened as if to speak, but nothing came from her quivering lips. "God loves you and your child" I said, squeezing her hand, and turned away. I could not bear to see the question in her eyes: if God loves me, why do I feel so abandoned?

How do you say to someone in her circumstances that though God is love, and loves all alike, the problem is *our* refusal to share the bounty of the Mother? *We* must be that love in the world. And so far ... we have failed to do so.

Naomi and I walked on in silence, a counterpoint to the deafening noise of the crowds. It was a relief to enter the gate to Joseph's small compound.

James grabbed my arm and pulled me over to a group standing near the kitchen door. "Joseph has been waiting for you," he said.

"Veronica!" he shouted. "There you are! Come. I was telling them about the great storm that greeted you and Miriam on the way to

Penzance."

"To this day I cannot think of that without feeling queasy," I answered, grabbing my stomach. "Can we jump ahead and speak instead of the gentle ride across the lake?"

Joseph laughed and nodded. "Yes, that is where I was going." And his voice turned suddenly serious. "The events of today are the culmination of that day."

I felt ill at ease as my uncle told the group about what he called our initiatory experience around the sacred pool at the bottom of the great Tor. Except for Jesus and James, I don't think either Miriam or I had ever spoken to anyone of the events of that day ... not even in full to mother or Mary.

When he had finished, everyone turned to look at me. I looked around for Miriam, hoping to have her at my side to field any questions. But she was nowhere to be seen.

"What did that mean ... 'seeding the dispensation of grace?'" asked Thomas.

Uncle stood patiently while I thought how to respond. Miriam and I had been told that was the purpose of the ceremony, indeed why we had been brought to that far northern land.

"I am not sure I understand it fully, even now. It is something that only the heart can know." I stalled. They waited. "My heart tells me that Miriam and I were brought there for two reasons. One is our connection, through birth and circumstance, to the ancient prophecy destined to play out here in our own land."

As I said those words, I felt lifted out of myself, almost as if I stood alone in a cave, cool and quiet. My own voice echoed back to me from out of the stillness.

"The other is that the Goddess had drawn us to her, as parts of Her very self, to prepare us to stand in her stead as the bride to the bridegroom." I was shocked to hear myself say such things. Where had it come from, I wondered?

"Just so," said a man's voice.

"None can stand alone within the light. At least not until we stand shoulder to shoulder with the One who carries the waters of life in the age to come."

The heat of the night closed in around me and I knew myself again, standing between my uncle on the one side, and my cousin on the other.

All eyes moved to Jesus. He put his hand lightly upon mine, steadying me, while he continued. "Our Father and Mother exist together in the heavens, neither one complete without the other. Yes," he said, answering the unspoken question, "even our Father in heaven. In perfect union they claim sanctuary in our hearts." His hands rose to cross over his chest. "Will you invite them in?"

I looked around at the men who stood with Joseph, and wondered what they thought hearing such words. To the Sanhedrin it would be considered blasphemy. Tradition speaks only of the Father. Our women's circles always include the divine Mother, but I knew this was not spoken of among men, except perhaps an esoteric reference to the feminine Shekina. But even then, some rabbis chose to ignore the allusion and instead speak of Shekina as 'a place' – telling us that God is complete only when He is in His *home*.

"The son of the Father and Mother sheds light on the lessons of his divine birth. He is the issue of both, in equal parts. And both are in him. These mysteries are played out again and again within our world."

I wanted to move back into the shadows, except my cousin's hand now held my wrist. There were too many eyes upon us for comfort.

He went on: "Veronica and Miriam stood together under the down-pouring of the waters of life, to serve as a surrogate womb for the divine Mother. What happened there, and now here will resound throughout the whole world. The Mother is mother to all, uniting us in the golden thread of her love. These women are Her daughters, as I am the Father's son. And so are you sons and daughters of the All."

I would be surprised if there were more than a handful of men or even women who understood a word he said. How does one speak of such things? I knew in my heart that my cousin's path was being cleared by the women who went before him, and that he would never reach his destination without us. He had said as much, many times, that he depended upon us to do what he came to do. I resisted that at first, even argued with him. But then, one night in vision, the divine Mother came and showed me that what he said was true. We were to him as the night sky is to the stars, or as the moon is to the sun. Together we keep the earth and the heavens in balance.

Joseph broke the silence by calling Rebecca over to refill our cups.

Nicodemus took my hand from Jesus and led me away.

"I am sorry, my dear, that you were placed in such an awkward position. These are young men, mostly unschooled in the ancient teachings. Joseph is trying to give them a condensed course, hoping to bring them understanding. But to suddenly throw the Goddess at them must be a shock!" He chuckled.

"Thomas, I have no doubt, will understand, but even some of the twelve will resist the call to accept you as equals. Everything in our tradition argues against it, unless they have come under sway of the Brotherhood in one form or another."

I loved Nicodemus. He and my uncle risked everything by standing with us as they did. Somehow – no doubt it had something to do with their wealth – they managed to retain their standing within the Sanhedrin even while quietly supporting a group as unorthodox as ours.

We did not seek revolt against the Romans, nor did we wish to force radical change upon the Sanhedrin. I knew my cousin did not reach for political office, or even a position in the priesthood. He had told us countless times all he wanted was for each of us to awaken the divine spirit within us.

I hated being put on display, by Joseph or anyone else. And while he was a kind and just man, he never hesitated to use others to accomplish his objectives. The object in this case – I realized later – was to prepare us for the trials to come. Those present at his house that evening were being challenged to find tolerance and courage within them. And I was offered a taste of what it was like to risk everything by standing in front of a potentially hostile gathering.

Chapter Seven

PASSING THE TORCH

The morning winds had died down. Soon the heat would drive us indoors. There were few trees on our side of the hill, and the sun was robbing us of the little shade we had.

We sat quietly meditating together after morning prayers. Our numbers waxed and waned, depending upon the political climate. Scores came to walk with us for a time, most of them eventually returning to their everyday lives. It wasn't easy sustaining interest in something they didn't really understand. Many joined our group expecting Jesus to rise up against the Romans and their Jewish underlings, usurping Herod as King. The rest didn't really know what to expect, outside a vague hope their personal circumstances might be improved.

Few were interested in searching their hearts. Had they done so, they might have discovered the very sins for which they sought to blame others. It was easier to sacrifice an animal at Passover or Shavuot, and be done with it.

Fewer still gave serious thought to his words, which continually challenged us to follow his example – entering the personal fires of purification, rather than expecting him to solve all our problems for us. He taught us the way of the heart, which is the way to God. Truth be told, my own understanding of what this means still falls short.

That morning I had finished my meditation and sat looking out toward the horizon, to Bethany. I looked around at the men and women sitting here and there on rocks, or the rock-hard earth. Though most had by then opened their eyes, none had yet moved, each luxuriating in the silence, enjoying the morning coolness.

I absentmindedly counted those gathered. My cousin aside, there were twelve men and twelve women. Having learned the significance of numbers while in Egypt, I was struck by the natural symmetry. From that day forward I made a point of counting those who came to study with him. And even though some who were among us that day left the group, others took their place – and most of the time *we numbered twelve and twelve*. I could not imagine this was by chance. Twelve was a master number, and the same number of men and women meant perfect balance at the highest level. When Naomi, Miriam and I studied sacred architecture in Egypt, we learned that numbers rather than aesthetics underlay the orientation and proportions of the temples and other consecrated buildings not just in Egypt, but across the breadth of our world.

That day out on the hill, the men and women had begun to rise while I sat pondering this new mystery, their voices muted like buzzing bees hovering around my thoughts. A hand on my arm brought me back, and I looked up into Naomi's smiling face.

I stood and hugged her. "It is so wonderful having you back among us. You must promise never to leave again."

"Sister, I can promise no such thing," she laughed. "We come and go as we must. You know that."

"Ah, yes, I do. Well then, I shall ask you something easy. Promise never to forget we love you." She laughed.

Jesus came up and took my free hand and the three of us were walking down the hill together when we heard a woman's voice call from below. Even before I could make out the words, I saw it was Mary, sister to Lazarus and Martha.

"I was afraid you had left," she said, out of breath. "Martha's servant said she'd seen you pass through the gate early this morning while she was out on an errand."

"We are leaving soon, but wouldn't do so without saying goodbye," said Jesus, kissing the older woman's forehead.

"Come to dinner tonight then. There are some people I want you to meet."

Mary wasn't the only person looking for us. A large crowd had gathered just inside the city gate and set upon Jesus the moment he came into sight.

"Master, my daughter fell and hit her head," a man shouted over the crowd. "She has been in a swoon since yesterday."

Jesus turned to the man and the crowd parted so he could approach. My cousin reached out and took the man's hands in his own, holding them in silence. The intensity of his gaze caused the man to flush and look away. But Jesus would not release his hands. With a sigh he turned back, opening his mouth as if to speak – but it hung slack when words escaped him. Suddenly his whole body began to tremble and his knees buckled. But Jesus held him with his eyes. I could feel the man's tension in my own body. Finally Jesus said, "Go home to your wife, and child," letting go his hands. Without a word he turned and ran back through the crowd, which immediately pressed in against my cousin.

"Rabbi, the priests say you have sinned. The other day, on the Sabbath, you healed a woman of fever at the well. And you stood outside the inn and spoke to a crowd of things that should not be said to women, and then only *inside* the synagogue."

"You mean I spoke of God."

"Well, yes, you were talking about forgiveness, forgiving the Romans and the Samaritans," he agreed, and spat on the ground at their names.

"The woman with the fever had drunk from the well," said Jesus. His accuser nodded. "And that which gave rise to her fever might have gone to others who likewise drink from the same source."

The man nodded again, only this time he did not look so certain. And I wondered who had sent him to say those things.

"And you are saying that God should not occupy our thoughts and words except inside the synagogues, or maybe that God lives only inside temples and not in people's homes or hearts or on city streets or mountaintops. Further, you say that God does not speak to women, but only to men! And that we should take care not to become ill on the Sabbath, because on that day God will not care what happens to us." He looked at the man with a mix of frustration and compassion, understanding he believed only what he had been taught.

"If your wife had broken her leg on the Sabbath and leaving her for the following day would make her a cripple, would you ask me to let her lie?" he asked one man, who shook his head no.

"And you, sister, if your child was bitten by a snake, would you let that child die for the sake of the Sabbath? 'No,' she whimpered, shocked at the question.

"God is here," he said, pointing to his chest, "and here and here," he added, putting his hand over the hearts of others standing in front of him.

"Where we stand, God is. There is nowhere God is not."

Just then the man whose child had lain in a coma came running towards us, his daughter in his arms. Again, he tried to speak, but could not.

"Papa, why are you crying," the girl asked him in alarm, struggling to get down. "And why do you carry me when I can walk?"

"They are tears of happiness, that is all," said Jesus, stroking the girl's forehead.

"Be joyful, all of you," he said to those assembled, "for today you are reminded of God's love which can heal all things."

"How dare you speak as if you know the unknowable? Who do you think you are?" growled a man in priest's robes, standing at the outside of the circle.

"And you, do you not speak for God?" countered Jesus.

"I read from the Torah, and do not presume to know Him whose name should not be spoken." And he turned and walked away. The people looked back to Jesus, awaiting his response.

"Our Father speaks through me, it is true." Some gasped at his impudence. "But any of you could say the same."

"You blaspheme!" someone shouted.

He calmly replied, "I am His son, as are you. He longs to speak through you, and you, and you. The Mother breathes life through us in every breath we take. We are never divorced from our holy Mother and Father, nor because of Them, from each other. You and I are sons and daughters of the one eternal God."

At this he turned and walked away. But when we tried to follow he said to us: "I go now to be alone. But there is great need here and it is time you each begin your own work, attending to those who suffer in body and in mind. It is not enough to follow me. You know this already but still fear the power that lives within you. This power must be released into the world. The one who surrenders to it will walk at my side."

From that moment on he no longer allowed us to stand in his shadow. From the beginning, even from our childhood together, he had insisted we were no different than him. But I don't think I ever really believed it. Even today I sometimes falter, taking refuge in my inadequacies. But then or now, he has never indulged me my fears.

*

No matter where we went after that day the crowds gathered around him and he would stop to comfort and heal, often from sunrise to sunset, for days on end. Now and then someone appeared to challenge his authority, sometimes threatening him if he continued to heal and preach so indiscriminately. But still the crowds grew, following us on the road from city to city, infringing on our meals and sleep.

Once, in Nazareth, someone threw a stone, laying a cut across the side of his head. In moments a furious mob appeared out of nowhere, stones in hand. I had noticed a Roman soldier watching us from his horse across the square, and ran in his direction, desperately hoping for help. But before I could reach him his horse reared and charged into the crowd, shouting for people to disperse, threatening to put anyone to the spear who would harm us. The mob scattered with sullen looks, not waiting to see how serious the threat was. The soldier left the square before we could thank him.

But I have never been able to forget his face. His expression confused me. It was not anger or simple loathing of the rabble. I realized later he was frightened – and not for his own person, but for us. *For Jesus.*

"Cousin," I asked, as we sat round a campfire on our return to Capernaum. "Why would that Roman have come to our aid?"

"Do you think our Creator smiles only upon us Hebrews ... that others are incapable of hearing and responding to His will?"

"No, of course not. But why would *he* have come to the aid of a Jew who is being threatened by other Jews? It would have made more sense for him to just turn away and let us settle the matter among ourselves."

I was a little embarrassed at my own question. Marcus and Julius were sitting nearby, and I had known other kind Romans before them. But this man was a Roman soldier, *in the employ of Rome.* How could he reconcile what he did, I wondered?

"In part because it is his job to keep the peace, and preventing a stoning would accomplish that. But I saw something in his eyes," said Jesus. "I know you did as well."

"Yes, but what?"

"He *knew* me, Veronica. He recognized that the light that shines in my heart shines also in his. He, a Roman, understands the one thing that most of you still resist. The light cannot prevail unless Jews and Gentiles learn to stand together, unless men and women recognize that in their differences they complete one another, unless we forget our ancient grievances and forgive our own trespasses and those we imagine committed against us.

"You," he said indicating Miriam and myself, "helped plant the seed for the time to come while on the Holy Isle. But it took an age before that for the seed to be fashioned, which was the work of our entire Brotherhood. It would be wrong to think this seed was planted only in my heart."

I *had* thought so, and also that we were there to support him when he offered salvation to ... to whom? I am not so sure I fully appreciated the universality of his mission before that, even though I had been taught it from childhood. And if I found discrimination in my own heart, what of the many that hadn't been given the same privileges I had?

"Veronica, do not judge yourself so harshly," he said, knowing my thoughts. "We work together to root out the old hatreds, and we do this with love, with love's forgiveness – and nothing else. We have only ourselves as examples. As you rise above the old way of thinking, you should be heartened to know that just so each man and woman can rise above theirs."

He told me that one of my roles was to serve as an example to others as they became aware of their faults and weaknesses. My openness to him allowed me to risk public exposure, and while that was could be painful for me, he said others were often inspired by my courage. While people sometimes refused to see his failings – and he insisted he had many – they would benefit from seeing the rest of us overcome ours.

I wasn't sure if his saying that made me feel better or worse than before. But he assured me people would trust me because of it. And from that place of trust would accept what I offered to them – the teachings I had been given: healing, love, forgiveness.

*

"He should have known better," came a whisper from the crowd.

"He said nothing that hadn't already been said a hundred times by other men."

"But those others did not have so many followers, and with Herod's spies scattered among them."

John, called the Baptist, had spoken out one too many times against Herod Antipas and his new wife, Herodius. And now he had been arrested. The real surprise was that it had not happened before then.

It was the only topic of conversation that morning in the marketplace. We had been in Capernaum a few days when the news hit. Everyone, it seemed, knew that we were somehow associated with John, even though he had stayed far south of Galilee until recently. Why he decided to travel north, I could not imagine. In going to Tiberius he was placing his accusations at Herod's doorstep. The king could no longer pretend not to hear.

I am embarrassed to say I was relieved when I heard what had happened. With all the stares and whispers I wondered if Jesus and the rest us were ourselves in danger.

"His life is at risk," Rachel said, her eyes rimmed in red.

"Did they tell you that?" asked Helen. My old friend had recently arrived after many years in Alexandria. Sequestered in the school there, she'd had little contact with political intrigue.

"Herodius will not rest until her accuser is dead," Rachel answered flatly. "That is what they are saying. We must go to him."

"What? Are you mad? We would only draw attention back to us, to Jesus," said Miriam. "We cannot do that."

"But he is his cousin, and our friend! It is he who cleared the path for Jesus, and pointed to him as the chosen one. We owe him much," insisted Rachel.

"I will accompany you, if you insist on going." It was Arturus.

"Oh, thank you! Can you be ready in the morning?"

He nodded. "My lady, I will go with you, but I ask that you pray for guidance whether it is a fool's journey. I would not see your head on the block with John's."

I heard a gasp from behind us and turned to see my sister Elizabeth, who had arrived from Nazareth just the day before. She'd stayed behind when we left, helping with the younger children.

"Please do not go," she pleaded to no one in particular. "Arturus is right. They will not let you see John. There is nothing you can do."

That night many gathered in the home of Simon and Miriam for dinner. We borrowed a table and extra chairs from a neighbor, as there was not enough seating for everyone.

"Where is he?" asked Thomas.

"The stories conflict, but I believe he is chained in a dungeon on the Bitter Sea, as Herodius did not want him anywhere near her."

"What was his sentence?"

"No one knows for sure. I do not think he has been condemned to death."

"The dungeon will be worse than death for John."

"We must go to him," Simon shouted into the night sky. He and Andrew, as well as John and Philip had once traveled with John, as close to him then as they were to Jesus now.

Many spoke that evening, some for and some against going to his aid. But the one for whom we waited to give his opinion said nothing. Later, with just a few of us left lingering in the darkness, Miriam asked Jesus what he thought should be done.

"His work is finished," he said. "If Rachel or another feel called to go, I will not stop them. But there is nothing to be done."

Though his voice was gentle, his words sounded harsh in my ears. I even considered he might be afraid for himself, but realized later I was putting my own thoughts on him. He was right, of course. There *was* nothing to be done.

Rachel was talked out of going, but only because Simon and Philip said they would go in her stead, along with Arturus. The three were gone from the new moon to the full, and each day Rachel fretted she had sent them to their death. Only Jesus was able to comfort her, as she trusted his vision that they remained unharmed. No one asked him about John's welfare though, afraid of the answer.

"We were not allowed to see him, not even once," Philip said on their return, his voice quavering. "We spoke with him on several occasions through the bars of a high window, and for that privilege we had to pay handsomely."

"We talked," said Arturus. "John listened."

"How do you even know it was he?" asked Rachel.

"We heard his voice just twice. Once he asked about Jesus. We spoke at length then about his travels and ministry. He wanted to hear it all. And on our last visit he asked us to give his cousin a private message, which we have done."

"And that was it? Has he been beaten? Does he eat? Is he well?" asked Rachel desperately. I had only recently learned the reason for Rachel's personal distress. After their parents died, Rachel had served for a time as John and his sister Martha's step-mother, and thought of him as a son.

"Despite that, we were never close," she told us that evening. "He had no friends, in the usual sense. John thought of nothing beyond the destiny that had been laid at his feet.

"Jesus is right. There is nothing that could have been done to stop him … and nothing to be done now." With one hand she brushed the wisps of white hair back from her forehead, and with the other the tears that streamed down her face.

Chapter Eight

THE WOMEN GATHER POWER

A deep thrumming moved across the dark, silencing the night creatures. The past two nights had been filled with the sounds of crickets and owls and the occasional wild dog or night hawk. It had been some time since I'd been out of the city, and longer still since I had slept so close to the land.

There were no beds, no stuffed mats. Those who chose to sleep indoors threw their shawls onto the tamped earthen floor. I spent the first night inside. But the air was stale and I decided to brave the cold the next night, sleeping under a star-splashed sky. The soil had a faint spicy smell, leaving its scent in my hair and clothes.

I often dreamt of people and places unknown to me. My old teacher Zebedee used to speak of our night journeys, and showed me how to arrange them in advance when there was great need. Once I tied to visit my cousin in his travels, but in the morning the many fragments of sights and sounds and emotions overwhelmed me. Nothing I recalled made sense. When Zebedee quizzed me about my dreams that morning -- which he often did – his brow furrowed.

"I have told you not to do this for selfish purposes. You gained nothing but confusion."

"But dreams *are* often confusing," I protested. "And besides, I only wanted to know how he was. How could that be harmful?"

"Dreams are mysterious. They help us learn to read signs and symbols, to speak the language of the soul. But if you seek to travel beyond the body for the sake of satisfying curiosity alone, it is little different than peering through someone's window without their knowledge.

"Your cousin already shares with you what he wishes of his travels, and confides in you as seems appropriate to him. Night travel is for helping others in need, or to enhance your knowledge and daytime training. Your soul is the master of your dreams."

As the years went by, I realized the most important lesson to this was learning to recognize the call of my soul. Responding to its call ultimately becomes as natural as answering a knock on the door.

That night in Carmel out under the stars, the knock was forceful and unequivocal. But instead of being drawn to aid someone in need or to an exposition on an earthly lesson, I found myself propelled beyond the world I knew. At first I felt overwhelmed by nausea, though that made no sense since I was quite certain I traveled in spirit and not in my body.

The first thing I saw (once the nausea had passed) was a group of men and women who were taking seats around a long table. Except for Jesus the others were only vaguely familiar to me. He waved me over to the group, and indicated a particular seat at the table. The chair looked heavy, but I found it almost weightless when I pulled it back to sit down. My cousin sat at one end of the table, and a woman sat at the other end. Otherwise we alternated male and female all around, twelve and twelve. The woman at the end seemed very queenly to me, though her robes were simple enough, and she wore no ornamentation beyond a single large blue gemstone at her throat.

No one opened their mouth to speak, and yet I heard words in my head – real words and not just thoughts (as sometimes happens in visions). The speaker said that the end was not far off, and that the end would be the beginning.

A woman's voice then spoke of ascending a mountain slowly, going round and round until we reached the top. She said it would often seem as if we were making no progress, and nodding at me, warned us not to become discouraged. Our way was true and assured of success only if we kept our family (seated round that table) foremost in mind, never ceasing in our support of one another. If one of us forgot our purpose or began losing sight of the goal, it was up to each of us to remind them.

When all of us had renewed our pledge of mutual support, the table transformed into a mighty tree, with huge, leaf-filled branches. We circled the tree holding hands. I do not recall what lay behind us, but had the feeling the tree grew at the very center of our world, and that its roots held everything in place.

We sang songs of gratitude for things that had passed, and for things to come, for pain as for pleasure, for joy and sadness alike. It doesn't make much sense that we would thank the Creator for pain and sadness, yet when pondering that tree and the holy family singing our praise and gratitude, I only recall tears of joy.

Once back under the stars (instead of being out among them) I knew I must at all costs recall the joy I experienced around the tree, no matter what may come.

After a time I fell asleep, awaking at dawn curled into a tight ball. There was frost on the ground and I was stiff with cold. Someone had lit a fire in the hearth set against the outer wall. A few women were speaking in quiet voices.

I recognized Jania and Edithia in the shadows, and Mary and Mary Salome, my mother, and Naomi, all wrapped in heavy shawls. A dozen of us had come together in the ancient building near the school where at one time or another each of us had trained. The building was rarely used, except by women and then only for vision questing.

Jania handed me a large cup of steaming tea, filled with mint leaves. The leaves had been partially dried; those on the plants growing next to the house were wilted with the frost. Pots of boiling water kept the tea flowing and our hands warm, until the sun reached over the walls.

We did not speak of our night journeys until all the women were up and gathered. We knew each would bring a different piece to help unravel the mystery of what lay ahead of us. We had gathered at sunset the night before to ask our angels and other guiding spirits to bring us to our knowing -- and then retired in separate directions, in the expectation our request would be honored.

We were witnessing the changing tides of time, with profound implications for us, and for all mankind. I had seen in my own earthly travels representatives of the Brotherhood that tied us together, and learned of others whom my cousin had met in other lands. And while they chose not to draw attention to themselves, I had since childhood witnessed an array of people with strange dress coming to our small town, who met behind closed doors with the elders, only to leave within a day or two as quietly as they had come. Uncle Joseph said we could count on our brothers – men and women, known and unknown to us – for their support.

"But support of what?" I once asked him. "We do not even know ourselves what we are doing, or why. If someone else knows, if *you* know, why aren't we told?"

"Each of us knows one part; none knows the whole of what is to come. You have received training in the language of the stars, and have had your own measure of visions. It is enough for now to point you in the direction of your soul's purpose.

"Your cousin is the guiding star, and when the time comes his light will ignite our own, and together we will fire the heavens and transform the earth."

My own light did not seem worthy of such an undertaking. But next to Jesus, James and our mothers, there was no one I trusted more than Joseph.

On that particular morning each woman spoke of her experience. Some had dreamed; a few, like me, had traveled far into the light, while others had been in prayer. After the sharing we sat together in silence. A picture was beginning to take form and what I saw did not reassure me.

After a time Edithia stood, took up her shawl and walked out through the gate. Mother nodded at me and we followed her. The air was still. Not a hint of breeze rose up to us from the sea below. "It is the calm before the storm," Edithia whispered when we caught up to her. Looking out over the water she sighed: "The lesson of John should not be lost on us."

She had been one of the Baptist's followers. But, like many, she left him to join my cousin after his anointing in the river. John had encouraged them to leave, saying his time had come and gone, while Jesus stood at the cusp of a new era. When she protested, John said Jesus would have need of people like her who were intimate with the unseen realms and strong enough to stand with him in his need.

"Surely you do not think *he* is in danger of arrest," mother asked.

Edithia shot her a look that seemed to say, 'surely you do not think he is safe.'

Mother flushed. "You do, then. And what of the rest of us?" She looked at me worriedly.

"John is lost to us," Edithia said." He has told us so." Her face seemed to me surprisingly calm. "We do not know what will happen, but we do know each of us will be tested, and for that we women must stand together. He will need our strength."

That night we built a great bonfire just beyond the walls of the cottage. Gathering within the flickering shadows we sang and danced, and danced some more until the very air vibrated with our power, and the darkness shone with our radiance. We did not sleep, but spent the long night of the dark moon recalling the divine Mother who moves through the world as each of us.

Elois had not joined us in our rites. Though she still headed the school in Carmel, she was then quite old and no longer went out, even so short a distance as that. So we went to her before beginning our return journey.

A young girl met us at the gate and led us to her mistresses' rooms.

"Thank you Maya," said Elois. The girl had recently arrived from

Hindustan, one of a continuing river of boys and girls that came to Carmel from all parts of our world, keeping alive the Brotherhood of which we were a part.

Elois looked from me to Miriam to Naomi and Helen, and laughed at our stares. "Did you think I would never get old? My dears, even the stars will one day die out. How else can we be reborn?"

It had been some time since I'd seen my old teacher and she looked small and frail with shawls wrapped around her shoulders and feet. She was right. It had never occurred to me she might one day grow old and leave us.

She had the four of us sit with her, while the older women stood back, encircling the room. It wasn't until later that I realized the mantle of power had been passed from the old woman to the four of us that day. Ordinarily the process of succession would have been a formal one, passed from one woman to another woman, rather than from one to four of us. And the new leader would already be wizened, having lived a full cycle of life, and ready to serve as head of the school on her own. (As had happened when Elois took over from Judy.)

But the four of us were young. And rather than remaining cloistered in the school, each of us would carry one corner of the mantle of power out into the world, holding it over the changing landscape, offering a salve to heal the wounds that occur during the struggles to come.

I think Elois understood the significance of our visit, though she chattered happily about little things. She never spoke of John or Jesus, or what lay ahead, but their fates, and ours, lingered behind her every word like the shadows of butterfly wings.

Nor did we speak of the events of the previous three days, knowing she had in some sense been with us, and knew the whole of it. We left with her blessing, and my heart told me I would not see her again. Though I loved her, I was not sad.

Chapter Nine

A LIGHT IN THE DARKNESS

"What happened there, in the river with John?" Zebedee's son James asked Jesus.

"Yes, what happened?" echoed Simon. Miriam's brother opened his home whenever we came to Galilee, and a group of us had gathered that evening out under the ancient olive trees by the back wall.

"You stood in the water in front of John," said James. "You were saying something to him, and then I thought you'd lost your footing in the fast-moving current. But then …"James' mouth worked as he searched for words, but none came.

All eyes were trained on Jesus, waiting for his answer. The men and women gathered there comprised the core of his followers. We had become close, though not all of us were necessarily friends. Some of us were opposites in every way, and except for my cousin would have had nothing in common with each other. I wish I could say this brought forth our higher natures, but more and more it seemed we fell to the other extreme.

Most often a simple look from him was sufficient to calm the situation. Instead of speaking to our suspicious, judgmental selves, he simply reaffirmed the best in us. He loved us without asking anything in return. I saw that as our capacity to accept such unconditional love increased, our ability to serve others likewise grew larger.

There were times he simply did not answer a question – for reasons of his own – but after an interlude, he responded. "I surrendered myself to the waters of life that day." His graceful hands began to move through the air demonstrating the churning motion of water. "Even as we stand here in Simon's garden, we are immersed in its livingness, ourselves alive because of it.

"You might think it is the actual water that sustains you, that without water you hasten your death. But water is only the carrier of life, as is our breath. That which sustains us cannot be seen or drunk or known by the body of flesh. *Life* ... is not dependent upon this body."

While a few of us had trained in the ancient teachings and understood his words, for many those concepts were unfamiliar. To them it seemed he spoke in riddles. Thaddeus stood behind him, rocking impatiently from foot to foot; the other Judas (Iscariot) sat off to the side, wearing a frown.

"We are born, live awhile, and die back to the earth. But *life* cannot die. Only the form dies.

"John is a lion among men. As many as are drawn to him, there are countless more who fear him, fear his message. He inspired many to enter the waters of transformation, challenging us to surrender our old ways that the light of life can flow freely through us. As symbol of my surrender, I immersed myself in the water at John's feet.

"He prepared the way for me, at great sacrifice to himself." Jesus looked at each of us in turn, and though I could not see him clearly from where I sat, I thought I saw tears in his eyes. "You who followed John, and loved and supported him – I am also in your debt."

"The light ... what was the light we saw around you there?" whispered Marcus.

"There is but one light and it is always with us."

As if in answer an arc of lightning shot up through the night and for a moment the sky shone brighter than day, startling sleeping dogs around the neighborhood into a noisy chorus. Some of the men leapt to their feet: Marcus drew his sword.

Jesus held his hand up, and the radiant light faded to a golden luminosity. A charged silence followed, and I knew that no matter the challenges to come, nothing would turn me aside from following my cousin as he went out to meet his fate.

"This light is what you saw in the river," he said, "reflecting the Mother's love and the Father's purpose, giving birth to the awakened son who knows himself. It is your destiny, as well as mine. In relinquishing earth's fortunes, you are granted the eternal treasures of heaven. In surrendering your little life, you are awarded eternal life. In serving the light, you will discover it serves you."

No one spoke after that. Words are pitiful containers for the riches they are sometimes called to carry.

Thaddeus and Philip walked away into the night, whispering between them, with Judas close behind. The others rose to embrace Jesus, and then retreated into the shadow of Simon's house, or left for their own home.

*

"He has been so quiet lately. I wonder if something's bothering him."

Susanna voiced my own concerns. People followed us everywhere, calling out to him for healing or a kind word. There were times he seemed lost in thought, not hearing them. It was not unlike when he first returned from the desert.

Miriam had not seemed herself either. I doubted they'd been fighting. Over the years she had come to a quiet acceptance of his life, and her part in it.

Others had been asking the same question, and my answer was always the same: I don't know.

Mary and mother were planning to return to Nazareth the following morning. Though I would miss them, in a strange way their plans comforted me. I knew Mary would not be away from her son if she thought he was in danger. I had a little time alone with them before dinner, and decided to ask if they knew something I did not.

"You know him almost as well as I," said Mary. "He has always had need of time to himself. The difference is he no longer has that luxury."

Her voice was quiet, and she did not look at me as she spoke, which was unlike her. Mary always gave people her full attention, fixing her luminous eyes upon them as if speaking to their soul as well as their person.

I glanced at mother who had sat down on a chair beneath the open window. She watched as her sister packed her few clothes into a bag for their journey. I could not read her face.

Having run out of things to occupy her attention, Mary stopped and looked at me. "It is almost impossible for him to go apart on his own – by ordinary means. And he is loathe to do as he can, as it will only increase unwelcome speculation."

She sat down on the bed, and mother went to join her. I knew what she meant. I had seen my cousin simply disappear from sight several times. He was careful not to display his unusual abilities in public; the confusion offered by crowds generally masked such a departure. (I wouldn't even notice him go, though once I had stood right next to him.) But of late his every move was scrutinized, his every word analyzed. No one seemed to take thought for the *man*. Indeed, if his friends did not create some boundaries around him on occasion, it is likely people wouldn't leave him alone day or night.

"Yes ... I understand," I said.

Mother put her arm around her sister. Mary leaned against her with a long sigh. I saw in that moment how the mother was carrying her son's burden.

"You also forget to take care for yourself," she said to me. "You and Miriam, and some of the others. He needs you, but he needs you to be strong and healthy."

"I am fine," said a voice from the doorway. It was Miriam. "You do not need to worry about me; I have long known the journey, perhaps better than he."

"This is true. Judy began preparing us when we were children, just as she did with you," I nodded to the two older women. "And much of our time in Egypt was given to readying us for our part – though I confess even now it isn't always clear to me."

"That is because the role itself continues to change," said Mary. "Though we preceded you, Salome and I are not the first to have undergone rigorous training. There is a long line of women, stretching back to the beginning of our history, without whom we would not be here today. My son would not be here today."

"And not just our own history, either," mother added. "Most priests think only of us Hebrews. Actually, they think only of those who believe as they do, whether Pharisee or Sadducee. Even we Essenes fall victim to such narrowness of thinking, saying this one is acceptable, while that one is not.

"Differences between Essene communities are sometimes nearly as great as those between Hebrew and Roman. Elois said once that what unites us is circumcision, and little else."

Miriam laughed dryly. "Today I heard Simon complain to James that Jesus spends too much time with the women. Worse, he said – and I could hear the resentment in his voice – Jesus actually asks our council when there are men about in whom he could confide."

"He said this to James? And what did James say?" I asked, incredulous. James had said nothing to me of this.

"He said he *often*, then changed it to *always* heeds your advice on matters of import." She grinned. "He added that since Jesus had lost his father early, both of them were accustomed to talking things over with women. I think he knew I was listening."

"But he always confided in Mary, even when Joseph was alive," interrupted mother.

"Yes, I am sure James knows that, but it's something Simon would understand. I'm guessing the real reason for Simon's anger was probably not any of that. It was me."

"You? Of course, if he were jealous of anyone, it would be you," I said to my friend.

"I have heard grumbling before, but mostly it was done to tease him, as men do about women. But there was bitterness on Simon's tongue."

We would later learn that Simon Peter's father had taught his son to mistrust women, pulling selective quotes out of the Torah to support his own harsh views on that and other subjects.

Later that night Miriam confided her concerns.

"He is not so different from us, you know." She spoke of Jesus. "Anyone in his position would wonder at the wisdom of the path he is taking. He worries much about us, his followers, and what will become of us. He never expected the way to be easy, but it is becoming evermore apparent that the consequences of his acts will affect many people."

"We walk with him willingly."

"Yes, you do and I do. But maybe half our group does not really understand what he is about. They think, or at least they hope he will one day take up arms to lead them into battle – or at least sanction their doing so."

I knew he would never do such a thing. He had told us, told everyone over and over that the kingdom of which he speaks is not of this earth.

"I wonder why he has let Simon and some of the others who are sympathetic with the Zealots into the group," Miriam asked. "Why would he draw the Romans to him in such a way?"

"I have wondered the same thing myself at times. But we know that the kingdom of God is for all people, Jew and Gentile alike. I guess if our Creator does not discriminate, he believes he too must embrace all who come to him."

Miriam nodded, her eyes troubled. "He told me he embraces Simon and Peter and Judas and others who would take heaven by storm if they could, because he cherishes their passion, their desire to bring freedom to Palestine."

"I asked him once *why Matthew*, why bring a tax collector into our midst, one who associates with the Romans and takes money from the poor. And there are the Romans themselves, Arturus, Marcus and Julius."

I understood my friend's concerns. "But again he reminds us we are all the same in God's eyes. How then should he treat them differently? And he is right. I do not know Arturus or Julius well. But I would trust my own life, and that of Jesus, with Marcus. We've also seen how important it is for us to have uncle Joseph and Nicodemus among us, they who know the Sanhedrin and can help mediate for us when there's trouble. It can only help to have Romans and publicans and businessmen around who love him as we do."

We were an odd assortment of men and women, rich and poor, educated and illiterate. Some within our group were intimate with the ancient Brotherhood and its teachings, while others were as innocent of the prophecies as a newborn, or a Roman.

It was our differences that often drew attention to us, which didn't seem helpful to me. But Jesus said he was not here to hide in the shadows. He was here to be a light in the darkness, to give comfort to those who fear, healing to those who suffer – to serve all alike in his Father's name.

A few days later Miriam and I were walking arm in arm along the lakeshore. It was a beautiful warm morning, with only the hint of a breeze. "I asked him yesterday about our group's destiny," she said. "I really wanted to ask about him and his destiny, but sometimes I am afraid to hear those answers."

I understood her reticence. "What did he say?"

"He did not know for certain. He said that man's interpretation of the prophecies and what is written in the stars is imperfect. And more, that what is written is not fixed. He said that each of us is as powerful as God, because God works miracles *through us*. When we turn ourselves over to a life of service we become the hands and the words of the Divine. And just as we were talking about the other day, this cannot be withheld from one, and bestowed upon another. When we learn to love in this way, we gain the right to move heaven and earth to change prophecy.

"He stopped there, but I pressed him, finally finding the courage to ask: 'What is *your* destiny?'

"'I know the final destination, but not all the steps along the way. I have set my feet upon a path and while it is my choice to continue or to turn aside, I am committed to walk it to the very end.'"

There were tears in my friend's eyes and I tried to comfort her, but she would have none of it. "Until my beloved knows peace, I turn my back upon it for myself," she said.

"Very well then." If she could be so brave, then so could I. "The prophecies speak of sacrifice for the good of all. Is he to be sacrificed? Why would he accept this? *And why would God allow it?*"

"I asked him the same thing. He told me it was true, the Son was sent into the world as an offering upon the altar of matter. Through his sacrifice the world will be transformed." Her voice shook as she continued. "But the nature of the sacrifice is not foreordained. If you ask me, it is sacrifice enough for him to walk among those who will not hear his words, to put up with our ignorance. But he has chosen to honor his destiny, to walk the narrow path from darkness into light. He will lead us, those who choose to follow him from the unreal to the real. And this is the way to immortality, our final goal."

"But will he die in the process?" I bit my lip so hard it bled, but I could not help myself.

"I do not know," she said, and together we wept.

Chapter Ten

AWAKENING TO A HIGHER LOVE

"Master, what is prayer? You have said we should pray ceaselessly, but how can we care for our families and our work if we are constantly praying?"

I sat close by, listening as Jesus spoke to a small group of men and women on the steps of a building next to a large synagogue. We had been in Jericho seven days and each day the crowds grew larger.

The sun had not long risen, and my cousin chewed thoughtfully on the dates given him by one of the women. A plate with fresh-baked bread sat on top of a chest-high wall next to him.

We never knew what to expect from the people, even when revisiting the same town. At times it seemed they could not do enough for any of us, opening their homes, offering food, or even a new robe or pair of sandals. And then, usually without warning, someone would turn on us and we'd have to make a quick retreat.

We were in Hebron just before the last full moon. Late one night a man brought his son for healing, only to discover that Jesus had already left. Anna and I offered to do what we could, but he waved us away. Thinking he might be closed to the idea of women ministering (as some were), James offered his assistance.

"Ha! I would not let you touch my son – any of you!" The attack was sudden. "You are charlatans, agents of the evil one, here to deceive us."

"But your son appears ill," insisted James.

"I came to test your Jesus. But he has run away, afraid to be exposed as the fraud he is. He will be punished by God for his deceit."

He went on like this for some time, shouting obscenities and making threats while his poor son continue to suffer from some sort of malady. Jesus returned during the night and we prevailed upon him to stay in the background the following morning. Thanks to God we did. There were Roman guards posted in front of the synagogue, where none had been seen before.

Later Miriam and I were in the market buying provisions for the day's meals when the same man jumped out in front of us with one of the guards in tow, shouting, "There they are! They are sorcerers, apprenticed to the Nazarene who calls himself King of the Jews. They are spreading lies, practicing witchcraft, healing on the Sabbath ...." As he ranted he pulled, then pushed the guard toward us. The Roman stopped an arm's length from me, his eyes searching mine, then Miriam's. Finally he turned and walked away without a word to the fanatical Jew who was left sputtering to himself.

Here in Jericho, at least, we had been welcomed as kin. Even the priests usually received us without the usual suspicion or jealousy, some standing among the crowd listening to Jesus' words with respect.

"Prayer is communion," he began. "Prayer is an attitude, a feeling that cannot be feigned. God will not be fooled by false piety or public devotion. God hears only the heart, and the heart cannot lie."

A woman approached with a small crock of honey. She opened it, pulled a piece of bread from the loaf lying nearby and dipped it into the honey, shyly handing it to him.

Barnabas, standing next to him, made a move as if to intervene. Jesus held his hand up to his friend. "Stay. This woman approaches in an act of prayer. Through her kindness God sees and hears her." Barnabas backed away, his face flushed.

To the woman Jesus said: "You have not asked for a blessing, nor have you spoken unkindly of the one who has so often harmed you, not even to your closest friend. You have seen his pain, and know his anger is at the world, at God, and not at you. You have answered his attacks with forgiveness."

The woman's jaw dropped, her eyes trained on this man who had read her deepest thoughts.

He turned to the crowd and said, "No one is required to bear such brutality. God does not require victims. There is no shame in turning away from abuse, no sin in self-respect. It is not fit to judge the man or woman who makes one choice over another, for none know the prayer within their heart, the purity of intent, the form their love takes.

"I do not rebuke, but honor you your choice," he said to the woman who had offered him the honey. Taking the bread from her, he took a bite and closed his eyes, savoring the gift. I heard a soft moan escape his lips, and could taste the sweetness in my own mouth from where I stood.

"Your kindness is returned to you a thousand-fold. Go home. Your husband is looking for you, eager to make amends. God has helped him see love's true nature, and this he will never again forget."

Tears streamed down the woman's face as she turned to leave. The crowd silently parted to let her pass. Even those of us who did not know the man and woman could see the bruises on her face and arms and knew what she had borne.

To us he said, "I do nothing. I have not brought healing into her life, or her husband's. It is she who, in her forgiveness, opened the way for the miracle. She already was whole. And now her husband can begin the long process of forgiving himself so they may learn to live again in love.

"You have watched me here, day after day, offering healing to one after another of your family and friends. I am like the flute through which the music passes, but I am not the music. The music comes from the angelic realm. It is not given to this one and withheld from his brother. The music is for all, each according to their ability to receive.

"But first you must ask."

"Master, that woman did not ask you to heal her husband," said a voice from the crowd.

"No, she did not ask me. But in each morning's prayers she has asked God to take care of her husband. And she asks with the same sincerity for blessings upon you, her townspeople, that each may be well. You must know that what you ask for another will be given to you."

Jesus took another bite of the honey-soaked bread, washing it down with the cup of water Miriam handed him. He smiled at her his thanks, and love shone between them.

"Bless those who curse you. Love those who do you harm. How can your own shortcomings be forgiven if you cannot forgive others? It is all one. *You* are all one, a part of each other. You have shown my friends and me great kindness. *This is prayer*. Our Father has heard your prayer and marked it well.

"And so my brother," he said, turning to the man who asked the question on prayer, "to pray ceaselessly is to train yourself in the habit of kindness in all things, large and small. God cares not for animal sacrifice, nor is He interested in the amount of money you give to the synagogue. Seek ever the kingdom of heaven and you will find it."

I noticed one of the priests who had been standing next to James stiffen, then turn and leave with his robes fluttering. James leaned over and whispered "I am afraid his words transformed that one from friend to foe."

"Yes, you are probably right." It made me nervous, but there was nothing we could say to convince Jesus to be more discrete around the priests.

"They are most in need of what I have to say," he had told me the day before. "Their ignorance comes from what they have been taught. It is hard to resist when told often enough they are superior in every way, and deserving of special treatment from men and God alike. They must be reminded that all are the same in God's eyes. In fact more is expected of them because more has been given."

The next day would be our last in Jericho, and the most memorable. A man who had been paralyzed for twenty years was brought before Jesus. My cousin bent down and whispered something in the man's ears, then called Miriam and me over. Out of hearing of the crowd, he told us the man had agreed to allow us to stand with him as he drew down the healing power.

"Are you sure," whispered Miriam. "The crowd is here for you, not us."

"I am nothing," he reminded us.

He turned to the crowd and said, "Healing does not come from me, from any of us. This man's heart has opened in prayer, and it will be done to him as he has asked."

Miriam placed her right hand over the man's navel, and raised the left into the air, closing her eyes. My left hand slid under his upper back and my right hand moved onto his chest, the man's emaciated body held in between. Immediately I felt an intense heat coursing through my hands. His cold body began to warm until I was afraid he would be burned with the healing fire. I knew someone was speaking, but I could not understand the words. I wanted desperately to remove my hands, but could not. There was nothing I could do but allow the process to complete itself.

The next thing I knew I was laying on the ground, my head in James' lap as he stroked my forehead. I still could not understand anyone's words, but felt the tumult around me. The air shimmered and it was hard to breathe.

At last my senses began to clear and I heard the uproar. James helped me to my feet and I saw the man who had been paralyzed standing before me. He seemed to be in shock, not understanding what had just happened. The two people who brought him there were talking excitedly, and at last a faint smile formed above his quivering chin.

Miriam stood on the other side of him, behind Jesus. While she and I had worked together often over the years, serving as instruments for many healings, this was the first time we had stood together in such a public arena. She looked as nervous as I felt.

Those were times in which women were required to remain in the outer circle of the synagogue, never allowed to approach the Holy of Holies. In fact no man of tradition would even acknowledge its existence in front of us. It was expected we accede always to the will of our father and brother and husband, never presuming to have or wield authority. But Jesus had told us from the beginning that he would have us stand at his side, equal to him in every way. And we had long trained for this time of service, as had our mothers before us. In the end it would prove to be one of the main grievances held against my cousin.

Some days later we arrived back in Bethany. It was good to see Mary and Martha again, and others of our friends. I felt safe with them, though I could not say safe from what. We were becoming more exposed and vulnerable with each passing day.

"My husband tried to discourage me from coming here," said Martha.

"Why?" I asked. I had the impression he was also tiring of the misuse of power within the Jewish hierarchy, and would welcome Jesus speaking out against it.

"His old friends have been pressuring him. He won't tell me exactly what's going on, but I think your feelings are right, Veronica. It would be better if your cousin could hold back a little from casting blame on the Sanhedrin – at least in public."

"You know he will never do that."

"Yes, I know," she sighed.

"But aren't you concerned about him finding you here?" I asked, speaking of her husband.

"He can say and do what he will, but this is one time he cannot decide for me," she said, clamping her jaw shut in emphasis.

We hurried through our meal preparations; there was much to be done before sundown to make sure we'd have enough for everyone to eat over the Sabbath. All the women had gathered to help, and even John and Andrew were pitching in. As Jesus brought us more and more into the center of things, more of the men were taking his lead and treating us with respect. That some would now and then help in the food preparation was an enormous show of support.

Still, there were those who resented the natural intimacy that some of us enjoyed with Jesus, a result of having known him our whole lives. Above all they hated Miriam's special relationship with him. Everything shines brighter close to the sun, and at times the competition for this position was intense, though none would admit to it.

After the ritual washing of hands, we gathered around the long table heaped with pots of slow simmered food. Mary had set out her best dishes, though they were nowhere near as fine as what would be seen on her sister Martha's table. Martha's husband thought his position required they buy the best that could be imported from Rome and Greece. I did not much enjoy Shabbat at their home as his prayers would drone on and on, especially if other members of the Sanhedrin were present. Instead of fish, Samuel served red meat, intended to impress his guests.

Mary had opened a new cask of wine just before sunset, and a full pitcher sat at each end of the table. "You are welcome here anytime," said Lazarus, smiling warmly. "Let my home be a refuge for you."

When the sun had set Lazarus stood and said a short prayer over the wine: "Blessed are you our Lord Father, who creates the fruit of the vine."

Mary lit two candles, drawing down the power of Shekinah, and added, "Blessed are you, our Divine Mother, who creates the light and warmth of fire."

Before we broke the sweet bread, Jesus looked around at each of us, and said, "It is good to come together with true friends such as you. We seldom have the luxury of undisturbed time any more."

What I remember most of that evening was our laughter. It filled the night air, reaching over the walls and into the village. A small group was encamped just beyond the gate, hoping for a blessing of some sort from my cousin. Their fires and ours had died down, since rabbinical law dictated we should not lift even a log on the Sabbath. But I was glad for the dark, as nothing impinged upon the brilliant starry sky. Even the wild dogs seemed quiet that night.

We went to sleep late, very late, yet arose refreshed. Mary hummed as she set out clean plates and the unleavened bread, honey and fruit for breakfast. I noticed a difference in people's eyes, a luminosity that was often hidden in the shadows of daily stresses.

Jesus did not go outside the walls that day, but still the people waited. He had been censured many times by the priests for healing on the Sabbath, but nothing would prevent him from responding to urgent need. He always said that all days are holy, none more than another. And what could be more appropriate than to honor the day by doing God's work.

Unlike the previous night we spoke little that day, opening a door to deeper communication among us. When we used to meet out in the desert during the early days, Jesus occasionally called for a day of silence. For some this was more difficult than fasting or other privations. Words come too easily, often without forethought. In our silence we begin to notice our thoughts. It seemed to me I became more aware and concerned with other people as a result, listening more carefully to what they said when they did speak. I think it made us kinder.

That particular Sabbath ignited in me a new way of seeing the people who had become my family. It would be some time yet before I understood this was how my cousin always saw those of us who are close to him, and more importantly, it is how he saw *everyone,* stranger or friend, beggar or king. It did not matter what we did, how foolish or selfishly we acted, he always looked through all that to our true heart. Of course, there were times he couldn't help but be annoyed with us precisely because he knew the truth of us and what we were capable of, while we too often saw only the worst in ourselves and each other.

But his frustration quickly reverted to patience as he directed our attention away from what was on the surface, so that we might become aware of the Holy Spirit dwelling within. It took no effort to see this in him, or James or mother or Mary or my dearest friends, but that day I actually began to sense the spirit within everyone, even those few men with whom I had had difficulty in the past. Each person appeared innocent and pure and beautiful, just as they were created.

From that day forward, what was then a new revelation became increasingly natural. There were exceptions, to be sure, especially with those who intended us harm. I was to have many opportunities to learn the important lessons of non-judgment and forgiveness.

That evening when we had finished our prayers we found a messenger waiting. He carried a note from uncle Joseph, asking us to come to Jerusalem as soon as possible. He gave no reason.

Before we left the following morning Jesus went out to spend some time among the crowd that had waited so patiently over the Sabbath. Several of us went with him, while a few went on ahead to Jerusalem. I do not know if he actually spoke more eloquently that day, or shone more brightly as he offered healing to those in need, but it seemed so to me. I could not take my eyes from him, even when he asked my assistance with an elderly woman who was in excruciating pain, her back bent almost in half.

We took to the road around midday, after a bite of bread and cheese. Miriam fell behind to talk with Naomi. The others were absorbed in silence or private conversation when Jesus asked me, "What happened to you yesterday?"

For a moment I did not understand what he meant, but he persisted. "You are changed, Veronica. You are not the same person you were before Bethany. Can you tell me what is different?"

His question sent a shiver up my back. I was sure he understood the transformation far more than I, but now the man at my side spoke to me not as my kin, but a rabbi asking his student to explain the unexplainable. He had told us many times that we are each of us teachers. One day our own students would ask us the very same questions, and in order to help them understand their experiences we must first understand our own.

"There have been times when I felt a sudden shift, or a new understanding," I began tentatively. "Once or twice I even felt I'd been hit with lightning, the shock of sudden knowledge was so powerful. But this was different. There was a slow awakening that went from sunset to sunset. Maybe it was my first real Sabbath."

"What do you mean?"

"Is this day not meant to be a day apart, to be spent not just thinking about God, or reciting prayers, but to actually rest with God?" I looked at my teacher, who nodded.

I felt the thrill of understanding. "*With God*," I repeated to myself. "I think that being in the company of people whom I love enabled me to open my heart to love itself."

I stopped and looked at Jesus. "God loves us through each other. We cannot even recognize God's love if we have not first learned to love each other." The words came slowly as I pondered each one in my heart before giving it voice.

"But now ... now that I have seen that love and know how it feels, I can begin to perceive that greater love. My heart has been broken open and made bigger so that God can use me to bring love and healing and comfort to others. To do that I must be able to see the face of God in other people, knowing He is already alive and working in them. That is why you tell us, why all our teachers have told us, it is not we who heal, but God within."

My cousin smiled at me, and nodded.

"That is what I saw yesterday, what I felt in you. Those of us here to teach can only plant the seeds of such knowledge. You have heard these words from my mouth before, and from your other teachers, but now they live in your heart. That makes all the difference."

And then his smile left as quickly as it had come. "It is none too soon. The need is great and increasing daily. I will have need of you at my side, you and the few others who have awakened to this understanding."

He took my hand, squeezing it as he looked deep into my soul. Had he not held me, I might have fainted at what I saw in his eyes. But strength flowed from him, buoying me.

*

Joseph met us at the gate. The others who had gone ahead already sat at the table eating.

"Thank you for coming," he said, embracing each in turn.

He did not mention his summons over dinner. When we had finished, he pushed his chair back and began to pace in the garden. I felt my stomach tighten. At last he turned and looked at his old friend Nicodemus, then back at us.

"John is dead.

There were gasps all around, but no one said a word.

"Three days ago I received a message from Tiberius, one of our brothers who serves Herod."

"Serves Herod!" Simon shouted, jumping to his feet. "I don't believe you. How could one of our brothers be in the service of such an evil man?"

"Sit down Simon, please." Joseph's own eyes were filled with tears, and some others had begun weeping openly. I might have been one of them.

"This man sits at Herod's table at great sacrifice to himself. If we are honest with ourselves, each of us would rather see the king suffer that which he has done to so many others. But this is not the time to indulge our own passions. Through this man who serves at Herod's side we receive information that is of enormous assistance to us."

"But why could we not help John? Save him? What good was this man ....?"

"John came to light the way. You know this; he spoke of nothing else. John knew his fate from the beginning. He never questioned, never feared. He is the bravest man I have ever known."

PART TWO

Chapter Eleven

TRANSCENDENCE

"They said he had been beheaded," Joseph told us the following morning.

"Beheaded!" Edithia ducked at the word, as if the blade had come at her own neck.

Her eyes were rimmed red, and tears began to flow anew. Rachel pulled the woman to her, stroking her hair. No one among us -- except maybe Simon and Andrew – had known John as well as Edithia. They had been among his followers before meeting Jesus.

Simon paced angrily, while Andrew sat on a bench alone, away from us. He had not said a word since the night before. The light seemed to have gone out of him, while it flared in his brother.

We were all in shock. I had known John long, but not well. Yet, in his death a part of us all had died.

"Where is Jesus?" Nicodemus called out from the doorway.

"We have not seen him today," someone said. He nodded and went back into the house.

Jesus must have known what would happen to our cousin, but still he wept when the news came. They had been born into different families some distance from each other, yet their fates were as deeply entwined as if they had been twins.

In quieter times Jesus and Miriam, James and I used to gather at James' and my home, talking late into the night about many things. On one of those nights Jesus told us that the four of us, together with John and other kin and friends had come into the world together again and again from the dawn of time. He said we are constantly changing positions in life's dance and just as John had come to clear the way for him in his work, Jesus was preparing the way for us in ours.

John had been held for nearly a year in the fortress of Machaerus in Perea. As reviled as Herod was, I do not think he intended to have John murdered. More likely he had sent him across the Jordan hoping his wife would forget about him if John's rants against them could no longer be heard. But her hatred held no bounds, and time only increased her desire for vengeance.

If John was right in calling their union wicked, then surely Herod was paying daily penance in his life with Herodias. From our source within the palace we learned that it was she who demanded his head, and Herod who gave it to her in hopes of finally winning a peace.

And now he was gone. John ... was gone.

I felt sick to my stomach at what had been done to him, and sick with fear for Jesus.

"Uncle, is he in danger too?" I asked Joseph when I saw him alone that afternoon.

"Veronica," he said, putting his hands on my shoulders and

compelling me to meet his eyes, "I must be honest with you. If you do not know the threat, you will be powerless against it. There is danger all around. And just as John intentionally stirred the pot, exposing injustice and personal vice, so is Jesus here to shine a light into the gathering darkness.

"No one, not even he knows what will be revealed in the shadows, nor the consequences of his words and deeds. But there are others even closer to us than Herod who will strike out in fear of such exposure. They fear losing control -- though control is an illusion, born of a false perspective."

"What is this perspective, uncle?"

"They believe they own power, which is theirs to wield against others. They believe worldly power can exist apart from the sacred, instead of being the two sides of one hand. But until they come to know the indwelling spirit, they are nothing. Their power will melt away like the snows of Mt. Hermon when exposed to the sun's light.

"John's death has cast a pall over us all, and we will mourn our loss. But you know he does not suffer, and so we must rise from our own suffering to continue our work. We cannot indulge in fear. There is no time for that."

His smile brought a flicker of light back to my heart. "Now it is your job to remind the others of this," he said as he walked away.

I noticed how Joseph had called me Veronica, instead of child or daughter or niece, or even dear one, as he had always done before. And I knew it was his way of telling me I had assumed a higher level of authority within the group. Some of that was due to my age, of course. I was now, what? I forget sometimes … thirty, I think. But it was more than that. I knew he was asking me to take on the role of protector. Some of my early teachers had hinted at some such function, yet I still did not understand what it meant. I wondered where I might find the strength to help shield others.

*

No one asked where Jesus had been when he returned that night. His presence brought a needed salve to our shared wound. We hovered around him all the next day, as if he too might suddenly disappear forever if we did not keep a close eye on him.

On the third day he told us we should begin preparations for the journey back to Galilee. But before we went to gather our things, we met one last time in the courtyard to pray together for John (as we had been doing both morning and evening), saying the requisite words to help him complete the transition to spirit.

The death rituals were even more exhaustive among the Essenes than with the Sadducees and Pharisees -- especially when the death was a violent one. We took solace from the ritual and prayers, and drew strength from our meditations upon the light as we took up the path opened for us with John's passing.

A quiet laughter returned to our table that night. Joseph brought out the best wine, and Elizabeth had ordered a feast. We'd just stood to clear the table when we heard a shout at the gate.

"Jesus, come quickly!" a woman's voice called into the night.

My cousin did not appear surprised at the summons, which calmed my fears. He tapped Miriam, James, Ruth, Edithia and me on the shoulder as he made his way toward the gate, nodding for us to follow.

"He is dead, master." It was Mary, sister to Lazarus.

"Who?" asked Ruth, looking from Mary to Jesus.

"My brother. He is dead!" And she started to sob.

Jesus took her in his arms and gently carried her over to a bench, kneeling in front of her. "Mary, look at me," he said in a soft voice. "Mary, he is not dead, but only sleeping. Look ... at ... me," he repeated.

She looked into his eyes and stopped weeping. "But he is not breathing. How is it possible to live without breath?"

While this was going on, Joseph readied a sturdy cart with two of his fastest horses. They waited for us outside the gate. "Come," Jesus said, taking Mary by the hand. We all piled into the cart. James attended to the horses and, at his urging Mary laid her head in my cousin's lap as we rode into the night.

Martha and three servants heard our approach and stood waiting at the gate. The lantern light cast shadows across their faces. Martha took charge of Mary and led the way in. No one spoke. We gathered around Lazarus, who lay in a middle room, alight with lamps. The air was stifling and Jesus indicated that some lamps be extinguished. The servants complied, and then left us alone.

He certainly looked dead. There was no movement in his chest and I could feel no breath on my hand beneath his nostrils. At his insistence Mary and Martha went out to heat water. "Scent the water with oils," he said to Mary. He could have asked one of the servants to do this chore, but I think he wanted them out of the room.

The rest of us stood where he indicated and then, as we had been taught, we joined hands and said aloud an invocation to the light, the light which clothes the life. Twice before I had taken part in such a ritual, inviting the soul to return to the body, if such be the intent of the Holy Spirit. Once it did and once it did not. Jesus said it is the decision of the eternal Self which cannot be forced by any man.

But he had already told Mary that Lazarus was not dead. What if his soul did not choose to return? I forced such thoughts out of my mind, and stood emptied.

We then dropped our hands and stepped back in a wider circle; Jesus alone stood in the center with our beloved friend. He took the man's hands in his and held them, eyes closed. His lips moved silently, whereupon he bent and breathed into Lazarus' open lips. He did this three times, laid the man's hands upon his own chest and stepped back.

I closed my eyes and asked only that the Father's will be done.

The scent of precious oils filled the room and I opened my eyes to see Martha dabbing oil on the top of his head, his temples, the middle of his forehead, his throat and chest, and at other points of connection to spirit. When she touched the soles of his feet, I heard a gasp and thought it came from Martha. But another followed, and then the sound of someone clearing his throat – and I realized it was Lazarus who now took his own breath.

When he opened his eyes we all cried out in thanksgiving at his return to us. Mary, who had been standing in the doorway, rushed to her sister's side. Lazarus looked up at his sisters, who were alternately laughing and crying, and then at the rest of us standing round his bed. He looked bewildered.

"Sleeping," said Jesus, laughing. "He was sleeping, that's all."

Edithia and Ruth stayed behind with the sisters to attend to Lazarus who insisted he was fine and couldn't understand what all the fuss was about.

By the time we got back to Joseph's a new day was dawning. No one had slept, and once the exhilaration of the night subsided, we realized we were exhausted. Joseph had no trouble talking us into staying another day.

*

"What do you do, when you are together without us women?" asked Naomi. "We

have told you about our dance, both the formal ceremonies and our spontaneous expressions of joy. We have our first woman's ceremonies and rituals relating to our moon cycles."

"Naomi!" whispered Rachel, in what sounded like a rebuke.

"What? There is nothing wrong with such things, nothing to be ashamed of," she insisted. But Rachel came from an earlier generation and a more conservative community than our own, and I am sure it must have sounded terribly bold to speak of such things among the men. A few were quite young and unused to women's talk, by the sound of their giggles.

"Well, what *do* you do?" she persisted.

James laughed and said "Well, I guess I'll start. "We have our own dance, of sorts, though it is nothing so animated as your own, by the sound of things." He looked at me with a twinkle in his eyes. We had lain awake many nights while my husband peppered me with questions about our women's rituals and celebrations, and about our training in Egypt. Once he had me get up and show him the dance, though without the other women it held none of the fire of the real thing, and I am sure he was disappointed in what he saw.

He looked around the room and said to the other men, "Come, let's show them." Jesus got to his feet, but the younger men weren't about to be coaxed into a public display. But much to everyone's amusement, Joseph and Nicodemus got up and stood with them. I expected to see a shortened version of whatever they did, sure there would be certain things not meant for outsiders -- men or women -- as was the case with us.

Joseph left the room and returned with a small drum and a flute. Simon Peter shrugged and got to his feet, took the drum from the older man and began tapping out a simple beat. Thomas looked around, then rose and took the flute. "I don't really know how to play, but ...." If that was true, he had a natural talent for the instrument. It was a simple melody, but one filled with feeling.

James and Jesus, Joseph and Nicodemus put their arms around each other's shoulders, facing us. Seeing them standing thus brought a flash of memory of James' and my wedding, what seemed a lifetime ago. Though I had married late, I was a child compared to how I felt now. The innocence of that time was long gone from us.

The four men slowly moved their feet in unison with the music. Ah, if only life could be more like that, I thought to myself: slow, deliberate, without rushing to some unknown destination. A quiet chant broke through my reverie. Well, not a chant with identifiable words, but the men were making rhythmic sounds that seemed to convey purpose and meaning to them.

I was drawn into the music almost as if something inside of me played and danced with them, though I sat unmoving. Stealing a glance at the other women, I saw they sat spellbound.

Slowly, slowly they began to pick up speed, the playing and chanting becoming louder. And then something quite unexpected happened. The rest of the men who had sat watching from the sidelines stood and went to join the others, almost as if they could not help themselves. On his way to the front of the room, John took my hand and brought me to my feet. Seeing that, Andrew took Miriam's. Emboldened, the younger men followed suit until all the women stood in a line facing the men. Thomas and Simon Peter slowed the tempo so we could pick up the simple steps, and then slowly brought it back to a faster pace until we were all moving as one, voicing the chant in unison.

In our singing and dancing together I felt I had stepped out of a dense fog into dazzling clarity. And while everyone there was well known to me, it seemed I was seeing some of them for the first time. When the music finally stopped I saw a kind of rapture in the glowing faces around me. I blush to make this statement, but there was something mysterious being revealed, a love greater even than that I had known with my husband.

Eventually I understood that a unique bond had been forged which had up till then eluded us. The natural barriers between men and women -- which serve a purpose in ordinary times – had dissolved. A bridge had formed in its place, to serve us in times to come when trust would be in short supply.

"There are many other rituals and prayers and a few songs and dances specific to one occasion or another," said Nicodemus when conversation returned, "especially within the Sanhedrin." He laughed. "I'm sure some there would have been outraged at such a display, condemning us all to perdition! But nothing is as it once was" he ended wistfully.

Jesus leaned over and took the flute from Thomas' hands, putting it to his lips. It had been long, long since I'd heard him play and I doubt many there even knew of this talent of his. He began with a song I'd heard him play when we were children before he left for Egypt, the first of his many journeys. I could not help myself, and wept at the loss of our youth.

He played and played, seeming to lose himself in the music. The men's faces, hardened with concerns of the world, relaxed. The women's eyes turned within to visions of everyday pleasures, most of which had fallen beyond our grasp.

After a time he nodded at Miriam, who joined him in song. My friend had a beautiful voice that rose and fell with the flute like healing waters. She sang songs from Magdala, many of which were unknown to us. Sometimes when her voice soared high into the rafters it was easy to forget that the sounds came from a woman and not the angels.

"You must be exhausted," said Thomas when they stopped.

"No," they replied with one voice.

"It brings me back to myself," said Miriam. Jesus nodded in agreement, eyes on his beloved friend.

One of the servants approached, whispering in Elizabeth's ear. "Dinner has been ready, and already cold," she said, rising. "But Rebecca did not want to disturb us. I doubt anyone minds."

"Well, the only thing that could compete with the heavenly music we've just heard is Anna's cooking," said James, bounding for the table.

After we'd finished eating Joseph cleared his voice to speak. "Tomorrow you will leave early, and return to Capernaum. I wish we could join you there, but it is important Nicodemus and I remain where we can be of most use. I have spoken of this already with Jesus, and I think it well you know too."

What came next shocked me.

"Pontius Pilate is an unpredictable man. I know some of you think of him as your enemy. But it is not that simple. I have come to know him quite well, and he is not unsympathetic to your cause. More importantly, I have become something of a confidant to his wife. And twice that I know of she has come to hear Jesus speak, standing unrecognized among the crowds."

"I too have talked with her," said my cousin. "She has a kind heart, and is a good influence upon Pilate. She could not speak for us publicly, and if pressure were put upon him to act against us, she would have little power to interfere. But it is good for you to know that we have many friends, even in the most unlikely places."

"There are others within the Sanhedrin too, besides my old friend Nicodemus here, who are not caught in the web of dogma and fear. But like Pilate, there are limits to their power. Even Herod has told me that he is not his own man."

Simon spat at the sound of the king's name. Joseph ignored it and went on.

"Listen well to the words of Jesus, and not the clamoring of your own voice. Some of you think we are on a political mission, but we are not. Some of you hope to unseat Caesar's proxies in our land. Much as I would like to see that, it is not our goal. Ours is a mission much larger than Judea or Galilee, or Palestine or any of the lands we know so well.

"We are being called to the liberation of not just Jews, but all men and women, everywhere. My dear brother here does not serve any nation or race, nor one religion and not another. Think bigger, open your heart wider. We are about the liberation of souls.

"Listen carefully to his words, and remember always the brotherhood you experienced here tonight. *We are the Brotherhood.*"

Chapter Twelve

BEHOLD MY BELOVED SON

Passover had come and gone, and it was time to travel north. By the third day of travel, my cousin had begun withdrawing into his customary silence. Even from childhood he had done so, gathering an impenetrable cloud of stillness about himself, admitting no one. Though he walked among us, there were times he simply was not there.

It was evening and he was explaining the importance of really *seeing* the person in front of us, especially when engaged in healing of one sort or another. Miriam commented dryly on how he ought to listen to his own words. When she explained that James had three times asked him the same question without getting even a nod of the head in return, he burst out laughing. That laugh of his could defuse any situation that otherwise might give rise to anger or hurt or jealousy.

"Forgive me if I offend you," he said, bowing playfully to those of us present, "but when a Father calls his son, the son cannot refuse." And then, "I'm sorry, brother, what did you want?"

Unlike the rest of us Jesus never had to *think* about how to heal; it radiated from him as naturally as he gave his breath to the wind. He said the secret to healing lay not in technique, but in the purity of our hearts. Truly seeing someone created the bridge for it the transmission to take place.

We had stopped for the night in Nain. The small inn had few rooms and not more than two or three beds per room, so some of us had to sleep in the courtyard. It was a lovely evening on the brink of summer. A gentle breeze flowed over us where we lay, enticing me into a restful sleep.

During a lull in conversation during breakfast the following morning the innkeeper leaned in to Jesus and said, "Tell your friends about the boy and his mother." My cousin ignored him. But the innkeeper, whose name was Josiah, insisted, posing his question again.

"Yes, do tell us," said John. Then others chimed in, begging for the story.

Finally, he gave in. "It might have been about this time last year," he began.

The innkeeper nodded, well pleased with himself.

"Only Marcus, Matthias and two of Joseph's men were with me. We stayed at this very inn, a one-night stop on our way north, I think." He nodded to himself, thinking back. "Yes, we were headed north.

"That evening Josiah here knocked on my door. He said he had to knock several times, as I was sleeping so soundly. When I got up he asked me to accompany him. He was so agitated that I did not even ask where we were going, or why.

"It was very dark that night and I remember the wild dogs growling and baring their teeth at us. Somewhere ahead we heard the wail of a woman's voice. Josiah opened the gate without knocking. The house was ablaze in light."

He paused in his story, and I could see behind his eyes he was there at the house again. "The woman did not even see us enter. But Josiah pulled me over, and pushed me down to the ground in front of a rough mat on which lay a small boy. His mother alternated between moans and a plaintive wail, her unloosed hair falling over the child.

"You who know me well will understand," he said, looking up at us. "It is only the Holy Spirit within that knows what is to be done in such circumstances. I stand aside and life flows through me.

"The voice of authority spoke the boy's name, though no one had told it to me. 'Saul, breathe!" it called out. 'Consider your mother who mourns you. It is not yet your time!'

"Truth is I did not recall saying these words, though apparently I repeated them twice more. Josiah told me later what I had said, as well as what followed. He said the mother stopped her cry at the second command and looked at me as if for the first time. At the third command the boy's chest heaved and his eyes opened. In a small voice he asked, 'Mother, what is wrong? Why are you crying? What has happened?'

"Once again the woman saw no one but her son, Saul, come back to her. She pulled him to her breast and wept, this time with joy."

"Yes, that is how it happened, exactly like that," agreed Josiah.

The innkeeper did not want us to pay for our rooms, but we insisted. Somehow, there was always enough for our expenses. Besides, he was not a wealthy man. When we were ready to leave, he took a corner of Jesus' robe in his hand and raised it to his mouth to kiss the cloth. But the Nazarene turned and instead embraced the man as if he were his brother, saying, "God sees the goodness of your heart, Josiah, and has made a place for you at His side."

The man's chin quivered, and he turned quickly away.

Jesus often called one or another of us to his side when there was healing to be done. Miracles flowed from him like water, without need of anyone's assistance. But he often told us "You must know your own strength, awaken to your own wisdom and power. After I am gone, there will be much need of healing. Though I will stand with you unseen, the greater good comes not from me but the recognition of each one's connection to the Source of all good."

I could not bring myself to think about what life would be like with him gone.

We passed an uneventful day on the road, and it was early still when we stopped to rest. Jesus pointed out a rounded hill in the distance and said "We will pass the night there."

"But we can travel further before darkness falls, and arrive tomorrow in Magdala, or even Capernaum if we press on," protested Miriam. She was anxious to see how Simon fared, as she heard their older brother Eli had been making threats against him.

"Have you forgotten? It is the full moon of the bull, and we have not performed the ritual of water for some time. Mt. Tabor will be perfect for the ceremony."

Though we had taken that road numerous times, I had never given the small mountain much thought. A gentle stream ran at the base. Each of us carried a measure of water up the gentle slope with us, as we would spend the night at the top.

Of our companions, only James, Miriam, Thaddeus and I had taken part in the ceremony near Caesarea a few years earlier. There were twice as many people this time as then. As before, we found a large flat rock at the eastern end of the hilltop. It did not seem that could have been by chance, but neither could so large a rock have been carried to that spot. All other large rocks had long since fallen to the base of the mountain.

Jesus explained what he wanted each of us to do. Miriam and I set a large halved gourd on the rock and filled it with water, then took our places shortly before the sun set. Those of us who had participated in the ceremony previously began to sing the ancient chant which he had learned during his time in Tibet, when he took part in the ritual there. It was simple enough that the others soon joined in.

I felt the movement of sound in my body, warm and steady. The longer we chanted the more powerful were the waves surging through me, building, building, until a column of bluish light shot up from the center of our circle the very moment the sun dropped behind the hill.

As instructed, we turned to face the four directions. I faced west, while others faced east or north or south. I heard someone gasp and knew the full moon had broken the horizon. Fluttering robes shimmered in the rosy glow between setting sun and rising moon.

My feet were firmly planted on the ground, that I might endure the pulsing power of heaven and earth.

"*Now.*" Jesus' soft voice carried easily across the night air, and together we turned to face the stone to the east. He stood in front of the stone, arms raised into the air. It seemed to me his body and robes were transparent, the moon shining through him onto the hilltop. I did not think to notice if he cast a shadow.

Then, just as I'd remembered on the hill outside Caesarea, a sudden blast of light or power of some kind came down from two points above us, fusing in him. He lit up as a tree catches fire when struck by lightning, and I heard the same crackling sound one hears then. But instead of incinerating (as would the tree), he cast the lightning from himself into the bowl of water.

I wished I had stood closer. I imagined the water boiling as it once had when Miriam and I were seeding the light during the ceremony on the Holy Isle, when we were still young. I could not see but somehow knew the water was changed – as it had been then – aiding our own transformation to light.

But what happened next was something new. A glow remained in the air around him, an enormous halo of light from which flowed a chorus of the sweetest sounds I had ever heard. And from the heart of that chorus a powerful voice rang out:

Behold, my beloved son, brighter than all the stars in heaven, symbol of the way, the truth and the life held forth for all who wander in the darkness. In him I am well pleased.

When finally the light began to dissipate Jesus lowered his arms and turned to face us. Three of our companions lay in a swoon. But only after the rippling effect of the voice had stopped could I bring myself to go to their aid. Miriam, Matthias and I helped them to their feet. They were as if drunk on wine and had to be carefully guided to where Jesus stood waiting. When we had assembled he lifted a ladle and dipped it into the water, offering it to each of us to drink. His lips moved, in silent benediction.

One by one we drank, Miriam last. And then she took the ladle from

Jesus' hand, filled it and held it to his lips.

"What were the words you spoke as we drank the water?" Thomas asked him later. "You spoke so quietly I could not hear."

"The waters of life flow from you and out into the world. You are Light, Love and Life; three in One."

Afterwards, we lay down to sleep on the hilltop.

"It has only been two years since we took part in the ceremony of water outside Caesarea, but I feel much older," I whispered to James. "So much has happened. We stand on the edge of a cliff about to collapse, but I cannot run, even to save myself. It doesn't make sense, but I am not afraid. Are you?"

"Sometimes, yes, but not tonight. There were shadowy figures within the flash of light, but I could not make them out. It is just as well, I suppose. Whatever lies ahead, I will not abandon my brother."

"Nor will I."

I thought of many things that night, from past to future, and sleep did not come until shortly before the sun's return.

*

"This is right where we stood untangling our nets when we first saw him," said Andrew.

"You were untangling the nets because you were the one who had gotten them tangled in the first place," laughed Simon, who loved to tease his brother.

"And if I hadn't gotten them tangled, then we might have already gone home and missed him," retorted Andrew, pleased to have the last word.

"Nothing in heaven or earth would have prevented our meeting," said Jesus. We had not seen his approach. "Do you truly think there are accidents in this world? Some of you are strangers to each other," he said, gesturing out over the crowd that had begun to gather around him. "And some of us have known each other from birth, and beyond," he added, looking at James and me.

"But we are all brothers and sisters, and in knowing any one of us, you also know our Father in heaven, for it is He who shines from your eyes, and is the laughter on your lips. You hear Him in the cry of a newborn and the birdsong in the bushes that line the springs behind me.

"It is His great joy that we gather here. For the One who makes the grass to grow and the rivers to run, it is an easy matter to bring us together. And then it is up to us to choose the nature of our association, whether we are friends or enemies, whether we are kind or do each other harm.

"But know this: whatever you do to another you do to yourself, though many years pass before your deeds return to you. And what you do to yourself, you also do to me, your brother.

"Your Father in heaven hears your every word, sees your every act and knows your every thought, great or small, loving or hateful, and remembers it all. You hope He takes note of your sacrifice in the synagogue at Passover, yet overlooks the angry hand you lay upon your wife at night. Not so.

"But know this too. Ours is a loving Father, eager to forgive us our wrongs when we have forgiven ourselves and move beyond old behaviors." He looked out over the silent crowd that now pressed in upon him.

"But do not imagine that forgiveness of self is an easy matter. God has created in us the knowledge of good and evil, so we may know when we upset the balance of life. We have learned to judge ourselves harshly, bringing all manner of penance and suffering upon ourselves, and those closest to us. We have learned self-hatred instead of self-love, and then blame our heavenly Father and the great Mother for our weaknesses, holding them responsible for our suffering.

"We say that God rebukes us when things don't go our way, and pray He will hate our enemies. But such a thing is impossible. *God is love.* God can do nothing but love us, all of us, even when we do not. God is ever-ready to help us replace hatred with love, and our suffering with joy. If we will have it, our heavenly home is right in front of us, at this very moment."

Some laughed derisively and walked away. But another man standing nearby turned and took his wife's hand and placed it upon his heart: a tear was in his eye. Some few stared at the ground, perhaps ashamed; still others looked around and smiled. The lesson of love and forgiveness -- especially of oneself – was often the hardest for people to hear.

We had gathered, as we often did in those days, at Heptapegon, more commonly known as the Seven Springs. It was a lovely green place in a summer sea of bronzed hills, where water ran year round, one of the lake's many feeders. Some days there were no more than a handful of people beyond our little group, while on others there would be hundreds. Much depended upon the weather, and the events in people's lives. The last time we were there, we saw few Romans, and rarely any soldiers. But now, a day did not pass without one or more standing off watching us, fully armed.

"What do they want?" hissed Simon. He had awakened that morning in a foul mood, after a restless night. "Why can't they just leave us alone?" He had dreamt of evil things: Roman soldiers sacking villages and killing innocents. And there was worse, he said, refusing to give it voice.

Before joining Jesus, Simon had been active in a group of Zealots that carried out raids on a string of Roman fortresses to the south. He was among the few in our camp who sought to persuade Jesus to join them and take up arms against the occupiers 'before they destroy us all.' Jesus had asked him instead to lay down his arms and take up the more powerful weapons of love and forgiveness. Simon had reluctantly done so, though I think he believed my cousin would one day turn aside from his talk of forgiveness and lead them into battle and victory.

It is our nature to hear what we want to hear.

The following day we gathered further up a slope that spread out under a thicket of shade trees. It was a large crowd.

A young woman suckling a baby asked this question: "A priest at my synagogue told me that because my husband died our children and I will be lost to God until I remarry. It was hard enough to lose my husband, but why must I be punished yet again? My husband's family and even my own parents shun us. Our neighbors will not talk to me because I turned down a marriage proposal from an old man whom I never even met." She began to weep and could say no more

Jesus walked over to the woman and put a hand on the child's head which, distressed at his mother's tears, had begun to cry along with her. He bent down and whispered so only the two of them could hear. The mother stopped her tears and beamed up at the man, her whole countenance changed.

He looked up at the crowd and said: "This woman's heart still aches at the loss of her young husband. Will her heart heal more quickly if she is rebuked? Whom does the priest serve? Surely not the God of love. We are born in innocence and only learn suffering at the hand of man. What would you teach your children, and the children of this grieving mother? Love or hate?

"You who have listened to me before have heard that what we do to another will be done to us. Forgive and be forgiven; love and be loved; judge and be judged. It is up to you."

Across the stillness that followed, a well-dressed man called out, "Master, is it not better to be rich than to be poor, if wealth is gotten by honest labor?"

"Worldly wealth can be a stepping stone or a stumbling block. Of itself it has no value. If indeed money is gotten honestly, without harm to another, it can provide a means to achieve worthy goals. But once gotten, it has the potential to be an impediment to the fulfillment of good intentions. The danger is in believing that money is a sign of inner worth. With this belief comes fear of its loss, and the subsequent loss of one's sense of worth. From that arises a desire to hoard or even hide what one has. The moment this is done, money loses all potential usefulness. It becomes a jail keeper rather than a means to freedom from want for oneself and others. Instead of ending suffering, it increases it. Instead of bringing people together, it enlarges the gulf between us.

"And remember, that which separates us from each other also separates us from God. So, what is money worth to you? Are your hands open in sharing, or closed with greed? Does your wealth flow freely, or is it dammed by fear?"

The man nodded slowly, taking the words in. With his eyes turned inward he turned and walked away through the crowd, which parted silently to let him through. We never saw him again.

"I have heard that you asked these men to leave their families and follow you," said a woman, indicating those among our company. "How can this be a good thing, turning aside from their responsibilities? You heard the woman earlier who said she was condemned for being unmarried. How can it be right for a man to be unmarried and not a woman? If a woman cannot leave her husband, why then can he?"

Jesus looked at Andrew and Simon, Philip and James, who stood nearby, men whom these people knew from the lake.

"No one was asked to renounce anything for me."

Several of his closest followers looked startled. Philip said, "But master …."

Jesus held his hand up and Philip went quiet.

"Of anyone who wishes to accompany me on my walks, or to listen to my homilies, or assist in offering healing to those who suffer, I ask if they are willing to give up the temptations and attractions of the world, for something far greater and everlasting. Some have asked me if this means they must renounce their fortunes or their pleasures or their loved ones. To this I answer they must give up anything that stands in the way of their awakening into God. Though few actually understand what is being asked of them, all suppose they do.

"I do not force my view of things on anyone. But until you have discovered the pathway to your own truth you must ask so that your questions can be answered, and seek diligently after truth if you would find it. What good would it do to go to the home of your beloved and stand outside the door without knocking? Would you blame him for not opening the door?"

Many among the crowd shook their heads *no*, Philip among them. Jesus had not explained this before, and I was glad to hear him speak of it, as some among our own ranks had complained that he asked too much of us.

"You must give up anything that stands in the way of your awakening into God," he repeated. "God does not ask and I, his son, do not ask you to leave your wife or father or children. You heard the man who stood here earlier asking if his wealth would prevent him from entering the kingdom of heaven. The answer to that is also no. Neither should you judge those who are wealthy or poor, those married or unmarried, with or without children, thinking those conditions represent the approval or disapproval of our Father. Another's circumstances are nothing to you, except that you may alleviate suffering when it is in evidence and you have the power to do so.

"These things of the world prevent your entrance through the narrow gates of righteousness only if they prevent you from seeing the glory of that which lay beyond … only if they entice you away from your goal … only if they become more important to you than union with the Divine.

"It is God's will that you find joy in loving companionship with your family and friends as a reflection of His love. As you open your heart to others, even strangers, you will begin to recognize the signposts pointing to your true Home.

"We are given the things of the world in stewardship. They are never ours to have for ourselves alone. The riches of earth are on loan to us, so we may learn generosity of spirit. It is not right to pass by one in need when your own warehouses are full. You are worthy of all the gifts of the kingdom, but only if you are willing to share what you have. A mother would not withhold her breast from her infant. If she did so, it would soon dry up. Legs not used will wither."

"But these young men, not yet married, have turned away from a life contributing to our communities. Instead they follow you. This is not normal. And you, are you married? Do you have children? And these women, is it not immoral for them to wander the highways with unmarried men? How could their fathers let them do these things?"

It was a young priest who asked these questions. He stood respectfully, hands folded in front of him, in contrast to other priests who lingered at the edges of the crowd, mocking Jesus' every word.

I waited with the others, wondering how he would answer.

"Each of these men and women is free to follow their own conscience. And each is dedicated to serving God in their service to man. They may walk with me but they do not serve me. I am no more than they, no more than you or any other standing here on this hillside."

He had told us this often enough, but I knew there were some among our group who still thought him the *only* son of God. He had never made any such claim, but people condemn (or worship) him according to their own interpretation of what he did say.

"But who will support the community? The synagogue?" the priest insisted.

"We are few in number," said Jesus, "come together in common purpose, to feed the souls of men and lead them to the gates of heaven. Some are married, some have children of their own. We do not subject the youngest children to the rigors of the road, but once they have taken their mitzvah they are free to join us. The women pass through the same training women in the village do, so they may carry the sacred trust of motherhood if God grant them that. There are fathers and daughters among us, mothers and sons. And while a few of the women do not have their father's blessing, none has reason to be ashamed before heaven.

"You ask of marriage. What is marriage? Is it a promise made to priest, or to God? The former without the latter is without soul, and meaningless in the eyes of heaven.

"*And what of love?* If a union through marriage is built on empty promises, the woman so bound is little more than a prostitute, is she not? And if the union is nothing more than a political alliance, both husband and wife are the same as sheep bought and sold in the marketplace. Yet there is no power on earth that could sever a real marriage.

"Instead of holding fast to rigid ideas and legal standards, we ought to pattern our unions after the blending of soul and spirit which is the very same formula offered us for entering the kingdom of heaven. We should strive to love *and* honor each other, husband, wife, father, mother, sister, brother, the least of us and the greatest. Without that, it is all meaningless."

It had become quite dark, and he rose then and turned back to our camp, leaving many questions unasked. But the people would return the next day.

"There are none more devoted than they," I whispered to James as we lay together that night, speaking of Jesus and Miriam.

"Her brother will kill her if he thinks they have married secretly," James said, "as well if he thinks they have not." He sighed. "Eli hates him, believing Jesus has brought shame upon their family. It is better he avoid the issue, if possible."

"I do not know the real nature of their relationship," I confessed. "They are as close as any husband and wife, but Miriam does not share confidences the way other women do. She was taught, as well as I, the sacred marriage ways."

James and, I assumed, a few of the other men had also been taught the simple yet difficult exercise that brings together two people in spirit without their merging in the flesh. The main purpose of this exercise is to enhance the bringing forth of new life, rather than to substitute for it.

One of our most sacred duties is to serve as parents to our children; this we do for the children and ourselves, of course, but perhaps even more so for the community, serving as stand-ins for our divine Parents. The spiritual marriage has another purpose. But I did not speak with my friend about these things, at least not since our training in Egypt.

Chapter Thirteen

THE SHINING ONES

Mother would not leave her sister alone in Nazareth, and Mary said she wasn't prepared to leave the children. There were four yet at home, between the ages of twelve and sixteen. She wanted to see Ruth, the youngest, through her first woman's ceremony, and then she would join us, she said.

Ruth was just two years older than my sister Judy. I never really got to know Judy and John --Matthias' children -- after he and mother married. For that matter I had missed much of my blood sister's life, as James and I seemed to be perpetually on the road. Now that Elizabeth was older she occasionally joined our band of travelers during breaks from her schooling in Carmel. I looked forward to those times.

One day a dark-skinned man appeared on Miriam's doorstep asking for me. When I came out he bowed, and handed me a note. I was torn between tearing it open it in front of people I hardly knew (friends of Simon's) and waiting until I was alone to savor the message. I knew it was from mother... but who was the messenger? I had never seen him before.

"Come, you are tired, sit down," I said, remembering my manners. He started to protest, but exhaustion won over and he took a seat at the table under a pomegranate tree. I brought a pitcher of water, still cool from the well. While he drank, first one and then a second cupful, I set a plate of early grapes and fresh bread with honey in front of him.

Where was Miriam, I wondered? I did not want to leave the man sitting there alone while I went to my room to read the note, so I sat and waited with him.

Finally he spoke. "Forgive me. My throat was so dry I could not find my voice. Thank you for your kindness. I am Ephraim," he said, as if reading the questions in my mind. "Your aunt was kind to offer me a place in her home when my parents were killed," he said quietly. "I had nowhere else to go. My father had recently brought us from Nubia to work in the carpentry shop in Nazareth. The foreman of the shop had seen his work when he came to my country in search of rare woods, and offered him a powerful incentive to move."

Ephraim's face beamed when speaking of his father, clearly proud of him. I wondered how old he was, and what had happened to his parents, hoping he would continue his story so I wouldn't have to ask the personal questions.

"I met many of your countrymen when I studied in Alexandria," I said, refilling his cup. "Have you ever been there – to the school?"

"Yes. Father studied there too, in his youth. This is why he wanted to come here. Do you know Hebeny?" he asked.

"I do! Oh, *how is he?*"

"He is still headman at the school. He is father's older brother. Hebeny told father and me that we must come here, to meet the man called Jesus. My uncle said there is no one in all the world like him, and that at his side I would stand in the light of a thousand stars, igniting my own little light."

Ephraim's eyes shone with joy and hope and wonder at such a marvelous prospect. I put my hand on his and told him "You can meet Jesus this night. He will be here for dinner."

The boy's mouth opened, but no words came.

Just then I saw Miriam and called her over, introducing them. "See he gets a bath, and clean clothes, sister. Ephraim will join us for dinner." She nodded and I ran off with note in hand.

It was from Mary rather than mother. The date had been set for Ruth's celebration, and she wanted Miriam and me, and some of the other women to come. Two days later we were on our way to Nazareth.

"Why don't you stay in Capernaum?" I asked Ephraim. When they had met over dinner Jesus embraced him as a younger brother.

"No, I promised auntie I would bring you back safely."

His words made me smile. Simon and Peter had trained most of the younger women who traveled with us to protect our own persons. I knew how to wield a club and even a sword, though I could not imagine ever using them for the purpose of harming another.

"But you will return with us later, won't you? With you I feel like I have a part of Hebeny with us. He is beloved by all who know him, and already we have come to love you too."

Ephraim would return to become a part of our troupe, staying with us to the very end.

*

The sands of our world were shifting, though the extent of change was difficult to recognize back then. Soon we would not have the luxury of traveling all the way to Carmel for such rites. Ruth would be one of the last to celebrate her coming of age ceremony there. I think we all sensed this, and savored each moment of our time together.

It was our tradition that only those who have reached their first moon are allowed to take this journey. Judy, the youngest of our cousins, was devastated when reminded of the custom. She would be the last to reach this important milestone, and already felt left out of much that went on around her. Knowing her disappointment and recognizing she may never have the chance to go to Carmel in the future, the older women gathered the night before we left and reached a compromise. She would travel with us and take part in everything except for the final ceremony, known as the covenant of womanhood. She was ecstatic.

"Salome," Rachel called out, "come back here and sit with me. And Judy, you and Veronica come too." I had been walking since early morning, and the idea of riding for awhile appealed to me. Rachel patted the cluster of fat pillows next to her in the cart. As I settled in I noticed with a shock that her hair had gone almost entirely grey. Time was going by so quickly, and with each moon I felt I had less and less control over my life. I thought too about the coming of age rituals for men, which were too often shaped by the blood of war and death. Ours, on the other hand, was marked by the blood that brings forth life and thus hope for the future. Most of the men I knew had risen through the Essene traditions, and shunned this bonding through blood loss as far as was possible. But there were times it could not be avoided.

My own ritual seemed long ago. Miriam and Naomi had stood with me as my sponsors then, just as Elizabeth and Martha would for Ruth. A sponsor was a sister by blood or heart bond, one who had undergone her own rites within the previous few years. This ensured a never-ending chain of women connected by the ancient bonds of sisterhood.

Our party represented three generations of women; Rachel was slightly older than Mary and mother, Judy was then around ten, and my friends and I were in between. We talked of the rites to come and those past, how things had changed or stayed the same from generation to generation. We talked about many things, while carefully avoiding the uncertainty of the times. Eventually the others fell asleep in the afternoon heat. I saw Mary and Naomi walking together at the front of the procession, and climbed out of the cart to join them.

I loved Mary as my own mother. The two sisters were much alike in thinking and temperament, though quite different in appearance. Mary was raven-haired with startling deep blue eyes that turned almost black with intensity when she turned her concentration on something. I shared mother's coloring, hair bronzed with the sun and eyes blue-green like the moss I'd seen hanging from trees in Britannia. Mary was smooth skinned, the color of seasoned ivory, which darkened when she spent time outdoors in the sun. Mother had passed her freckles on to me, which were sprinkled liberally across my chest and shoulders. I had always been self-conscious about them and the fact I did not brown under the sun as everyone else did, until James convinced me they were a part of what he called my *mystery*.

Mother and Mary were capable of spending an entire day together without saying a word, anticipating thoughts and needs in ways that unnerved people, as if they were reading each other's mind. There were also times they talked non-stop, finishing the other's sentences.

In some ways it was like that with Naomi, Miriam and me. We three had traveled to Egypt together and shared many marvelous experiences over the years. First was the school in Alexandria, staffed with the greatest teachers from around the world. From there we went to Heliopolis where we learned the science of form and numbers, taking part in rituals within the great pyramids. We ended our novitiate in Mareotis, where we studied the sacred art of healing through movement, sound and the use of plants and other medicinals. In Alexandria and Heliopolis we had much the same training as Jesus did, though the studies in Mareotis were devised for women.

Only those who have passed through the portals of initiation in the great pyramid will know the bonds that form between fellow initiates who have stood at death's door.

We used to joke about which of us was the wisest, which one sat at the peak of the pyramid and which the base. Eventually wisdom began to emerge from our youthful competition, and I came to understand that the greater honor lay in quietly helping others attain the heights.

We had leisure to recall those times while on our journey to Carmel, and to share our stories. There was no direct route through the Levant from Nazareth, unless we wanted leave behind the carts and scramble over rocky hills on foot. Since there were several older women among us besides Rachel, it was not an option. Besides, James said it was too dangerous. And so we had to travel somewhat north to the port city of Acco, and turn south from there to Carmel.

Acco had a large Hellenistic Jewish population, but also many Romans and Egyptians and Nubians and people I had never heard of before. It was a major center of trade, with many languages and varieties of food; one of the most sophisticated cities in all of Canaan. While our accommodations were usually very modest, the inn that night bordered on the luxurious. It was the only place available that seemed safe enough so near the port.

There were many unfamiliar dishes on the other tables when we went in to eat, and a wondrous mix of smells. We decided to experiment, asking the inn keep to bring us food we would not find in our own country. He looked at us as if we had gone mad, and would not leave the table until Julius and Arturus nodded their assent. Turning away, he yelled something in a language I didn't understand to a middle-aged woman who was probably his wife. Without looking up, she yelled something back, and thereafter took care of our needs.

We didn't think to mention our dietary restrictions and were brought two dishes we started to refuse, though the men called them back. "I wondered if you could be coaxed to try the mussels," laughed Arturus. Though he called himself a Jew, he had been raised far to the north where the rules were decidedly more relaxed than in Palestine. And so he did not let those delicacies, as he called them, go to waste.

There were a variety of sauces for the fish and vegetable plates -- a few too spicy for my tastes. And the sweets ... ah, creams and honey pastries that brought to mind the journey north through Gallia that Miriam and I took with uncle Joseph so many years before.

There was a large fireplace in the inn with big comfortable chairs stuffed with wool that overlooked the sea below. The night air was chill and the wine so satisfying that we stayed awake talking half the night in front of the fire – until Marcus reminded us we needed to get an early start and had best be off to bed.

We were greeted with a hot barley drink at dawn, and bread left over from dinner. The sun had barely broken the horizon when we were already on the road. We huddled silently in our blankets, walking or riding in carts. But in the afternoon warmth we resumed our conversation from the night before.

"Tell me about your mother," asked Miriam. "Her name was Anna, wasn't it?"

The sisters smiled at her name.

"She died before Veronica was born, so she knows her only from our stories," Mary began. "It saddened me our mother would never know any of Salome's children, and only Jesus of mine.

"They say she was old, too old to give birth the first time. Some said she and my father Joachim had found displeasure in the eyes of God, and that was the reason for their many barren years together. Even the priests said these things, and would not accept the sacrifices Joachim brought year after year to the synagogue in Jerusalem. Mother said it nearly destroyed him, and seeing that nearly broke her heart.

"But only one who is himself without blame is fit to cast judgment against another. Clearly those priests did not qualify," said Mary, without a hint of bitterness.

"I do not know if our parents were being tested by God, but I think not," mother said, looking at her sister. "Just as it is perilous for an infant to be born before the tenth moon, so too must all the stars in heaven be in their right place before a new age can be birthed. God surely smiled upon this elderly couple in granting them their first daughter.

"Mother told us father was at first disappointed with the birth of a girl, and though it was unlikely at their age, he held out hopes for a son – especially as the priests had begun accepting his gifts to the temple.

"But his time was finished. And before I was old enough to know my father," said Mary, "he unexpectedly died, leaving mother and me alone."

"But …." Miriam started, looking from Mary to Salome.

"So how did I get here?" laughed mother.

Miriam blushed and nodded.

"When Joachim died, Cleophas, his brother, came to mother and offered to take care of her. As Joachim had not been a poor man, mother did not want for anything and at first declined his brother's offer. But as time wore on, she realized her fondness for him and as it was not suitable that a woman raise her child alone she accepted his offer, which by then had changed to one of marriage. I was the result of that union," mother added with a laugh.

"He was a good man," offered Mary. "And I had a new sister, for which I will be forever grateful."

"Mother said she knew even before my quickening there would be two girls, and no more. And she knew the reason for it," said mother.

"Reason?" asked Miriam. "What reason?"

"Only after many years of training in Carmel was Mary chosen as the vessel for *the Shining One*." Mother's voice had fallen to a whisper.

"I have not heard that term before: the Shining One," I said. "Not even from Judy. I like that. It suits him."

"Shining One, the Light of the World, the Christos as he is called by the Greeks. It is all the same. Though I would suggest you not call him these things to his face," Mary laughed.

"I would not!" said Miriam. "I think he would never speak to me again if I did. He is in fact the most ordinary of men and at the same time, the most remarkable. People often ask me what he is like, *really like*. And they think I am being coy by not answering. But I do not know what to say to such a question."

"Nor do I," the three of us said in unison.

"Well," Salome continued, "mother said she had known from the first time she laid eyes on Mary that she was the one who had been anointed from the beginning, and that I would come to stand alongside her so she wouldn't have to bear her burden alone. Still, she was shocked when she realized I would not be returning home to her after our initial training. She had hoped I would only join my sister in later life. This is why she named me Mary as well, thinking one way or another she would have her Mary with her."

"Mary? But your name is Salome … isn't it?" Miriam asked.

"*Mary Salome*. Salome was Anna's own grandmother's name. But there are enough Marys around without it being the name of two sisters who were almost inseparable. So everyone has always called me Salome.

"I am not sure how old she was when I was born, or when she died," mother went on. "But she always seemed so vital. Cleophas died when I was quite young, after which mother married their youngest brother. By then we were both away at school, and hardly knew these men. When I did see them, it seemed to me they were in awe of her, their own wife."

Mary nodded agreement. "Not just them, but all men. No one, especially the priests, seemed to know what to think of her. She knew the scriptures better than they and took care to abide by the laws, though she found many of them foolish. You can imagine how hard it was for a woman who had been thrice widowed and who had only produced daughters to find acceptance in a world ruled by men. But she never complained. I have thought about that often now I am older. We were much too young to appreciate it at the time. Besides, we were away, living in a world of our own, and did not see all she went through.

"I am glad she lived long enough to see her first grandson. But their time together – *our* time together was much too short. She was gone before we returned from Egypt."

The shadows were growing long on the road, and Marcus dropped back to ask if we wished for him to ride ahead to the next village in search of an inn. The two sisters said yes, thanking him,

"I do not know what we would do without Marcus," said mother.

"His father was also named Marcus," added Mary thoughtfully. "I never met him, but he was devoted to mother. She never spoke of him herself, but I heard many stories after she died. Some thought there was impropriety between them, but I do not think so. Besides," she laughed, "how would she have had time with three husbands in a row!"

Miriam said, "Even in Magdala we had heard of Anna the healer."

"Or Anna the witch," said mother dryly.

"Witch?" I asked, incredulous.

"People always judge what they do not understand. She was a powerful healer, always crediting God with the results of her efforts. But she spoke of God as both Mother and Father, giving tribute to the Mother for many healings, especially those that came with the use of herbs and poultices, things of the earth. The priests would themselves speak only of the Father, suspicious of anything that reminded people of their ancient devotion to the Goddess of the earth."

"Why do the priests hate the Goddess so? She is the moon to the sun, neither of which shines upon us without the other." This had always galled me. "It is the same as their insistence that the presence of women would contaminate the Holy of Holies."

Mother put her hand up to silence me. "Daughter, *we know*. That the priests pretend to understand the mind of God, asserting that He considers some of His children more worthy than others, is an affront to the Creator. But that is between them, and has nothing to do with us. We know who we are."

"And yes, Anna was a great healer," said Mary, changing the subject. "While she used herbs and other medicines to aid in her efforts, her greatest work was accomplished through her insistence on seeing her patient without blemish, as created by God."

"That is what Judy taught us, and what we learned in Egypt," said Miriam. "But our teachers also cautioned us to be inconspicuous in our efforts on behalf of others. They knew well the dangers of being a woman drawing attention to herself."

We had reached the inn. Marcus arranged the dinner before our arrival, which sat waiting for us, already warmed. That night we went to bed early, to make up for the night before. Rachel had us up and out on the road early, as she was anxious to reach our destination. The sea breezes kept us alert and on our feet, and there was little conversation. We arrived at the edge of Carmel in the late afternoon and came to uncle Joseph's house before the sun set. He was rarely there, holding it in trust to be used for such ceremonies as these. It was very near the school where Elois took over as head teacher, after Judy retired to Egypt. I looked forward to seeing her again.

As we unloaded the carts I noticed the older women watching Ruth as she wandered off alone. It brought to mind my own walk out on the high cliffs that overlook the sea when I arrived for my first rites ... and I knew they were thinking of their own coming of age, long before mine. It is the tie that joins us to all the women in our land, before and after our times of exile.

Late that night, after everyone else was in bed, I walked out under the stars. I recalled the powerful explosion of light that night so long ago, when I was transported into the heavenly realms. And I remembered the painful return to my everyday world, which felt dark and heavy in comparison. And I wondered how Ruth had fared out there on the cliffs alone.

My thoughts strayed unguarded into the unknown future, and. I felt a momentary chill of fear, and a childish desire to run to mother for comfort. But I kept my place, knowing there would be no refuge for any of us.

Chapter Fourteen

A DEEPER WOUND

Ruth's ritual was little different than any I'd attended over the years. Mother had made and embroidered the robe I wore for my ceremony. But Mary was not one for the needle arts, so Ruth's robe was a joint effort by mother, Mary and their friend Susanna.

Susanna was visiting Mary when she went into labor. Ruth's birth went fast, and she breached before the midwife arrived. While Susanna had no experience in midwifery, there was little choice but to take over, tending to mother and daughter. She always said that having been a part of her birth created a powerful bond between them.

When Ruth entered the room that night with her sister Martha and my sister Elizabeth beside her, I marveled at the transformation. There is something about the long ritual – first with her two sponsors in private, and then with the larger group of women – that utterly changes a girl. When the circle opens to receive the neophyte, we draw her in and embrace her as one of us. And then we join to sing to her, the songs and chants ranging from sacred to playful, hinting at her new spiritual role and that to come in the marriage bed.

After this each woman approaches the initiate and whispers her vision, for her ears alone. While those closest to the girl might give a gift of something crafted specially for her, the sharing of aspiration or prophecy is the most cherished of gifts. By the end of the night, another woman has joined the sisterhood.

As we were of the Essene tradition, the ritual also marked the point when another soul joined ranks with an ancient Brotherhood that spanned vast tracks of land from east to west and north to south, comprised of men and women of all races and beliefs – vessels of light in a world of darkness.

It is no wonder then that the woman who leaves Carmel shines like a thousand stars, no wonder she turns heads as she walks the long road back to her home. Upon her return she takes up a new role in her community, sharing in the collective spiritual and civic responsibilities.

From that day she is free to marry, though few women do so immediately ... especially in such uncertain times. Many young men and women had been putting off marriage and children until they were older, some foreswearing it altogether. The priests were haranguing parents, blaming them for shirking their duty in finding husbands and wives for their children. They stood on synagogue steps, pointing fingers at young people walking by, cursing them for not fulfilling their God-given roles. As a result some of them had begun avoiding the synagogues altogether.

"Pay them no mind," Elois told Elizabeth, who would stay behind in Carmel to continue her studies. Elois had married when she was very young, and was widowed before she bore any children. She had herself been the target of many a priest's public rant, and learned to ignore them. When she took over the school after Judy left, the priests finally left her alone. "Your time will come; do not rush it," she said.

My sister was beautiful, more so than I had been at her age. There was no lack of men interested in her, but she set her standards high. Her husband would be an Essene (though obviously not from the reclusive sects that practiced celibacy and shunned women), treading the way laid out for us from ancient times by the Brotherhood.

"Finish your studies as quickly as you can, then come join us," I told her during our goodbyes. "You will find your path, and somewhere along the way, a man worthy to walk with you."

"I will miss you, sister," she said, "more than anyone. Somehow, when others say such things, it seems they are talking down to me. But not you. I can trust you to speak the truth."

Though Elizabeth was quite a bit younger than I, and though we had been apart many years by that time, we had somehow managed to grow close -- and I loved her dearly. "I will see you soon, I know. But we must leave. James and some of the others wait for us in Tyre. From there we will travel east to Caesarea."

"But *we* are returning to Nazareth," said mother, walking up behind us. "The time approaches when we will leave our homes to join you," she said, and it won't be long after that, my dear Elizabeth, when you'll be finished here and can join our little band."

*

We traveled together as far as Acco. There, most of the group turned off toward Nazareth, carrying letters for Miriam and Naomi's families. Helen, Martha's sister Mary, and Ruth, sister to Barnabas, together with Miriam, Naomi and I traveled north, with Arturus as our guide. Julius, Marcus and Ephraim went with Mother and the others.

At first I missed the noisy camaraderie, but in the quiet I fell back into my thoughts. I liked Arturus. He always seemed to know when to drop behind, leaving us to our silence or private conversation. And yet at meals or around the evening fire he was an amiable companion, ready with stories of life on the road, or his youth in Rome.

Those were the last days of summer, not overly warm but with a honeyed stillness. Flies glided by, barely bothering to buzz. I lost all sense of the day, until the coolness of dusk settled upon us.

Arturus' voice reached across the growing shadows. "It will be full dark by the time we reach Tyre. There is an inn on the outskirts that I know. We can stay there, or press on to the city. The men do not expect us until tomorrow and won't worry if they don't see us tonight. Which would you prefer?"

He looked from one to the other of us. It had been a long day's journey and I was tired. If we pressed on, James would want to hear all about the trip, and I was not ready for conversation.

"I would like to stay outside the city," I said, speaking first.

Ruth looked surprised, but nodded.

"I too need a night of quiet," agreed Miriam.

The inn was most agreeable. There was bread just out of the oven and bowls of honey with a faint scent of herbs. A spicy stew had small bits of lamb, and the last fruits of summer swam in fresh cream. After dinner Miriam, Naomi and I retired to our room and fell quickly to sleep.

We were on the road by daybreak. The noise of the city assaulted us even before we reached the gates of Tyre. By the time we got to the inn where we'd arranged to meet the men, I wanted nothing more than to retreat under a quilt until night's quiet returned.

"What is wrong, my love?" asked James, when they returned a short while later. "Are you ill?"

"No, it is nothing," I tried to smile. "It was just so peaceful in Carmel, and this city … is not."

"Come," he said, pulling me away from the others. "I know a place."

He led me back to the city wall and we followed it around until we came to a quiet street where several women were hanging their wash, talking quietly among themselves. They looked at us curiously, saying nothing. We continued on to an opening in the wall, which revealed a stairway. Climbing, we made our way to the top of the high wall looking out over the sea. The clamor of the port below was muted by the sound of the surf. I could see guards posted at different intervals along the wall, but there were none close by. If they saw us at all, they made no sign of it.

James pulled me into his arms and kissed me, gently. He knew me well, knew I needed time to readjust to his presence before asking anything else of me. We sat down on the wall, leaning against each other. Eyes closed, I breathed in the salty air mixed with James' scent, and felt content.

After a time, I opened my eyes and looked at my husband as he lay dozing. Where had all those lines on his face come from, I wondered ... and the grey in his hair? When had he begun to age? I rarely saw a mirror, but imagined I too must have changed. My fingers could not sense the lines in my own face, nor tell the color of my hair unless I pulled it out in front of my eyes. But my hands belied my age. Not old of course, but no longer young.

James' eyes opened suddenly. "I felt you watching me," he said. "I do that sometimes, when you are asleep. I love to look at you when all the cares of the world disappear and you are my Veronica, the girl I loved from the first – before you even knew I existed."

I started to protest, but he smiled and put his hand over my lips. "No matter. You are here now, with me." And he kissed me again, then stood and pulled me to my feet.

"Better now?" he asked, as we descended back into the city.

I was disappointed not to find Jesus among the men. So were Miriam and the others. "He went ahead to Caesarea," said the other James, son of Alphaeus.

"You know how he is," John said to Miriam. She nodded, her grey eyes reflecting the gathering clouds.

There were so many demands upon my cousin that he needed time alone now and then, even from us. Even from Miriam. It was something I understood about him, often craving such silence myself. James never really understood this. He sometimes took my reticence personally, trying all the harder to fill my needs himself. This of course just intensified my need to be alone. But all in all, it was a small matter between us.

We left Tyre the following morning. On the third day we crossed the beautiful cedar-covered mountains northwest of Galilee. It was one of those perfect days and we slowed our pace to take full advantage of it. Arturus had tried to prod us to move faster, and I could feel his anxiety as we made camp, stuck as we were in the middle of nowhere at nightfall.

"What is wrong?" I asked him. It had been such a peaceful day I could not find it in me to feel concern.

He took my arm and moved me over to James, who was gathering wood for the fire.

"We should not be out here alone like this," he said through clenched teeth.

"Why? What is wrong?" asked James, looking quickly around. We were in a wide clearing, nearly surrounded by tall trees. The moon was just large enough to dampen the stars without casting any light itself.

"I don't know for sure. The feeling has been growing all day. I do not want to frighten the others, but we must take turns tonight keeping watch. Veronica, maybe if you suggest it to the group...."

I tried to laugh. "Of course. They will agree, to humor me, thinking it only a woman's worry."

"I didn't mean .... "

"It is alright, Arturus. It serves nothing to bring fear into our midst. But what do you think it might be?"

"There is always the danger of thieves on major trade routes. But it should be obvious to dishonest men that we carry nothing of value."

"We carry nothing at all," said James. "Not even beds to sleep upon."

Together we gathered a large pile of wood, enough to keep the fire going all night. It would be cold at that altitude, and we had little else than our shawls and the robes we wore. We had just one donkey, whose single blanket was thin. That we gave to Zacharias, the eldest among us.

Our dinner was spare, leavings from the previous night's table, and a few nuts and dates. But thanks to Andrew and John, there was wine to warm us.

"It is from Rome," said Andrew, who bought it in Tyre. "I had hoped to share it with my Sophie when we returned to the lake. But I'm sure she will understand."

I was glad it was dark, for Andrew's sake. He blushed easily, especially when teased by the men about Sophie. He hoped to marry her, he said, when things settled down. I feared the peaceful time he looked for might never come. "What better time than now?" I asked later that night. "Why don't you marry when we get back?" The others were already asleep around the fire. He had volunteered the first watch, and. I wanted to make sure the fire was strong before leaving him on his own.

"But everyone is spread far and wide. Who will come to our wedding? We don't even know where everyone is."

"There are ways to send messages, relayed from one person to the next. Why wait? You could marry before the new year."

"But what then? We marry, and Jesus calls us to travel south, or east. And then? We would have to part, and I could not bear that once....once we have been together."

His voice quavered in the flickering light, and I reached out to him. "James and I are usually together. Sophie loves you, and would go wherever you go. She understands your love for him, and seems to share it."

Just then the donkey's bray ripped through the night, and we flew to our feet. The others had awakened, and voices called across the flickering light of the fire to ask what had happened.

But no one knew. We could not see into the darkness beyond, and so we waited, tense. The beast's hard breathing was the only sound to be heard except the crackle of the burning logs. *Something* had agitated it, something that was still there.

A scream cut through the night, followed by scuffling sounds and curses in the dark. I froze where I stood. Several of the men circled round us women, pressing us close to the flames to protect us. At that moment I had more fear of falling into the fire than whatever it was that might come at us from the darkness.

"Watch out!" screamed Helen, grabbing hold of Ruth and pulling her close. Ruth's hair had been singed, the acrid smell encircled us.

It was not long before the noises stopped, and the limp forms of two men landed with a thud at our feet. Iscariot, Simon and Thomas stood above them, their faces grim.

"Your arm is bleeding," Mary said matter-of-factly, wrapping her scarf around Simon's arm above the wound. It was bleeding heavily, quickly saturating the scarf and dripping to the ground. She calmly took the spear from Judas' hand and thrust it into the flames; then without a word she touched its tip to the wound. A single cry pierced the night air. Simon's jaw clenched, his eyes betraying the pain. Mary handed the spear back to Judas, took another piece of cloth handed her by someone and tied it directly over the wound.

"There, the bleeding has stopped," she said, all this before any of us had come to our senses enough to act. Simon swooned. The men laid him down upon the one blanket, and Helen sat to give her lap as a pillow for his head.

One of the strangers groaned and Judas stood at their heads, glowering over them. He was a tall man, and sturdily built. Feet planted widely, spear in hand, he would give pause to either of them when they regained consciousness.

"Thieves, I think. I doubt the attack was planned, or there would have been more men."

"Maybe there are more," said Ruth, looking about nervously.

"No, the donkey is calm now, and I sense nothing further," I said, putting my arm around Ruth. "But do we have rope to tie these men?"

Thomas took a spare length of rope attached to the donkey's pack and with James' help tied them to a nearby tree.

I carried a small pouch of herbs, as did Naomi and Miriam. (It was an old habit from our time in Egypt that would many times come in handy in the days ahead.) I found some which I brewed into a tea to help Simon sleep. Ruth bundled one of her robes to put under

Simon's head, and Helen got up to stretch her legs. We built the fire up and huddled close together for warmth. No one really slept the rest of that night and by dawn we all sat with John during his watch.

In the morning Miriam removed Simon's bandage and was pleased to see his arm had not festered. She cleaned the wound and rewrapped it, then fashioned a sling.

"What will we do with them?" asked Judas, pointing his spear at the two men. They were by then awake, shivering with cold and fear. I would have given them something for warmth, had there been anything.

"Leave them as they are," said Simon, always the firebrand. "It is enough we are threatened daily from Rome, chastised by our own Sanhedrin, judged by our neighbors, without being attacked by animals like this!"

"No, we cannot do that. Have we not learned the lesson of forgiveness?" It was John who spoke. "It is allowed to mete a just punishment for those who do wrong to others. But what might that be here, for these two? Leaving them tied up is a death sentence. We do not have that right. And besides, no real harm was done."

"No harm!" shouted Simon. "They would have killed us if we hadn't sneaked up behind them unawares."

"Maybe. But that does not give us the right to take their lives, even indirectly." John spoke just loud enough for them to hear. His eyes were luminous in the early morning light, reminding me of my cousin.

"He's right," I agreed. "What say you?" I asked the two men, squatting down in front of them. "You decide your punishment."

"What? Are you crazy?" shouted Simon.

"Hush," said Mary with her quiet authority. Simon's jaw snapped shut.

"Well?" I waited.

"Let us go," the one said, hoarsely.

"Why?" asked Judas. "Why should we? So you can harm others who pass this way? We would then be responsible for what befalls them."

"Let us go. Please," he repeated.

Mary brought water to the men, and held the cup for them to drink. The man who had spoken began to weep.

"I would not blame you, no matter what you decide. But you ask, and I say if you let me go, and if you would allow me, I would follow you to learn the reason for your kindness, and to repay that kindness in my treatment of others. I cannot speak for my brother here. But you have touched my heart."

In the end we agreed to allow Hiram to follow us to Caesarea. He pleaded for his brother, that we might show him the same mercy. "He cannot care for himself, and does only what I tell him. He was born this way," said Hiram. "His guilt is mine."

Along the road we learned that Hiram's family home had been burned by Roman soldiers the year before, their father and mother burned alive. Though the brothers escaped, Hiram was tormented with guilt at not having rescued them. They were hungry, starving, and attacked us in the hope we had food or money.

While Hiram would never leave his brother to follow with us in our ministry, his life was changed that day and he became as devoted a student of the teachings of life as any of us. They traveled with us to Caesarea and stayed a time, eventually settling in Bethsaida. There both men worked for Zebedee, and became advocates for the poor and oppressed who lived along the lake.

*

Caesarea reminded me somewhat of Alexandria, both cities more cosmopolitan than even Jerusalem. It had a Hellenistic feeling, despite the name. Rome's influence was limited to the political center. Herod's son Phillip had it built as the administrative center for Gualanitis – far away from his feuding step brothers.

But the best part was we were almost completely unknown there. We could disappear into the crowds, or walk in the hills outside the city unnoticed. Visits there offered a respite from the demands of our growing ministry. The burden carried by Jesus increased daily. Everyone seemed to think they knew what he should do to change or improve the world. Everyone thought he belonged to them, and them alone.

Though a Roman city, it offered us respite from the eye of Rome. In Galilee and Judea there were many who feared my cousin, feared the power he held over the multitudes that followed his every step. I did not understand why the authorities focused so much of their attention on him. There were other men who publicly claimed the role of Messiah to the Jews; each had their own following. These seemed a greater threat to their authority than Jesus did. But for some reason, both Rome and the Sanhedrin had come to believe that if he gave the word, the people would rise up against their oppressors, Roman or Jew.

The irony is he continually counseled *against* revolt. In fact he advised us to willingly pay tribute to Rome, and to tithe freely to the synagogue and directly to the poor according to each one's ability and the dictates of conscience. Jesus never asked anyone to take up arms or turn against another, but advised any who would listen to love their brother as they love the Lord.

All men, all women, all children are our family. There are no exceptions. None. How then would he call (as some say he has) for brother to strike brother, for husband to leave wife, for nation to attack nation, or anyone to enslave another? Such a thing would be impossible.

But because there was no apparent reason to fear him, they feared him all the more.

Chapter Fifteen

THE PERIL OF DESPAIR

"Does anyone know when he'll be back?" asked Martha. The crowds had been gathering ever since Jesus had raised Lazarus. And even though he had been gone an entire season, they continued to wait.

"He does not tell *me* such things," said Mary. "Though I am his mother, he never has – not even as a child," she laughed. "I do not think he knows himself what each day will bring, until it arrives. He has always said our lives are not our own. And yet," she paused, more thoughtful, "he says also we are masters of our lives, and that all the kingdoms bow down to our authority."

"Yes, and that is the kind of thing that gets him … and us … in trouble. People think they know what he is talking about, but they do not. They use his words to mean whatever serves their purposes." Martha sounded frustrated.

She turned and began putting the clean dishes back on the shelf. "The Romans think he is telling people the Emperor must bow down to *him*. Because they are hungry for power, they suppose he is as well. The poor also misunderstand, thinking he invites them to worship him – which they are glad to do. It confuses them when he gets them up off their knees, reproaching them for giving away their power to

141

him. And the priests hate him for refusing to bow down to *them*."

"He cannot win," said Mary. Though they had just finished cleaning up after the morning meal, the two women immediately began preparations for the next one. Martha's servants were all out shopping or cleaning the house or gathering firewood. There were many guests in the house, and much to be done. Besides, they enjoyed their time alone together.

Two boys ran through the courtyard, chasing each other and laughing.

"They must belong to someone staying here," Mary said, closing the gate behind her, "though I don't recognize either one. (This was the other Mary, sister to Martha and Lazarus.) It's good to have children around us." The boys had knocked over a stool, not even noticing it in their game. Mary picked it up and set it aright. The two girls who'd accompanied her to the market began putting their purchases away.

"I could barely make my way through the crowds that line the street out front. When *will* he be back?" she asked.

Before anyone could answer, Lazarus came out of the house with Nicodemus and two other men unknown to the women. They'd been inside all morning talking quietly. Lazarus gestured for the women to join them at the table.

He leaned over so they wouldn't be overheard. "Barnabas here has just come from Caesarea where Jesus and some of the others have been staying." Barnabas had many stories about how the crowds, once almost non-existent there, had been growing, and following Jesus everywhere he went. People were demanding miracles and signs of him, to prove he is the son of God. And when he did not respond to their demands, many turned against him, aligning with the priests already intent on destroying him.

Mary later said that as she listened to Barnabas that morning she finally understood there was nothing her son could have done to prevent the various groups from rising up against him. If he gave them the signs they asked for, some said it was the work of demons, others denounced him for some impropriety or other -- healing on the Sabbath was one of them. If he chided them for needing signs rather than going into their own hearts to seek the truth of his words, they accused him of speaking to them like children. Yet if he gave the higher teachings, as he did with his followers, they became confused and left.

The priests frequently challenged him on matters of the Law, expecting him to give the simple answers. But when he offered deeper truths, they turned on him as jackals would a kid. But he was no submissive lamb to be led to the slaughter. Barnabas reported that whenever the authorities closed in on him, he just disappears.

"Disappears?" asked Rachel, coming out of the house. "What do you mean, he disappears?

"I do not know how else to describe it," said Barnabas. "One moment he is there, and the next he is not. I have seen this with my own eyes on more than one occasion. It makes them furious – the ones who hate him – as they are left grasping at air. They have now added sorcery to their list of crimes.

"He asked me to tell you, mother," Barnabas turned to Mary, deferentially, "that he will see you again soon. Winter approaches and he hopes you and the children will stay in Bethany rather than journey north to Nazareth. He will look for you here or at Joseph's."

*

Nicodemus and Joseph walked a narrow path, with dangers on either side. They never hid their allegiance to Jesus, their affiliation with his followers, or the occasional challenge to convention, especially as it related to the position of women. For that they had our undying gratitude. Of course, they could usually get away with it because they were major benefactors of the temple and its many priests. They also knew the Law better than most and took liberties in its interpretation when it came to protecting the Brotherhood, a Brotherhood that did not officially exist. There were few willing to challenge them. Even the Romans kept their distance.

Still, they were wise enough to know when to step back and allow others to believe they had won an argument, or gotten their way when it served long-term plans. It was sometimes better to lose a skirmish in order to win – well, we did not wish to call it a war, though it was beginning to look like one.

Some former followers of our cousin John (the one called the Baptist) had been arrested for planning an attack on a Roman garrison located just outside Jerusalem's dung gate. Two of these men, Saul and Heman, had often been among us when Jesus was in that area. They sent word to Joseph through an intermediary to say they had been set up, and asked for his help to secure their release.

It put my uncle in a difficult position. If they were indeed among Jesus' followers, then he must do something to help them. But those were difficult times ... the risks were enormous for Jesus and for the rest of us if we were associated with criminals. Joseph asked around and learned enough to believe they were Zealots who had been using my cousin to screen their activities. In the end he did not even respond to their request.

*

"Unless you are born again, you will not see the Kingdom of God."

"But what does that mean, master? How can I be born when I am already old?" asked a man standing off to the edge of the crowd, leaning on his cane.

"We are born from our mother's womb into the bondage of flesh. Being born of the spirit frees us for eternal life. John baptized me with water; I will baptize you with fire. You must open your hearts. Confess your sins, root out your selfishness, your greed, your anger, jealousies and fear, and surrender them to the flames of purification. God is spirit and those who worship Him do so in spirit.

"Gather your families about you and pray to God in this way:

"Our Father in Heaven, holy is your name. Provide for us this day our earthly needs. Lead us from temptation and deliver us from evil. Forgive us our transgressions, as we forgive those of others. And teach us your will, so it might be done on earth as it is in Heaven."

Jesus turned his back on the crowd and raised his hands up into the air. Those of us standing nearby saw his eyes look up to heaven as he repeated the prayer in a voice that blanketed the hillside. The power of his invocation sent a thrill through me, and I knew I would never forget it to the end of my days.

When he had finished he turned back to face the people and said in the same commanding voice: *"This is the Lord's Prayer. What you ask with a pure heart will be given!"*

He walked away then without speaking another word. Usually he was followed by some part of the multitude when he tried to leave, but on that day no one moved until he had long gone.

We had been taught in Egypt to pay close attention to dreams, since we learn as much in the night as we do during the day. I had one teacher there called Amoos (I think it was – some of those Egyptian names were difficult to remember). Amoos said that it is the night that is real, and the daytime the dream. I do not know if that is true or not, but I have come to believe in the power of dreams and try my best to remember them.

That night I had many dreams, but all I remembered was a dream in which I was crossing a desert with a multitude of my brethren. It was a difficult crossing, and we were hungry and had not seen water for days. There was little of it left, and that which we had was rationed out to the youngest and oldest of us. I recall some men arguing that we should not waste the last water on the elderly, as they would soon die anyway. Their words sounded harsh to my ears, and the looks I saw on their faces were harder still to bear.

I understood what they said, but could not allow this separation to take place, and so I went around to the women and assembled them into a group. We went off onto a low rise overlooking the ravine where we had camped and there we gathered into three circles. The inside circle was comprised of the eldest women, the most powerful of us who no longer bore children. The second circle was made up of those in the middle years, who already had borne children. The third circle was the youngest women who already had their first blood. A few were pregnant, while some were still virgins. Ordinarily this third circle would be the largest, but in those harsh times, their numbers were fewer than the middle circle. This was a dangerous sign that our people were at risk of perishing.

We gathered and joined hands, and began to sing. Our strength was not great and our voices did not ring out as they should when singing the songs of power. But our hearts were pure and one in purpose. Soon we began to feel the power moving through us, the power of Shekinah, the holy Mother. And when our voices reached a pitch of greatest intensity, we stopped. And in the silence the eldest grandmother moved into the center of the circle, whispering her prayer for all our people.

"Sweet Mother in Heaven, holy is your name. Bring to us food and water that we may survive our journey. Oh Father, lead us from temptation and deliver us from the evils of despair. Forgive us our transgressions, as we forgive those of others. Teach us your will, that it might be done among us as it is in Heaven."

The sun set then in my dream. I had not noticed the sky darkening, so intent was I in our songs and prayers. But as we started back to the men thunder shattered the air, and by dark it had begun to rain. We would survive.

*

I thought about this dream all the next day, and wondered at its meaning. We did not want for food or water at that time. It is true we had little money among us, but people were generous and we always had enough. On rare occasions Jesus used the miracle of creating food for the masses, so they might learn to trust their God.

That night James and Miriam and a few others gathered around a fire and I asked Jesus about it. He smiled: "Were you listening to my words today?"

Well, the truth was I had been distracted by the dream and did not listen as closely as I usually did.

He did not wait to hear my answer. "I spoke of a hunger greater than that of the body. I told my listeners that whoever comes to hear me speak shall not hunger, and those who believe in me will never thirst.

You understand that I was speaking of the inner teacher, the indwelling spirit we call God, and not my person?"

"Yes, you have always taught us so," I responded.

"As people begin to see and believe in the God within me, they will learn to trust the same within themselves. And then they will know that everything needed for sustenance in this world will be provided for them. The Father nurtures our spirit and our Mother sees that our bodies have the food and water we need, so we may survive and prosper.

"But there is more to your dream," he smiled. "You were remembering crossing the desert in those years after leaving Egypt, before we came to Canaan. Those were harsh years, long years, and many perished along the way. The gathering of women up on the bluff was a turning point. It was a time when most were giving up hope of ever reaching the promised land – and without hope we would have perished. But the women, you women, holding the children in your arms and on your hips, had in your hearts the conviction of survival. When it comes to their children, women will never give up."

I thought awhile, and asked, "And what does this mean now? Do we risk the same end as we did then? Is it possible we will perish?" My voice sounded small in my ears, afraid of my own question. Everyone was silent, waiting to hear the answer.

"Not in the same way. There is a serious risk that we give in to despair, and lose our way. It is you, the women, who are our strength and who will see us through."

I heard someone groan on the periphery of our group, someone unhappy with his words.

"It is true," he insisted. "You will see us through this time and beyond. Never underestimate your strength, your power." He looked up and out into the shadows. "Neither should any man underestimate it.

"But none can stand alone. You will have need of each other."

Chapter Sixteen

MIRACLES

"I didn't think he would agree to stay in Capernaum."

"Well, he probably wouldn't have if Miriam hadn't offered to stay behind with him. She has more influence on him than the rest of us altogether."

Some of his followers were talking among themselves, thinking I couldn't hear them. Or perhaps they no longer cared. They were conflicted not just about Miriam, but the rest of us women as well – despite Jesus' words about how important we were to his work. Or maybe it was *because* of that. Mostly we just ignored it, except when they interfered with what he wanted of us. And then my gentle cousin became like a lion protecting his pride.

One time Sarah came into the house where we were all staying with a message in her hand for Jesus. "He's resting," Michael said, physically blocking the doorway so she could not pass. Naomi and I had been talking nearby and heard the menace in his voice. She protested, saying Thomas had told her it was urgent. "I don't care. You women are always bothering him, distracting him from his work and keeping him from needed rest. *I'll* give it to him," and he tried to grab the message from her hand.

"No, Thomas said to hand it to him directly," she said, stuffing it back into the bag at her waist. Naomi and I walked up to stand with her, but Michael just squared his shoulders and glared at us.

When Jesus found out about the incident later, he banished Michael from the group. Had this been the first such incident he probably would have let it go -- but it was not. He rarely gave way to anger, but when he did it burned white hot for an instant or two, before he let it go.

It was our habit to share stories in the evenings after dinner. One night he told us that when he was still a boy the fire of anger had twice taken hold of him and he'd had trouble breaking free of it. One incident involved a supervisor in his father's shop where Jesus was apprenticing. A new worker had gouged a fine piece of imported wood, ruining the piece he was working on, one commissioned by a wealthy but cruel merchant based in Jerusalem. Now, one's reputation is everything in commerce, and the supervisor dreaded having to tell the merchant he would need to wait for the next shipment of cedar to arrive from Syria. In his anger, the supervisor began to beat the younger man. Without thought Jesus picked up a hammer and swung it at the foreman to get him to stop. While he did not break the man's arm, it was badly bruised and he in turn had to face his father's wrath and apologize to the foreman.

He never said what the second incident was; only that he taught himself to pause before acting upon his anger after that. He would actually take two steps back to demonstrate to his anger that he would not do battle with it. The physical act eventually became a game and the temptation to merge with the fire simply disappeared.

When we were children together I never saw him angry, but I often saw his joy and laughter. He was always making up games for us to play, inviting anyone who was around to join us. If someone was sad, whether a child or adult, he would find a way to make them laugh, or at least coax a smile out of them. Laughter brought the angels to us, he said, and since they were God's emissaries it meant God had come among us too.

"But what about frowns, or tears?" asked Adi, a neighbor child.

"Does God go away when I'm sad?"

Jesus smiled as he took her hand. "God is always here with us, whether we're happy or sad. He lives right here in your heart. It's just easier for us to feel Him when we are happy, that's all."

He always took time with the little ones, which was unlike all the other boys I knew. On different occasions I saw him take an infant from their mother when they were upset. The moment he did so, the baby would stop crying when looking into the vast calm of my cousin's eyes.

And now he was older, a man without family of his own, it sometimes seemed he gathered all the children of the world to him. If he had become impatient with Michael for keeping Sarah away, that was nothing if someone tried to prevent children from going to him. Many times I heard him say, "Allow the children to come to me" when they were about, taking them onto his lap or in his arms. He couldn't bear to see a child suffer, and would do all he could within God's law to alleviate that suffering.

One morning after we broke our fast he said, "It is time to go to Judea to join the others."

"But I thought you'd decided to stay here," protested Judas. I nodded in agreement. We were all becoming fearful of the authorities who were getting more and more aggressive in their efforts to arrest him.

A grim look flitted across his face, frightening me. "I want to be there for the Feast of Tabernacles. Besides, it is not yet my time, so no harm will come of it. I would like you to go on ahead," he gestured to the six of us standing around him, "and I will join you later."

It did no good to question him as to how he would get there or why he would not come with us. He allowed only Philip and Nathaniel to stay with him.

It seemed I had spent most of my life walking those same roads, in different seasons and weather. I know now that all that moving about was preparing me for the journeys to come. But it is a good thing we do not know too much about what lay ahead, else we might lose courage and diverge from the path that God has laid out for us.

As had become our habit, we went straightaway to uncle Joseph's when we got to Jerusalem. He had two homes, one inside the city walls, and a larger property just outside. We spent the first two nights at the larger home, keeping the noise and smells of the city at bay a little longer. Aunt Elizabeth welcomed us warmly, asking after our families. Joseph was away, she said, and might not be home in time for the holiday. But she sent servants on ahead to prepare the city house for us, knowing we would want to be there during the Feast itself.

All their children were at home. Anne and Naomi were the eldest of four girls and while Naomi was one of my dearest friends (with whom I had studied in Egypt years before), I hardly knew Anne. She was of a different temperament altogether, having already taken on many of the duties of a head of household, though her mother was not yet old.

In contrast Naomi was content to create her own modest home. Married less than two years, she and her husband Peter just had their first child. Barnabas alternately cooed, wallowing in the attention of so many strangers, and squalled when that attention was turned elsewhere. That small child controlled the tone and quality of our interactions the entire day ... but no one objected as we so seldom had the chance to enjoy ordinary family life anymore.

Several of Joseph's business associates came by the house, unaware he was traveling. Elizabeth had gone to market in the morning, taking with her the only two servants still at the house. To our relief Anne assumed the role of hostess in her mother's absence, seeing to their needs after their long journey. One of the men, Rufus, seemed overly demanding of Anne. I offered to bring the men more water so she could rest from serving them, but she brushed me off.

The same thing happened the following day, even though Elizabeth and the servants were about. "Why don't you let one of us take care of them?" I whispered into her ear. She ignored me, flushing red from ear to ear. It took me some time to understand the reason for her reluctance. *She liked him.* I was stunned. To my knowing Anne had never shown any interest in the many men who passed through their home.

"Are you sure?" giggled Naomi, when I said something to her later in the day.

"Isn't he Roman?" asked Miriam.

"No, his mother is Greek and his father Hebrew; both are Jews who lived for a time in Rome. I already asked Elizabeth."

"You asked mother!" Naomi looked stunned. "What did she say?"

"Well, I didn't say anything to her about Anne. But she looked at me strangely, all the same."

"What else could his parents have named him, with that red hair and beard?" Naomi giggled again.

"Who are you talking about?" asked Anne, coming into the room.

I shot a glance at my friends, who looked the other way. "We were talking about your father's business associates, wondering where they are from," I answered: not quite the whole truth.

"Hmmmm" was all she said, turning her back on us.

But I'd been right. Rufus stayed on when the other men left, asking Elizabeth to give their apologies to Joseph upon his return. He stayed to ask for Joseph's blessing to marry his eldest daughter. Of course he gave it readily, as he was very fond of the younger man and pleased his daughter had finally found someone she could care for.

Meanwhile, by the time Jesus arrived in Jerusalem, we had settled into the city house. Naomi came with us, rather than stay with her mother and sister. When the sun began to set, she gathered us outside around the communal table to light the candles. I had never seen my friend take the role of head of household before, but she handled it with grace and depth of spirit. I immediately felt the familiar tingling around my ears and across my shoulders that comes with the descent of the holy mother.

Peter stood with her and offered the first blessing. We lifted our cups with a sense of gratitude for all we had been given.

"Why, you are weeping," James whispered.

"Am I?" My hand brushed the tears away. "I had not noticed." I didn't want to disturb the others while Naomi ladled the soup. "It is not sadness, but happiness at being with friends."

"You are the only person I know who weeps when she is happy," said James, seeming oddly annoyed.

"I understand. I do the same," Miriam interrupted from her place down the table. "Tears are a woman's response when her heart is moved, whether by compassion, grief or joy."

"Not only a woman's," said Jesus, who sat next to her. "I am not ashamed of my tears."

It was true. I had seen my cousin weep on numerous occasions, once even when we were still children. One of his friends felled a brightly colored bird with a stone. The boy went over and kicked at it, pronouncing it dead. Jesus picked it up and stroked the creature's head, with tears in his eyes. The boy who had thrown the stone and some of the others began to taunt him, but he seemed not to notice. Leaning over the bird, a single tear fell on its tiny head. He held the bird to his chest for a time, and then squatted to set it down. It toppled over onto its side.

I could not bear to look at it, and started to walk away when I heard a gasp. Turning back, I saw the bird shudder. At first I thought it must be the wind lifting its feathers. But the shuddering increased until it lifted its head and tried to get to its feet. I couldn't believe my eyes. It was alive! I noticed Jesus whispering to the bird, though he did not touch it again. It soon came back to itself and flew away.

Stunned, I asked what happened, but he only put his fingers to his lips to silence me. The other boys ran off. Later there were whispers at school about magic and things that were unnatural. But it was never mentioned again between the two of us.

"Tears have the power to wash us clean, to heal and restore us to wholeness," Jesus said, but James had already begun another conversation with Saul.

Miracles 155

That evening we talked about Anne and Rufus. Everyone had noticed their immediate attraction to each other. And while Anne could at times be stern (especially for her age), we were all fond of her, and would grow to love Rufus as we got to know him.

Someone mentioned how odd it was for a Hebrew man to bear a name from Rome. "But you have a strange name too, Veronica," said Philip. "I mean, it is a Latin name as well." Philip blushed, and I saw he worried whether he might have offended me.

"You are right. I had never really thought about it until we (gesturing to Naomi and Miriam) were in Alexandria, and several people pointed out that it was not a Hebrew name. I asked mother about it when I got home and she said it was my father's idea. When he was a child a woman came to stay in their home for a time. All he knew was she came from someplace beyond Rome. She was beautiful and wise; everyone listened carefully each time she spoke. And since he was still too young to think of marriage himself, he decided if he ever had a daughter, he would name her Veronica."

James laughed. "I never heard that story before! You still have the power to surprise me."

As the evening wore on, I realized there had been no talk of things outside the compound. But eventually fragments of conversation began to reach me from the other end of the table. "We were in the middle of the lake ...." and "how did he do that?" Soon we all stopped talking, to hear the story.

Philip and a few others had gone out on the lake fishing. It was late afternoon, and a pleasant enough day. They had let the boat drift since there was little wind, but suddenly it all changed. A powerful wind came up, drawing in storm clouds over the water. They pulled in their lines and readied the oars to return to shore. But they had drifted far out to the middle of the lake and no matter how hard they struggled they couldn't seem to get anywhere. The wind battered them, pushing them further from their goal.

"The waves grew higher and began to flood the boat. We had to secure the oars and put all our efforts toward baling water so we would not sink. I was terrified," Philip said. "It was getting late and turning cold. We were all exhausted. The thought came to me we might die out there."

"And to me as well," added Nathaniel. "It was Philip who said we should stop and pray. At first I thought he was mad: if we stopped, we surely would die. But then I saw he was right. I don't think we would have survived by our efforts alone. So we stopped and called out to the Father and to the great Mother, who controls the seas, to have mercy on us. And still the storm raged, drowning out our voices. We could no longer hear each other, or even the sound of our own voice. I was shivering with the cold and fright in complete darkness when I heard *something*. It might have been a voice, but I could not tell. So I reached out into the blackness and grabbed the arms of some of the others to get their attention. I think we were all holding on to each other when the voice came into my mind.

"'Why do you fear? Why doubt?' And I realized it was the voice of our master talking to me. 'I have told you,' the voice said, 'you have the power to cast mountains into the sea, and to raise the dead. What claim has the sea over one with such power?'

"But this was no voice from afar. Jesus was suddenly sitting with us *inside* the boat! I do not know how he got there; he still will not tell us."

I looked over to see my cousin's reaction, and found he had left the table. Philip went on.

"He chided us for our lack of faith, not in harsh words, but more like a loving brother who has charge over the younger ones. Even though it was dark, I was able to see him lift his hand ... and the waves instantly calmed. Had I not been wet clear through to my skin, I might have thought I imagined the storm. The boat sat perfectly still. A few stars began to shine through the clouds. We could make out the shoreline, but still we sat there, unable to understand what had just happened."

"'Must I row the boat for you too?' Jesus asked with a chuckle, bringing us back to ourselves and the task at hand. As we began to row, he asked in a sterner voice, 'How is it you are still lacking in faith, that I must come to you across the waters? You shout at God, demanding His favors, and grow frustrated when they do not come in the way you think they must. Is this what I have taught you, what the brothers of old have taught? I think not.'"

"That night when we were safely back at Moshe's house the master spoke to us about the way of miracles," Nathaniel continued. "He told us that miracles are natural events that happen when we allow God to work through us. All of us are capable of doing what he does. Or at least that's what he said."

"Yes, he has told us that many times," agreed Matthew. "But I have yet to walk on water," he laughed.

"All I know is it is dangerous for him to be here," Thomas cut in. "He is safer at the lake. The more he does such things -- whatever they are called -- the more he draws attention to himself, and us. No one knows about the event at the lake, save us, but all have heard of Lazarus, of the many who have their sight restored, and the use of their limbs. These are good things, surely, and the work of the Lord. But in this city they are seen as a challenge to the authorities, Roman and Jew."

Chapter Seventeen

A MEETING WITH THE BROTHERS

"Why didn't he just stay away, and save us all this trouble? He has forced us into a corner and we have no choice but to act ... and act quickly."

"I am sure Pilate will back us. Antipas hates him.

"I know I wouldn't mind having this thorn taken from underfoot!"

"Let's just wait awhile. He'll go away again; he always does. If we detain him now, there is sure to be a riot. The Romans will blame *us* for the unrest, and not him. Pilate is a weak man, blowing with the winds."

"If Rome sees him as a threat, they will destroy us along with him. We cannot let our nation suffer for one man, and our temple devastated again! If one man must die that our people live, then I will not stand in the way."

The arguments could sometimes be heard outside the temple precinct, though mostly the priests and rabbis tried to keep their comments behind closed doors. Nicodemus was an elder in the Sanhedrin, and privy to much of the gossip there. Though increasingly, conversations ceased altogether when he came into their midst. They knew that he along with my uncle Joseph favored Jesus.

Nicodemus kept most such talk to himself, taking only a few of the older disciples into his confidence. He thought they should know about the death threats so they could help watch over Jesus and keep him safe. Of course, nothing could keep him from harm, except if he chose it. Those of us who loved him would have silenced him if we thought it possible – for his own good. We meant well, but we didn't fully understand his mission even then, and were unaware of the decisions he had knowingly made that were putting him directly into harm's way.

There were as always huge crowds in Jerusalem for the holiday. Jesus continued to teach and the numbers of people drawn to him increased daily. He told one particular gathering that if they followed his teachings, they could conquer death. A Pharisee who stood on the sidelines shouted out that all of the Prophets had died, even Abraham. Only a crazy person would say that death could be overcome. He must have a demon in him, he said; his words and actions were that of a sorcerer.

"Before Abraham was, I am," Jesus replied.

His followers were cast out of the synagogues and the temple, even as they were attempting to offer the ritual sacrifices demanded of observant Jews. Jesus said such judgments were of man, but he judged no one, not even his accusers. That only made them angrier, but still they did not arrest him.

There was confusion among his followers – especially the younger ones – as to the meaning of his words. "How could he have been there before Abraham," someone asked, "when Abraham is the father of us all?"

"He speaks in riddles," complained another. "I heard him say the other day that if any of us would be first, we must be last. Now what does that mean?"

"And that to save our life we must lay down our life."

It was evening, and we were gathering back at Joseph's compound. Shabbat had ended and we moved the cooking fires toward the front of the house, so we women wouldn't miss the conversation. Jesus had not yet returned from the temple.

"Most say – and I believe it is true – that we have lived before," said James. "We return to this world to right our wrongs from the past and to strive to more perfectly follow the law. It is possible Jesus lived before Abraham, and that when we die we will come back to live again. And maybe laying down our lives to save them is the same as saying that if we sacrifice ourselves for another person or a higher purpose, then our lives will have been worth living.

"Anyway, you should ask him your questions, rather than passing them back and forth among yourselves as you do. That will get you nowhere. Or better yet, learn to think for yourselves and come to your own conclusions."

"The smell of food met me down the road. It must be time to eat," said Jesus, standing just inside the gate. "Come, let us join in prayer first, and talk later." We hadn't even noticed him standing there.

"James was right," he said when the dishes were cleared. "There is no final death, only the passing from darkness into light and then back into darkness again. It is little different than the changing of the seasons when the flowers die out in winter, to be reborn the following spring. There is only life, though it takes different forms."

"And what does the first and last mean; how can we be both at once?"

"The values we hold dear in our world have little worth in the next. The Father does not care if we have position or wealth. If you wish to sit at His right hand, you will seek to discover what matters to Him."

"What is it that matters to Him?"

"That we care for one another, putting others before us, showing them honor. In so doing we will be lifted up when we are finished with this worldly life.

"James is also right that while you are free to ask me questions, it is more important that you train yourselves to seek the answers within. I will not be with you always, and it would serve no one for you to spend your days longing for something that is not there. Seek first the kingdom of heaven, which exists within your heart, and your questions will be answered, your needs met."

We spent several more days in Jerusalem, and each day was filled with crowds of people lining up to receive his blessing. The priests continued to stand on the edges of the crowds, taunting him and those who believed in him. But none dared approach. It seemed as if they were waiting for something, a signal perhaps. Each day some of us dispersed among the crowds so we might hear the rumors, to know the dangers. It was said there were secret meetings between the Jews and Romans, but he continued to assure us it was not yet his time and no harm would come of it.

Leaving Jerusalem, we began our journey north, not to the lake, but to Nazareth. I was thrilled to be going home. Word had gone ahead, and mother, John and Judy were at Mary's waiting for us. The two brothers embraced their mother. Mary responded the same as always with James. But there was something different in her attitude toward Jesus. I sensed a distance, a gap between them, as if this son no longer *belonged* to her. Something of that nature happens with all children as they grow older, of course – but I will always be my mother's daughter, James his mother's son. However, there was an inexplicable change in this mother-son bond that would continue to deepen in the months to come.

Seeing this helped me begin to understand other changes – especially since John's death. I hadn't given it much thought since there had been no dramatic shift. But after this homecoming I realized the easy intimacy I had always enjoyed with him had diminished. He had become more removed from all of us: no less loving, but less engaged. It would take time for me to appreciate that the personal claim we felt we had on him as family, friends and students no longer existed. He now belonged to all of us, none more than another.

Mary and mother had laid out basins of water so we could clean the dust of the road off our hands and feet before we sat down to a light meal. Dinner was planned for the evening with neighbors and friends. Our visits were always treated as celebrations, as we brought news from the city and surrounding areas, and stories to be shared late into the night.

Mother's husband Matthias had stayed behind in Jerusalem. (He had business with Joseph, who was expected to return soon from his latest journey.) I carried gifts from him, and a message for mother. I saw the disappointment in her eyes when she realized he had not come with us. "Never mind," she said, "we will be together before long. It is soon time for the gathering."

It was both easier and more difficult for Jesus here than it was elsewhere. The crowds in other cities were often oppressive, while there was none of that in Nazareth. It was rare to find someone outside the gate in the morning, asking to be healed of some infirmity or other. No one blocked our way when we went into the marketplace, hoping for a touch or a glance, or words of wisdom. Indeed, when he spoke people scarcely listened, seeming to shuffle off uncomfortably at the first opportunity. It seemed as if people were avoiding him, and possibly all of us who traveled with him. The first chance I had, I asked mother about it.

"You have seen him through all his changes, Veronica. You knew him as a child, not much different from other children. And then you grew with him in spirit, learning to know him as both friend and teacher. You studied in Carmel and Alexandria, were initiated in the lands to the north and in the great pyramid. Your life has paralleled his in many ways.

"But here they just know him as Joseph's son, the eldest who turned his back on his father's business and left his mother alone with many children. They might have forgiven him that, but then he spirited away the next eldest along with my own daughter." She meant James and me. "Rumors reach us here all the time about his travels, and the trouble he stirs up throughout the land, drawing unwanted attention from the Sanhedrin and the Romans themselves. It frightens them.

"And now he shows up here with all of you. Though he does not wish it, doesn't even think about it, they believe he expects to be treated specially. But I tell you, a prophet is never appreciated in his own town. Nazareth is too provincial to believe that any great teacher could come from such humble beginnings. The truth is he is not much welcome here.

"Mary does what she can to lead an ordinary life. And while younger people know nothing of the early days of the twelve chosen girls, the older people will never forget. And in some ways they will also never forgive her."

"But mother, she has done no wrong!" I couldn't believe that what she was saying was true. "And he asks for nothing for himself that he doesn't ask for everyone." I was shaking with frustration. How could people be so blind, I wondered?

"I know that. But people do not like change, and they fault him to some extent for the great changes they see coming their way. We cannot blame them. We have been trained to see things larger than ourselves, but they have not.

"We've asked the brothers not to visit us here at our homes, at least for the present. There has been an influx lately from various quarters, and it was drawing unwanted attention to us."

"Why are they coming now?" James asked. He came into the darkened room where we were sitting, stomping the dust off his sandals.

"You know the answer to that," she replied, looking evenly from one to the other of us. The discomfort I'd felt the day before returned. We knew, but said nothing. In fact we mostly avoided the subject even when alone. "If you would like to go with us tomorrow to Sepphoris, you can meet them."

That afternoon some of us accompanied Jesus to the synagogue. We women waited outside while the men went in for their prayers and when they came out, he stopped on the steps. A small crowd had been watching us at a distance, and approached cautiously when he began to speak. They came just close enough to hear his words, but not so close as to be associated with him should any questions arise later.

"What do you seek?" he asked of no one in particular. "Is it riches you want, peace, security? What are you willing to give in exchange for such things? Your time? Your honor? And what good will any of this do you when your time here is done? If you seek riches, you will find them a weight upon your soul, keeping you from your heavenly home. You will have gained the world, but be lost in eternity.

"We are here for each other as brothers and sisters. I have come to show you the way, a shepherd to his sheep, that you might discover everlasting life."

"No one can live forever," someone shouted.

"Show us a miracle," another yelled.

"Blessed are those who believe without signs and wonders. Furthermore, it is not I who offer up miracles, but the Father who works through me. The light has come into the world, but you ask for tricks in the darkness."

The hecklers finally left, while others stayed to hear what he had to say. When he was done they shook their heads in amazement at his words, talking among themselves as they walked away. But few dared speak of it to others, lest they be associated with him in the dark days to come.

*

We left early the next day for Sepphoris. I was eager to meet the brothers who had gathered there, curious whether I would know any of them. There were only six of us, as we did not wish to draw attention to our party. Mother led us to a small mud house not far inside the city gate. No one would suspect anything of significance in such a modest hut. The furniture was simple but solidly-built, covered with beautifully embroidered pillows. Two women were in a small alcove tending to pots over a fire. They did not turn when we entered.

"Welcome," said a tall, thin man. His hair was tightly curled and he wore large gold hoops in both ears. I could not place his country either by appearance or accent. He gestured toward the outhouse and showed us where to wash up from our journey. This was the sort of thing generally offered by a servant, and not another guest.

When we'd reassembled, he and the others sat down with us in a circle, a few on benches and the rest of us on cushions on the freshly-swept floor. There were two men and two women, each dressed quite colorfully. Shortly afterwards the two women who had been cooking set down cups and pitchers of water on a low table, and then joined us. I had taken them for servants, but neither do servants join with guests.

The tall man (who had not yet introduced himself) asked that we close our eyes to receive the blessing of the one God. The thrill of that blessing blew over me like a strong breeze until I felt awake in every part of myself.

"Thank you for making the journey," said one of the women who had been at the cooking fire. "I am Rachel." She laughed at our reaction. "Yes, we have met before. It was my house that sheltered your aunt here," she said, gesturing to Mary, "when the Roman soldiers had her cornered in the alleyway nearby. That event changed my life."

Rachel went on to say how, in getting to know Mary she learned about my cousin and the Brotherhood that stretched across many lands, even to the farthest sea. She started to study, late in life she said, but worked all the harder for it so she could understand why we were all so committed to the one God. Her sister Sharon had joined in her quest. "It is an honor to see you again, and to have you all gathered here in our humble home."

"I am Chidi, come to you from the black lands. This is my first time beyond Egypt, and I am honored to be among you." His hand included all of us in the circle, but his head bowed to my cousin.

"And I am called Femi. I met Chidi in Alexandria. My people are Yoruba, not so far distant from his people.

"We are Aara and Gaspar," said the other woman, touching her husband lightly on the arm ... "newly married," she smiled. "We are from Persia."

We in turn introduced ourselves, and when we had finished, Chidi turned to Jesus and asked "What do you intend to do?" His directness startled me, but my cousin met his gaze, taking his time to answer.

"It is not up to me," he said quietly. "It never was … really. But it seems to me that events have gotten out of hand and are now beyond anyone's control. I long ago gave myself over to the Father's will, and have done my best to follow through on His plan, the plan for all His children. But instead of listening to the teachings, and learning how to transform their lives, they will now be given the harder lessons of death and resurrection." He paused. "I fear the lessons will be too harsh for most to bear." My cousin's eyes glistened, and I saw the pain behind his tears. But he squared his shoulders and did not look away from his Brother.

Chidi and the others nodded. "I share your concern. But I trust you to do your part. We have come to bear witness, though we must stand to the side. I hope you will understand. It is not for lack of courage …."

"I know that. We will be scattered, but we will survive," said Jesus. Then gesturing toward us he added: "These women have come together to take the secret teachings within and guard them until the time comes again when it will be safe to bring them forth into the light of day. I charge you and all our brothers everywhere to keep them from harm." The brothers gave their word, using an ancient vow known only to those initiated into the mysteries.

We talked at length about the increasing violence in the cities, and the fear and mistrust that we felt everywhere around us. The crisis, however it would show its face, was rapidly approaching.

During a lull Rachel and Sharon got up and announced it was time to eat. The food had been simmering on a low flame while we talked but I'd been so intent on the discussion I hadn't even noticed the wonderful aromas that filled the room. I got up to help, but Sharon waved me away. "It is our honor to have you as our guest. Allow us to serve you."

Though the conversation never returned to Jesus' dark words, they left a deep impression. From that moment I put all my thoughts and efforts toward strengthening myself that I might not falter when the time came, however events unfolded.

Chapter Eighteen

STARS TO LIGHT THE WAY

"The time is fast approaching for us to gather in one place. You heard him. That was the first he said it for everyone to hear. You and I and the other women have been trained to stand firm in the heart of the world when everyone else gives way to fear." Mother's words tumbled out of her mouth, keeping time with our rapid pace. I wondered where we were going in such a hurry. We wouldn't leave Nazareth for several days yet.

"Mary and I have put together a small group of men and women, trusted friends and servants to care for the children, so we can join you. Elizabeth will arrive soon with her youngest. Joseph believes they will be safer here than in Jerusalem – at least for a time. Elizabeth would have preferred to come with us, but she knows she is needed here to supervise the care and protection of those too young to ...." She did not finish her thought aloud.

"My heart is happy at the thought of having you and Mary at my side. But what of *our* Elizabeth, and the other young women? They are still very young. Do you think it wise to have them with us?"

"Some will join us, and some will come here. We are still discussing this. But look for us after the next moon."

*

I worried about my cousin. Jesus slept little during that time, retiring late and rising early. I sometimes awoke during the night to see him standing off in the shadows of the courtyard looking up into the sky. In those rare moments during the day when people weren't clamoring for his attention, he'd steal away for a solitary walk in the hills near Capernaum. We knew to go among the crowds ourselves then, so they would not see him go and follow him. Even Miriam kept her distance, unless he called her to him.

I was surrounded by people, both strangers and friends. But I often felt alone. James spent almost all his time with the other men, and rarely returned to our mat to sleep. I missed my husband, I missed Jesus, I missed our old life. But whenever I was tempted to feel sorry for myself I recalled Mary's advice to stop focusing on personal concerns, and the mood would lift. Instead, I reminded myself of what mother said: *this* was what we were born for.

The crowds were sometimes so vast he had to make his way above people on one of the hills in order that he might be heard. The place he liked best to go was shaped like a natural arena. For a time we went there every day, even the Sabbath.

On one of those days he stood a long time without moving, as if transfixed. The boisterous crowd slowly quieted until there wasn't a single sound. Even the children and the dogs had settled down. Flies buzzed and birds sang in nearby grasses. It was easy to forget the recent cold that had us huddling in front of fires, and the ill will some in the town below held towards us. For a short space I drifted in the blessed peace.

A rustle passed through the crowd like a breeze through the trees, and I saw he had sat down. His eyes scanned the scene in front of him, and he smiled. Dear God, how I wish I could have held onto that moment forever. His eyes reflected the blue of the sky and the sun shone out from them, warming my heart. I looked around and saw people smiling back at him. He had spoken often of loving our neighbors. People nodded when he said such things, but I wasn't sure they thought it possible to actually live that way. It was just too hard, an impossible ideal. But that day I saw the possibility in their eyes.

"Blessed are the modest in spirit," he began, "for yours is the kingdom of heaven." He paused, allowing his words to find their place in us.

"Blessed are you who mourn, for you shall be comforted." In the silence that followed I heard weeping and saw a woman sitting alone, face buried in her hands. Immediately two strangers rose and went to her side.

"Blessed are you of gentle nature, for you will inherit the earth.

"Blessed are you who bring beauty and harmony into the world, for you reveal God.

"Blessed are you who hunger and thirst after righteousness, for the gates to the kingdom will be open to you.

"Blessed are you who do not hide your light under fear or jealousy or anger, for all will find comfort and healing in your presence.

"And if any persecute you for my sake, I will call you to myself.

"Being pure of heart, you will see God. This is my Father's promise to you."

Some of the children had risen and begun to run among the people while he spoke. Simon went over and tried to hush them so they would not interfere with the sermon. But Jesus raised his hand and said, "There can be no lovelier music than the voices of children at play. They remind us to live with a glad heart. The problems of the world will always be with us. But if we remember to laugh and reach out to others, then enmity can be put aside and our fears will vanish with the morning mists.

"Our Father in heaven has no need of our gifts, our praise or thanksgiving. He does not require of us the sacrifice of living things, or gold and myrrh." People turned to see the reaction of the priests standing nearby. But Jesus continued, ignoring them. "Our heavenly Parents ask only that we love one another as we love Them.

"If we have harmed our brother or sister, or hold a grudge against them believing they have wronged us, then we must go to them with the gifts of love and forgiveness. *This* is an offering worthy of heaven.

"You must not judge another, as such judgment will then be meted out to you in equal measure. If a child becomes angry and throws his cup to the floor, breaking it, does his mother consign that child to the dung heap? Of course not; she loves him all the more so anger will find no place in his heart.

"If a girl shows little talent for the hearth, would a father consider her an unfit member of his household and send her out into the streets to find her way?" His eyes locked onto those of a man standing not far from him. The man's face reddened and he turned and ran out through the crowd. "No loving father would do such a thing," he said softly. "There are skills and talents lying undiscovered in each of us. Condemnation will not bring them out; only love and patience will.

"We have the law to guide us, and it is good we follow this law so the least among us is cared for, and counsel is given for the tempers and appetites of those whose passions run strong. Our Father gave us these laws not to bind us, but to free us. It is the job of the priest to help us in their interpretation, but the priests are men like you and me … are they not?"

The drone of dissent rippled through that part of the crowd where most priests had congregated – and I felt the thrill of fear rise up my back. I wanted to shout at him to watch his words in such a public forum, but knew better than to do so. It sometimes seemed to me he courted danger.

"We know the commandments, but do we really follow them? Oh yes, you have never taken the life of another. But what are the thoughts you carry in your heart? Do you give in to anger or even hatred toward others? Your hatred and evil words will cut them down as surely as will a sword. And in the Father's eyes they are the same.

"To whisper licentious words to a woman in the marketplace is no better than sleeping with another man's wife." I stole a glance at Miriam, who was looking at the ground. My friend had been a victim of men's wicked comments on more than one occasion.

"And you who follow the harlot are the maker of that harlot. And yet you profess to despise such women who often have no other means to provide for themselves or their children.

"To defraud or use deceit to take another man's livelihood from him, to charge too much for your services, to take advantage of one who is desperate by paying them less than their worth are all means of stealing. Does the priest tell you this when he asks for your child's inheritance to support his lavish lifestyle? *I think not*."

I prayed fervently my cousin might turn his talk away from such direct assaults. Then, as if in answer to my prayers he said, "Yet do not think you will gain virtue by condemning others. For any judgment you send out into the world will return to you.

"To cast yourself in the role of judge is a bitter offense. Instead of exacting an eye for an eye (as the judges of old taught us), offer your enemy your hand. If he strikes you, turn and offer him your other side until he can see in you a friend rather than his enemy.

"If someone should steal a loaf from your hands in the marketplace, chase her down and offer her the fruit in your bag, and the shawl from your back. She has need of them more than you. You do not know the burdens people carry and none of us is fit to weigh their wrongs. They are giving you the chance to be the hand of God in the world. This is a blessed opportunity.

"I have asked you to love your neighbor as you love your child or your mother. And now I say you must go a step further and love those who hate you, so that in you they may see God's love. What mother would throw her child to the dogs for words spoken in hurt or anger?

"*These* are as your children," he said, waving his hand over a crowd that stretched as far as the eye could see. "And you are their mother, and their father. The sun rises and sets upon us all alike. Thus is God's love for us. The rain falls upon the stone and the tree, caring not that one receives it appreciatively and the other casts it off. The waters of life are freely given, without hindrance or limit."

"But we are told not to consort with the wicked, and to stone a woman who shames her husband," shouted a tall man standing some distance away.

"Who tells you these things?" asked Jesus.

"Both Sadducee and Pharisee. We are told that if our eye offends us, we must pluck it out. These men of God tell us that if such people cause offense to the good citizens of our town, we must rid ourselves of them," he replied, quite certain of his answer.

"Men of God..." Jesus repeated, shaking his head. "To cause great harm to another by any means is to rob them of their life force. Do you think a man of God would really require this of you, that you would then have to stand before your Creator and tell Him you have broken His first commandment? This is no man of God," he said dismissively, and walked away, ending the day's discourse.

The following day I noticed a greater number of men wearing the local robes and head coverings that identified them as members of the synagogue, both Sadducee and Pharisee. Their faces were grim, though few opened their mouths to speak that day. But they passed dark looks among themselves.

"For whom do you do good works?" he began. "Do you walk into the marketplace and with a great show and loud words sprinkle a few shekels at the feet of a beggar, while kicking dust in the face of a woman who has been forced to sell her body in order to eat? Do you believe this has purchased passage for you to heaven, or for your wife or children? And what of the many others who have fallen on hard times?

"And do you pray loudly in the synagogue or when your neighbors are watching, so everyone will know what a good and holy man you are? This is nothing but performance, for the benefit of man and not God.

"God sees your thoughts in the dark of night, and hears the soft words of encouragement spoken to one who is struggling. Thoughts written on your heart are as easily seen as the words inscribed on a scroll. Nothing is hidden. It is good to study the holy Word in the temple or synagogue, good to share prayers with family and guests.

But it is better still to pray within your heart, to pray without ceasing until all your life is a prayer."

"But master, how can we do this? There is so much work to do, and we must sleep...." The young woman held a baby to her breast, with two more children at her feet.

Jesus smiled and walked over to where she perched on a boulder, and sat down on a smaller rock before her. Her face reddened and she struggled to get up, embarrassed that he should sit at her feet.

"Stay," he said gently. "I would sit here with you, my sister."

He looked over the crowd and said, "We are all brothers and sisters, here to honor each other in everything we do. If you know yourself in God, you will know that to love God is to love each other. There is no other way to do that. Tithing is a thing we do for our own soul; God needs nothing from us. Singing the Psalms uplifts the heart of the one who sings and for that God rejoices in our song. Giving to the poor recognizes the face of God in the one who might for the moment be lost in misery. Such an act stirs the one who suffers to remember the Divine, and lifts them up.

"All such deeds are prayer of one kind or another. We pray through our actions, our unspoken thoughts as well as our words. When you help or heal or bless another person, the angels sing their hymns through you, and when you give yourself over to a life of service, *you become the prayer*.

"Your life, my sister, is a prayer." He looked into her eyes and it seemed to me their faces disappeared in brilliant sunlight – though clouds covered the sky. And then he leaned down to kiss the foreheads of each of her children and turned back to the crowd.

"If you have need of things to sustain you and your family, remember that God knows your needs even before you do. If your heart is whole and not moved by temptations of the world, then what you need will flow to you as surely as a river flows downstream."

"But my family goes hungry," called out a man in a voice at once angry and weary, "yet I cannot find work. What have I done – no, what have my children done to deserve this?" he ended in a whisper.

Jesus looked at the man standing before him, saying nothing. The crowd began to grow restless. "He must not have heard him," said someone near me.

"Yes, why are good people punished?" shouted another.

"What kind of Father lets His children go hungry?" called out a woman.

"These are hard questions," he said at last. "It is cruel to speak of future rewards when children suffer, and I will not do that." He called the man and his family to him. The children – who often had to stand on street corners and beg – were accustomed to being shunned, and did not wish to move into the center of so much attention. But he coaxed them with his sweet smile and outstretched arms, and they soon forgot their fears.

Jesus, who never carried provision of any kind on his person, pulled a loaf and ripe dates out of his pockets, handing them to the children. As they greedily ate, he reached in and pulled out another bag with raisins and almonds which he handed to their parents. The mother's eyes ran with tears, her hands shook as she took it in her hands.

"Do not think that God punishes such innocents, nor should you cast blame on their parents. There are some who are guilty of neglect, but these are good people who have fallen on hard times. This is an opportunity for us to consider the consequences of our acts, to examine our priorities. Does God need more sacrifices when such as these go hungry?" He looked up and locked eyes with two priests who stood off in the distance. One glared back at him; the other turned and walked away.

"Their poverty is a gift to each of you." I could see the look of confusion on some faces when he said that.

"If you have learned the lessons of the prophets, and know the laws, you will find a way to help those who suffer. Every one of us has something to give. Open your heart and ask to be led. A kind word can do more to heal a ravaged soul than all the riches in the world. Even the simplest food can ward off starvation. A loving touch, a job, a spare shekel are all things you can offer. And when you give, do not give thought to your reward, either today or in heaven – for your reward is in the giving. This is how we show our gratitude for all that we have. And as these people receive that which is freely and lovingly given, their hearts are healed, that more good might come into their lives."

He kissed the children and smiled at the grateful parents who moved back into the crowd. People opened to receive them, some patting their shoulders or arms as they passed, whispering words I could not hear.

Something shifted among the people that day, faces softened. I noticed they stood more closely together, as if taking comfort in each others' presence. Voices quieted, the questions became less urgent.

"Avarice is the father of selfishness; fear leads the mother to hoard. To gather and keep more than you need is little better than theft from those who do not have enough. Why would anyone keep ten times the grain their family needs, unless they are a merchant. What good are reserves of gold when there is no food to be had?

"There is no harm in creating and enjoying beautiful things in your life, but remember that things in themselves are not what is beautiful. A golden ring has worth only because of the hand that wears it. A silver tray hidden away on a shelf has no value at all, yet shines its light on the table around which a family gathers. Time will come when all will know the true treasures from the false, that which brings us together and that which separates us.

"The real riches are right in front of you. Our eyes can deceive us, but our hearts do not. Do not lay up your treasures here on earth. Even the hardest gemstone will one day return to dust. Only through kindness and love are the real treasures amassed in heaven. This then is the light of the soul, which shines throughout heaven and earth. It is what I see when I look into your eyes. It is what lifts you up and makes you whole, bringing joy to all who know you.

"Only you can decide which master you will serve, whether God or the things of the world. If the earth is so magnificently clothed in all the growing things, and if the rain and sun fall upon man and fowl, plant and animal in their own time, then how would the Father not know to care for you as befits your needs? Even Solomon in all his glory was not arrayed as perfectly as the hill upon which we stand."

All eyes followed Jesus' hand as it swept over the hill. "Whatever you need will be given you in its own time, if you have the faith. Seek first the kingdom of God, striving to be righteous in all things, and all that you give out into the world will come back to you multiplied. If you judge another, you will be judged. If you speak well of your brothers, if you give the shirt off your back and the food from your table, your name will shine like the brightest of stars in the book of life.

"Do not concern yourself with what others say you should do, and do not repeat pleasing words that don't come from your own heart, thinking to impress others – or God. God awaits your sincere plea, your honest prayer. And just as a loving mother would not give her child stones when he hungers for grapes, neither would your heavenly parents deny you your good.

"What do *you* bring to the world? Are you sowing anger and hatred, speaking false words, taking what does not belong to you – or are you planting seeds of loving kindness, sharing what you have with others, guiding them in the ways of righteousness? What you plant, you will reap. What you give to others will come back to you.

"Take thought before following the easy path, laid out by the hard work of others. Go first to the house of prayer (which is in your hearts) and ask your angels to point the right way for you. Many are the wolves in sheep's clothing, eager for your downfall. And others with good intentions will believe that what is right for them will also be right for you. But we were set upon this path that we might find our own way to glorify God. Through us His glory is shed over the world.

"By merely mouthing the words of priests or repeating what you hear from me, you will not enter paradise. If you call me Lord but do not see God in the eyes of your brother, I will not speak for you when you come to the gates of heaven. If you only give money at the temple but leave children and women to suffer in the streets, the riches of the kingdom will not be given you. But if you follow my words and care for strangers as if they were your brothers and sisters, if you open your hearts to Gentiles as you would the Hebrew standing in the temple, if you do not seek more than you need, but accept that which is given you with joy and a grateful heart, then you will walk with me in the Father's garden."

Such were the days when Jesus stood on the hillsides above the great lake, taking the empty words of the Scribes and Pharisees and turning them into stars to light the way for those who sincerely sought the kingdom. He spoke with such authority and truth that the spies who listened from the edge of the crowds could find little with which to denounce him. And so they made up lies, delivering them to the various authorities so they might receive their dirty money.

Chapter Nineteen

NO ONE UNSCATHED

"They think they can get away with anything they want."

"Well, they can. Since the Jewish court was abolished in Rome there is no tribunal higher than Herod's. There is no appeal."

I had heard of Romans even more cruel and unjust, but Herod ruled over us with an iron hand. And in the end, it was often a whim of his or his wife's that led to a new ruling or sudden enforcement of an inactive law that swept across us like a devastating wind. It did not matter if one was guilty or innocent in the matter.

"But now they have taken to stealing from us, not even attempting to hide behind their damned laws."

I had been listening to talk in the marketplace while pretending to look at cloth. While I did not like the deception (allowing the merchant to think he might have a sale), we needed to know what was going on. The men did not even notice me.

"But you are not a Jew," one said to another, "so you are not such a target as we are."

"Maybe not directly, but all the new laws affect me as well. I am not a Roman, after all. It used to be the Gentiles who lived here were little bothered by the Herods of our world. But now my business has the same tariffs and other taxes on it as yours does. Tiberius must be blind or a fool to think he can do this forever without the scorpion of the desert rising up to sting him."

"*Quiet*. I would not be so bold, if I were you," said another, looking furtively over his shoulder. Their voices had been getting louder as they vented their anger. Indeed they had begun attracting attention to themselves, so I left.

The men were sitting around a table behind the house where we had been staying in Tiberius. They looked up when I came in and asked what I'd learned. After I had spoken, Peter glanced at John and said: "It is becoming too dangerous here. The Romans do not differentiate among us, and will believe those traders speak for us. And since we stand out more than they do, they will come for us ... for *him*."

"I agree," Miriam said, closing the gate behind her. She came over and took my arm.

"As do I." I did not look forward to leaving the lake, but it was clear the time had come.

Peter gave us that familiar look which said he had little interest in what we thought about this or any matter. He was never overtly antagonistic toward us women, but simply dismissive. But some of the other men did listen, as we had both the perspective of the marketplace (which they did not), and a unique bond with Jesus. For myself, I did not think our relationship superior to theirs, though I might once have done so. But I expect he spoke differently with us than with them.

That evening after the first blessing, the subject came up again.

"Yes," agreed Jesus, "I've been thinking about Caesarea Philippi."

Some argued we should leave right away. Nathaniel said he'd heard there were plots to arrest us, but couldn't say who was plotting or what the charges would be. "It doesn't matter the reason," he argued. "They do not need a reason!" He looked frightened, and I wondered if he wasn't holding something back.

Some among our group so hated the Romans they refused to call the place we were going by its new name, preferring the old Greek *Panias*. Despite it being the Roman capital of the area ruled by Philip, the fourth surviving son of Herod the Great, we were usually left alone there. Because of the hostility between Philip and Herod Antipas, Philip was eager not to appear subordinate to his older brother and took great pains to leave the Jews in his city alone. (There were so many mothers to Herod's children that I do not recall if Philip and his brother had the same mother, but I think not.)

A robust spring at the edge of the city settled in a cluster of pools, which together birthed the river Jordan. It was a true oasis in a broad desert. Mt. Hermon loomed over the spring, peppered with caves. The name *Panias* comes from the Cave of Pan, the Greek god who watches over fields and springs, ensuring fertility in the surrounding lands.

It was several days before word got out that Jesus had returned. Even then, there were never the crowds that followed us about in Galilee or Judea. People there were less interested in what he had to say than his ability to heal their physical ailments. If there was any theology behind their rituals to appease Roman and Greek Gods, it was well hidden. James and Thomas, and a few others thought Jesus should make more of an effort to spread his teachings in Philip's tetrarch, but I am sure he'd weighed the gains against what would be lost by doing so.

I loved the springs, where we often had him to ourselves. Those were the times of greatest intimacy, with only his closest followers at hand. He never forbade others to come; it just worked out that way. And best of all, mother and Matthias, my sister Elizabeth and of course Mary had finally joined us.

Mother caught up with Elizabeth and me one day when we were out walking. We talked about small things, happy to be together. After a time we fell into a comfortable silence, continuing our walk next to the sighing river.

Without slowing her pace, mother asked, "What is happening with you and James?" I was so surprised by her question that I stopped dead, not knowing what to say, nor even what to think. Though our problems were not new, I had put them in the background of my mind. There had been other more important things to consider.

"I think you need to talk about it, dear," she added.

I noticed Elizabeth looking from me to mother and back again, a quizzical look on her face. She probably hadn't noticed a change in my relationship with James, since she was so rarely with us. I wondered if others had.

"Mary and I were talking about you last night. She's worried, about both of you."

I sometimes forgot that she is James' mother, as well as Jesus.' In fact I usually thought of her as *my* second mother.

"Veronica, *say* something."

Mother had led us to a patch of grass on the river's edge, where we sat. I hadn't even noticed the tears running down my cheeks until Elizabeth reached over to brush them away. My dear sister looked so worried for me. I wished I could tell her that everything was alright. But it wasn't.

"Well …." I cleared my throat. "I … I don't know what exactly is wrong. There is so much going on that we hardly have time to think about ourselves. It isn't easy …. "

"No, it isn't easy," agreed mother. "Not for any of us. But still we do the best we can. He needs us," she said, referring – I knew – not to James but to Jesus. "I wish it weren't so, but some things will suffer for the greater good. And some exceedingly."

"Mother, how do you and Matthias do it? How do you keep a home an' a family when you too are pulled in so many directions?"

"We have our problems too, daughter, do not think otherwise. And maybe because we have the responsibility of our children we are forced to find our way through those problems, for their sakes."

Her words started me weeping again. I rarely thought about our childlessness; I just didn't have time to mourn something I did not have. But in that moment I felt the hole in our lives and knew the truth of what she said. Everything would have been different if there had been children. Different. But would it be better? The work we were doing, the circle we held for Jesus was my reason for being ... and the same was true of James.

"Yes, I do forget that every one of us has given something up of this world, for something greater. Even you, Elizabeth, you cannot hope to lead an ordinary householder's life. It may yet be a wonderful life," I hastened to add, seeing the tears spring to her eyes, "but it is not likely to be a peaceful one."

"Difficult times like these have always strengthened our people. They will make you two stronger, wiser," mother's voice was quiet. "If I could, I would have wished for you that peaceful life. But it is good we do not always get our wishes, for we too often think small instead of big, which is what our spirit calls us to."

"What will you do?" asked Elizabeth, her voice strained.

"I don't know. I don't blame James. I've tried to talk with him about it, but he either does not see there is anything amiss, or he cannot bring himself to think about it in light of the greater problems we all face. We have become so distant, not even brother and sister anymore."

"You have given your lives over to the work of the Brotherhood. Everything else comes second to that ... even our children," she said, stroking Elizabeth's hair. "And our husbands. Even our own well-being."

I stood and leaned over a small pool that formed at the edge of the river, and had to giggle. "And our appearance. I can't remember the last time I had a new robe, and this one is impossibly stained. It's no wonder James doesn't look at me anymore."

"You know it has little or nothing to do with that." Mother laughed joylessly. "It is actually better if we appear to others as peasants, as they will not be so inclined to molest us."

Somehow we managed to keep good hygiene, even when living on the road. It was part of our covenant with God. But it was sometimes a struggle when we were not near natural bodies of water.

"I have no promises for you, my daughters," said mother sadly. "Nor do I have words of wisdom that will help you resolve your marriage, Veronica. That you must do, or not do, yourself. How long have you been married now?"

I thought a bit. "Approaching seven years."

Suddenly I knew why she asked. In our tradition the contract of marriage existed primarily for the sake of the children born of it. Of course it is hoped that husband and wife will find a loving bond to sustain them in the world and enhance their standing in the eyes of God. That is, through loyalty to each other and the family they will have fulfilled the promises made in the marriage ceremony.

If, however, the marriage does not produce children and increase their service in the temple and the community at large, there are other choices. They can dissolve the marriage, and seek another means of fulfilling their earthly obligations. A few retreat to the desert where some of our brethren give up the things of the flesh, even living in caves or fasting for long periods of time as our brothers in the Brahmanic lands do. Others remarry. Some few stay within the world and remain unattached. But that is a path especially problematic for women, as it is said a woman's first duty is to bear children.

In that I had already failed – or James and I had failed. I do not know if we were unable to have children; if in calmer times they might have come to us. My moon time was always unsettled when we were on the road.

But many couples stay together after the seven year divide – even without children – especially if they are yet young. I was then just thirty and James a year older. I wondered what he would choose, if asked.

Chapter Twenty

STANDING TOGETHER

Three rabbis from Jerusalem had traveled north to join us. One I knew to be sympathetic to uncle Joseph, but I was surprised at the other two. I had only seen them in the presence of certain members of the Sanhedrin who appeared hostile to our teachings. Now, as the dangers around us increased, we were beginning to see who our friends were and who not.

We gathered in one of three homes located in different quarters of the city. One belonged to a business partner of Joseph's – a Greek Jew – and the other two were life-long members of our Brotherhood. One family had come from Persia, probably around the time Jesus was born, and the other was from Upper Egypt, as dark skinned as our dear friend Hebeny. Caesarea had become such an international city that no one stood out, a great advantage to us. As long as we moved about in small groups, we did not attract attention, and were never bothered by the authorities.

James and I stayed in Joseph's associate's home, a man called Alexander. Having a Greek name opened doors in his business with Roman traders. He said the question of religious affiliation simply never came up – though he was a devout Jew within his own home.

Mother and Matthias also stayed there, as did Jesus, his mother and Miriam.

When later I traveled with Thomas beyond the Indus, he told me it was Alexander who had opened his personal treasury to support our travel. I have often prayed that he did not suffer for his generosity.

On occasion we assembled near or even in the caves outside the city. Those gatherings reminded me of the early days when we used to meet in the desert the other side of Jerusalem. Even then, Jesus had been cautious about drawing attention to us as a group. Rome is a nation jealous of its authority and suspicious of anyone who appeared to be building his own power base. They could not imagine anyone could be disinterested in worldly power.

I looked for any excuse to go to the caves. It felt to me I stood in the womb which gave birth to all the lands between there and the Salt Sea through the power of the great river. Without it, no one could have survived in those otherwise arid lands. The Red river in Egypt was just as important to their survival. Such bodies of water are powerful channels for the divine Mother, a symbol of her generative power – and that of all women.

We women gathered in the caves at each new and full moon. The men knew we held ceremony in rhythm with the moons no matter where we were, and never questioned us about what we did or even where we went. These were things for women alone, just as men had their own conclaves and rituals (though they were not so regular in their going apart as we were). I have already spoken of the first woman's ceremonies, which are the cornerstone of all our rituals. But there are also ceremonies for when a woman first lay with her husband, for conception and the birth of her children, and again when our moon cycles have come to an end. And there are rituals when any of our community passes from earthly life into the life of spirit, whether man or woman. We serve as vessels for the Mother, for the good of all.

The rituals are passed on from woman to woman, mother to daughter. When we learned the ancient secrets in Carmel, or during our stay in Egypt, Miriam, Naomi and I had to commit each word, each movement and ritual undertaking to memory. There is a sacred trust associated with the learning. These things carry power, and are almost never written down. (The rare exceptions are when certain words are embedded within ordinary text – financial accounts or chronicles of war, for instance – so that only those who have been trained by the Brotherhood will be able to recognize the message or teachings.)

I can, however, say a few things without betraying this trust. We know that the power to create life lies dormant with the woman and that it awakens at first blood. But it only brings forth fruit by joining with man. And so we reenact the original creation by our heavenly Mother and Father in our own marriage beds. In speaking the *words of power* at the moment of joining, the hearts of those aligned in love are ignited. The flame thus lit in each one's heart transforms both in spirit and in body. This is prayer of the highest order. And it is this same flame that signals the spirit of one who is ready to be born into the world that the way has been made clear for them.

At birth the Creator breathes Life into the infant, which enables him to take his first breath on his own. This takes place even if the words of power had not been spoken at the quickening. But a child brought forth through ritual is thrice blessed, with the mark of the Holy Spirit above his or her head. Some of our brothers are trained to recognize this mark, and whenever possible the child is given special instruction, preparing them as spiritual leaders of their community.

There are many levels and kinds of training. Pharisees and Sadducees teach differently from each other, and each differs from us. Many Hebrews are influenced by the Greek, Roman or other traditions -- especially in our land which sits at the confluence of major trade routes, which lend themselves to the merging of many beliefs and practices.

We are taught that each of us has a personal spirit which, even when we are born to flesh, remains one with our Creator. With the higher quickening, our spirit moves into the heart of the infant. If we train ourselves and are conscientious in ritual and prayer throughout our lives, we will not lose connection with our Source. We will be able to *hear* Him speak to us, and we will be able to hear the spirit of others who have likewise experienced the higher quickening. This is the way of the prophet. It is a difficult thing to understand, I know. But once you have heard the Word of God, you will know what I am saying. And once heard, you will never forget.

But even if your own mother and father were ignorant of this, and did not say the words of power at your quickening, you may yet learn of it on your own, and awaken. But of this I can say no more.

The new and full moons were joyous times. We women gathered a short while before the sun set, carrying new fruits if they were available, or dried ones, along with wine, honey and bread, and cheese if we had it. Lamps were lit around the outer edge, so that the moisture on the walls of the cave shone like starlight. We sat together and prayed, silently and then aloud. We prayed for each other, our families and friends, for people known and unknown to us personally. We prayed for those who considered us their enemies; as time went on these last prayers became longer and longer.

There was no set pattern or duration for our prayers, but eventually someone started to sing and the rest of us joined in. There were songs of praise to our Creator, and songs of ordinary life, stories old and new. Now and then a new prophet would arise among us. Such moments filled us with awe and thanksgiving.

During that particular stay in Caesarea and at that full moon, a young woman named Martha rose during the singing and began to dance as if she were the Mother Goddess herself. Her body moved as a young sapling in a storm, sinuous and strong. The power and resolve in her movements reminded us of the many storms we each had weathered, and hinted at those to come.

When the dance stopped she stood motionless in the middle of us. She was like a bonfire, the candles a mere reflection of her light. I was spellbound. And then she began to speak. Even now as I think about that night, the hair on the back of my neck stands up and I feel myself expanding. Her words were both terrible and hopeful.

"The light of the world has come among you." She looked slowly around at us, with eyes from another world. *"You are the most*

blessed of women, as you have seen the light and known it is of God.

"Just as you watched this form turn upon itself, around and around, so too do the ages circle ceaselessly. Night becomes day ... becomes night; we are born, live a time and then die, only to be born again, and again. Man becomes woman ... becomes man; the ages pass and yet we remain.

"The light is born among us, but it cannot be sustained. It illuminates our world and gives us hope, revealing a higher path and the true way of being. It shines upon us until we can bear it no more."

Again, Martha turned in a slow circle, eyes open wide, sweeping us into an ocean of love and compassion.

"He is come ... but the world sees him not. He opens his arms and the children go to him. The rest are afraid of what they see in him but cannot find in themselves. In their shame they turn their backs upon him. He calls, but they can no longer hear.

"You hear him. But it is not enough. And so he leaves us until the stars make their slow journey through the heavens, and far into the future comes again to remind us of our promise. From now till then you will come and go with the tides, remembering and forgetting and then remembering again the light that you have seen ... igniting the fire within your heart.

"Keep the flame alive. One day you will be called together, one great soul to serve as kindling for the bonfire of God's eternal love."

Martha stopped speaking then, and slumped to the ground. Several women rushed to tend to her as we each pondered the prophecy. When she came back to herself, she asked a little self-consciously, "Why so solemn? Surely if God sent one of His own to speak, they would be words to hearten us in these dark times." And she began to sing an ancient song that all women knew well.

"If dark clouds of war and want circle overhead, our

Mother takes us into her arms, that we not give in to fear.

If our enemy calls us out to battle, the Lord sends his

Angel Michael to protect us, a bolt of lightning in his hand."

The song made me weep, both in sorrow at what was being taken from us, and in joy that I had my sisters to stand with me in such difficult times. Soon we all joined in, to sing with her.

"If all we cherish is taken from us, our very lives forfeit,

Our Father says forgive them, they know not what they do.

If each one stood alone, the load would be unbearable,

But under heaven's shield we'll stand together ...and together overcome."

*

A few days later we were gathered in the inner courtyard of Hakata's home. Hakata had gone to school in Alexandria, before my time. He was a prosperous trader, but lived simply. Without the eyes of Rome upon him, the brothers could come and go unnoticed.

That morning we heard a rumor in the marketplace that a detachment of soldiers would arrive from Rome by evening. It was said they were on their way to Jerusalem. "Salome," Simon called across the table to mother, "tell us exactly what you heard."

"Mary and I were there with the girls," she began, indicating the two servant girls. "Standing in the shade of the sweets stall was a group of soldiers, talking quietly among themselves. Mary was negotiating with the seller while I stood off to the side, listening. They did not appear to notice me ... an advantage of growing old, I guess," she said without a hint of regret in her voice.

"I did not hear everything they said, but what I did hear indicated at least one and probably more centuria were arriving from a large base somewhere in Anatolia. One of the men had a brother in the Praetorian Guard, who says there is talk about sending further troops by sea."

"Here?" Simon asked, his eyes bulging. "They are coming here? Why?"

"They did not say why, and only that the first group would be going on to Jerusalem. We left after completing our purchase."

The courtyard erupted into noisy debate, each one offering his interpretation of what it might mean.

"Quiet!" Hakata had stood up on a bench. "Quiet," he repeated. His authoritative voice could be heard without shouting. "We cannot afford to draw attention to ourselves. Not now."

Jesus came through the outer gate just as Hakata was climbing down off the bench. James went up to his brother and spoke to him out of earshot of the group, his hands gesturing vigorously. The group watched in silence, waiting for his reaction. But he just turned and went inside.

Jesus always told us we leaned on him too much. "I am here to point the way" he said once when I had gone to him hoping he'd settle an argument ..."but I cannot walk the road toward redemption for you. Each one must do it for himself. Through me you may learn of the way, the truth and the life, but only through your own efforts will you find your way Home."

He could be so exasperating! All I wanted was for him to settle a simple dispute, not give me a sermon. I could see arguments for both positions. One of the men insisted Jesus preached first of all the virtue of self-sufficiency and the other said no, the greater virtue was to help others. The first responded that if we were to offer our help, people would not learn to help themselves. And so it went back and forth. After his sermon about finding our own way – which was no answer at all – I persisted, asking him what I could say to the two men to resolve the impasse since others had begun joining in the argument, taking sides. All he would say was, "You know the answer."

"I most certainly do not!" I retorted, feeling my face redden. "I would not have come to you if I did."

"Cousin, I mean only that if I were to give you the answers to all your questions, they would only be *my* answers – and not necessarily the best."

"Well, I don't know about that," I said, somewhat embarrassed. "But it's easy to forget I am responsible for my own soul's journey ... and hard to stop hoping someone else will stand for me in the halls of judgment. Besides, this is not so important as all that."

"Then you will have no trouble deciding what to say," he smiled.

James had gone into the house after him. A few of his followers started to follow, but Mary held up her hand and they instinctively complied. Even if they would not have admitted it, all the men deferred to her ... except perhaps Peter.

Conversation slowly returned. Some thought we should leave immediately. But to where? There was no agreement on that count. We all knew that in the end Jesus would decide where he would go, and the majority of us would follow ... since, no matter the dangers, we would not forsake him.

By the time he came out, there was little food left on the table. The servants brought out a fresh loaf which he gratefully accepted, waving away the offer of wine. Mary sat off a ways, with Miriam at her side. James came over and sat next to me, squeezing my hand. For some reason the simple show of affection frightened me.

Jesus' eyes were turned inward as he nibbled the food in front of him. Judas had been sitting nearby. Without taking his eyes off his plate, he said, "Judas, you have guarded our resources well, and I thank you for that. No one has ever had to go without as long as you've been around." He looked up and smiled at the beaming Judas. It had been his function to keep our little treasury safe, accepting such donations as people wished to offer, and watching that no coin was spent unnecessarily. Some complained he was excessively tight fisted, but I'd always found him fair.

People began fidgeting in their seats, but no one got up to leave. They were probably wondering, as was I, why he had brought up the subject of money just then.

"We each have our role to play," he went on when he had finished eating. "Some will be lauded for their efforts and others – not understood – will be condemned. But God knows our hearts, better than we know ourselves. Most of you have seen the Greek plays in our travels together, and know how sometimes good is portrayed as evil, and evil, good. So it is in our own world where Roman and Hebrew, Greek and Egyptian (gesturing toward Hakata at the head of the table) come together struggling to find a common language and way of seeing things, that we might stop our eternal fighting and make our way to higher ground.

"Take care not to judge early or too harshly." He looked out over the courtyard, across sunlight and into shadows, scanning everyone so that each person would understand he spoke to them directly. "None of you is free from this temptation, thinking you know the right way to think and be ... that somehow you know the will of God better than any other."

He sounded like a parent, disappointed yet again in his child's behavior. I felt a knot in my stomach, and knew that in my unguarded moments I was as guilty as any other in making judgments.

With a deep sigh he went on, in a voice now tender. "Love, as our Father in heaven loves you. Judge not, if you would not be judged."

His shoulders sagged. "All that you see before you will soon be swept away, changed forever. Do not try to hold on to anything of this world ... least of all, me.

"I go ahead of you to prepare the way. It is not time for you to follow, but in your own time you will join me." He looked around to make sure we were still listening. I felt myself trembling. James squeezed my hand again: I had forgotten he was even there.

"I can hear the Father's voice even now, whispering to me, calling me Home."

"What do you mean, master?" It was my friend Naomi, Joseph's daughter. "You do not plan to leave us, do you?" her voice plaintive.

"But this is ridiculous," said Andrew. "You talk as if you are going to die. We will not let that happen!" he practically shouted. Others joined in, saying they would all protect him with their lives, dying in his place if need be. Some quietly wept. I did not dare look at Mary, could not imagine how she felt hearing her son's words.

He quieted us with a simple gesture. "I know you would each lay your life down for me, or so you believe now. But it is not so easy as that. If you study the prophecies carefully, there are hints of what is to come.

"If you really knew me, you would know I am more than you see here before you. If you knew me, you might then know yourself, that you are far more than what you believe yourself to be.

"The time draws close for me to leave and return to Capernaum. Some of you will stay here, some will journey with me and others will go on ahead to Jerusalem and prepare for us to join you there at the Passover.

"You must discover your own path. Do not blindly follow another – even me – until you have heard your heart speak."

*

He left the following day, asking us to wait where we were until he returned. He would not tell us his destination and I assumed he was going out into the desert as he had done before. He took with him Thomas, James and John, and no other. I felt comforted that he did not travel alone this time.

Only after he left, when a small group of us women came together for our sacred moon ritual, did we learn the truth. I realized then that he had shielded his true intentions from us until he was far enough away there was no danger we would try to stop or to follow after him. He had gone to Egypt.

He came to us during our ritual, similar to what he had done over the years of his travels but which I had seldom seen since his return. Some of the women only felt the comfort of his presence. A few thought they heard his voice, though were unable to understand what he said. All of them saw a light of some description.

But mother, Mary, Miriam and I saw him within that light, standing among us. He told us where he'd gone, and asked that we not speak of it to others. "The sun has nearly come full circle," he said.

PART THREE

Chapter Twenty One

THE FINAL JOURNEY

The four men returned and we continued as if they had never been away. None of them ever spoke of the purpose or destination of their journey, deflecting questions until people simply stopped asking them.

Hardly a day went by without someone new joining us in Capernaum. Jesus welcomed them all without question. Paul, on the other hand, took on the role of gatekeeper for himself, interrogating newcomers on the road before they even arrived at the lake. No one knows how many had felt the call to join Jesus, but were turned away. There were rumors that some had been beaten when they tried to go around him, but I find that hard to believe. Paul could be blunt, but never cruel.

He wasn't the only one. Thomas (not Didymus, but the other, from the mountains) openly confronted those he suspected of being spies. I walked into the middle of an argument one day, and heard a man say "spying ... I'm not a spy!" Thomas and Reuben towered over the young stranger. They shouted a steady stream of questions, hardly giving him time to answer. Then Reuben shoved the man, knocking him to the ground.

"Stop!" I yelled, positioning myself between Reuben and the stranger. I pulled myself up to my full height, though I am not very tall. His shoulders -- twice the breadth of mine -- shook with the effort to control his impulse to knock me down as well. I do not think I had ever looked into the eyes of one who hated me before that. It terrified me, but I stood my ground. But then I don't think I could have used my legs just then, even if I had wanted to.

I heard the stranger scramble to his feet behind me, and run off. Still I held Reuben's gaze. It seemed a very long time but Thomas finally muttered, "Come, leave the woman alone," and the two walked away. When they rounded the corner, I fell to my knees, trembling uncontrollably.

"Veronica! What happened?" Miriam's arms were around me, lifting me off the ground. And still I could not stop the shaking. "That's alright ... you are alright," she cooed quietly, seeing I was in shock.

When at last I could stand, she walked me back to her house. It was a good ways and by the time we arrived at the gate, I had begun to feel myself, enough to notice people staring at us open-mouthed. Her servant Adi came running and seeing me, gasped and ran away. Still too numb to think, I realized later I had been weeping and my face and clothing were mud-stained. Miriam said I looked as if I had been in a battle, and it certainly had felt like one.

"Why do you do this?" Jesus asked Thomas and Reuben later that day. He spoke softly, but I knew he was angry. Seldom had I seen that look on his face. He was the most patient and forgiving of men.

I had not wanted to be there, had not even wanted to tell him what happened. But Miriam went to him straightaway. She said he must know all sides of those who called themselves his followers.

"Why?" he asked again. They stared at the ground, not daring to look him in the eye. He stood with them in silence, waiting. He was not going to let them go until he got a response.

The other Thomas stood nearby, keeping people away. Though each one's behavior affected all of us, my cousin was a conciliator, seeing the best qualities in everyone, even those two. Only twice had I heard of him turning someone away. There was the incident with Michael awhile back. And the man from Tyre who had been with us just two days when he pulled a knife on Delius in an argument over who should pay the bill at the inn where we were staying. We'd all gone to bed, but the two of them had stayed up drinking wine, arguing about politics and women, and just about everything else, apparently. Fortunately Delius suffered only a small cut on his cheek, and his wounded pride.

Reuben broke the standoff. "He was a spy."

"How do you know? Who was he reporting to?" asked Jesus.

"I don't know. The Romans. Caiaphas? He asked too many questions!" he sputtered. "He's spying for *someone*. Or else he would have answered me."

"He was terrified," I said, stepping forward. "You gave him no chance to speak before threatening him." There was that look of hatred again.

Thomas ignored me, "You are in danger, master. Don't you see that?"

"And you think harassing people will keep me safe? Can you truly tell our enemy from our friend? Often the traitor does not even know himself. More importantly, there are many yet-unknown friends waiting to join us, yet you frighten them away. Thomas and Reuben, my brothers, you have first to master the demons within yourselves. Only then will you will be ready to slay those around you. Go now, it is near the Sabbath. Prepare yourselves, and I will see you back here at sundown.

"He should have banished them," Peter said later. "Thomas and Reuben are a greater danger to us than the Romans. They draw unwanted attention to Jesus, to us."

There was much grumbling those days. Few could agree on anything, and no matter what my cousin said or did, there were some to question it. It seemed to me the greater peril lay in our pettiness. We were all on edge, at times erupting into anger and other times giddy with laughter. Everything seemed larger than it was.

I was not immune, having that day argued with mother. Later, I couldn't even remember what we'd argued about. James and I had also been quarreling, about the meaning of Jesus' discourses, about whether it was alright to eat before prayers, and who should or should not accompany us when we left for Jerusalem in a few days' time ... about everything, it seemed.

But once we were on our way the tension evaporated, replaced by joyous anticipation. While we had lived in town, people came and went, stayed in different homes or camped along the lake, and we rarely saw everyone in one place. But out there on the road we were gathered into one company, a patchwork of color and sound, spilling over onto the hillsides, men and women and children.

We were on our way to Jerusalem for the Passover celebration. That day brought back memories of the early years when we traveled there before father died. Thoughts of father used to leave me feeling melancholy, but that had long since been replaced with a quiet contentment, in seeing the happiness mother found with Matthias.

I looked at James and wondered how well we would weather the coming storms. I'd largely put my conversation with mother in Caesarea out of my mind. But even so, the strain between us remained. There were so many unresolved issues, some large, some small.

I know he longed for children, and there were times I did as well. Some in our group were parents, though usually the mother stayed behind with the children. But I would not abandon my cousin as long as I had breath, and Jesus gave no sign of changing his way of life. James said he felt the same way, but he seemed increasingly impatient with his own brother, questioning his decisions ....

"What are you thinking about?" I hadn't even noticed Elizabeth walking in step with me.

"I was thinking of father." There would be no reason to speak of other concerns just then, especially as I could see my sister was becoming very fond of Gabriel, and probably considering marriage herself.

"I don't remember him," she said. "Matthias is my father. I could think of no better." She smiled.

I put my arm around her. "I know, and I am happy for you. For mother too. And I love him as much as any." It was the truth.

My sense of unease mounted the closer we got to the great city. Our lives were not all that different from what they had been since John's death. The ceremonies and feasts might be unchanged, but *we* were changed. I sensed a difference in Jesus too. He continued to preach and heal and embrace all who followed him, even finding time for the children that were always around. But with each day he became more pensive.

I asked Miriam what she thought was happening. "He is less with us now," she said, brushing off any further questions. I knew what she meant. I remember when we were children and I'd asked him where he went when he withdrew from us. He told me then he went to be with his Father. It was just happening more often.

The day was hot and dusty for that time of year. I'm not sure how many days we had been on the road, but it had begun to wear on me. The crowds were increasing and it seemed we were barely moving when I heard a voice call out ahead of us, "There it is. I can see the wall." We had come at last to Jerusalem. With renewed enthusiasm we pressed ahead, hoping to pass through the gate before it closed at sunset. But the crush of people could not be rushed, and finally we stopped altogether. Every Jew who is able makes the greatest effort to be in the holy city for Passover. Also, unknown to us, Roman guards had been posted at the gate checking everyone who entered. That had never happened before.

Night came and we set up a makeshift camp. We had planned to break bread with uncle Joseph that night, but we made do with what we had. It was a cheerful evening, with singing around the fire. Jesus held us in thrall with stories of his travels. We never tired of them, and that night there were many newcomers who hadn't heard the tales before. I lay back in James' arms and felt content. Just before I dozed off I looked up to see Elizabeth and Gabriel stealing off into the night.

We were ready to go at first light, hoping the delay would not be too great. When the horn blew signaling the opening of the gate, a family approached shyly with several donkeys in tow, insisting Jesus take one of them. I fully expected him to decline, but instead he silently lifted a leg over the beast's back.

I had never seen him ride a donkey before. He looked a little silly. My cousin was a tall man and his feet nearly touched the ground. A hush fell over the crowd as he began to ride toward the gate, and the rest of us fell in behind him. Before long the jubilant mood returned and the noise grew. Every now and then I saw someone steal a look at the man on the donkey, but no one tried to speak to him.

I left James and went to walk beside Jesus. I planned to ask why he was riding when everyone else walked, but once there, words just fell away. I was vaguely aware of the crowd's movement around us, but my attention was focused only on the two of us.

"Thank you, Veronica," he said. "You are always at my side when I need you."

His words sent a shiver up my spine, and I looked at him for reassurance. He went on in a voice no one else could have heard above the tumult. "Much will happen in the days ahead, and I ask that you stay close, if possible. The men will scatter, each to confront his own demons.

"But you, my sisters, will remain. Stay together and help each other." At last he turned his head to look at me. "Will you do that?" Before I could answer, he added, "Remember what you learned in Alexandria. Remember your training in the pyramid. I will need you all to stand with me, lest I forget."

The Final Journey 203

In that moment of grace I felt no fear. I nodded yes and he reached out and briefly touched my hand with a smile, then returned his gaze to the road ahead.

The spell had broken and the noise came crashing down around me, and I nearly fell. The crowd closed in and squeezed me out, and I realized the people were cheering Jesus, singing praises to him and throwing palm fronds in his path, to keep the dust down. At first I didn't know if they mocked or adored him. Perhaps there were some of both; many were sincere, some falling to their knees, reaching out to him for a blessing. Some who were lame tried to approach but were pushed back by the surging throng. Usually he would have stopped to attend to them, but not that day. More and more people came close, knowing only that something special was taking place.

All the while he kept his eyes trained on the gate. A group of Roman guards had come outside to see what the commotion was about. They warily eyed the strange man on the donkey, and two of them ran back inside to report. By the time he reached the gate it seemed a whole garrison had gathered. They said nothing, standing aside to let him pass. But it was clear everything about us was being monitored.

"What did he say to you," asked his mother, now walking next to me. I took a deep breath, and told her. She nodded her understanding. She too had been trained in the mystery schools and understood his request.

Once inside the gate, people began to fan out to look for lodging. Many who had traveled with us from Capernaum hoped to stay at Joseph's, but there wasn't room. Disappointed, they turned away to fend for themselves. Jesus dismounted the animal and handed the lead over to the family who had lent it to him. They smiled and left, content their gift had been well-received.

Joseph had been waiting for us at the gate. The courtyard was blessedly peaceful and a midday meal awaited us. We had not seen my uncle for some time and there was much to discuss, many stories to tell. It seemed strange being there without his wife Elizabeth, who remained in Nazareth with their younger children. Usually everyone would have made the journey to Jerusalem, no matter the distance.

By the next day Mary and Martha, Sarah and some others arrived. The circle of women that had been brought together in Carmel so many years before now assembled to bear the fruits of those early labors, and many of their daughters stood with them.

We made sure at least two or three of us were always with him, while the rest mingled with the men, our brothers and husbands and his other followers. After all, food had to be prepared, children cared for, and the Passover feast itself readied. As well ... we did not want to draw attention to ourselves anymore than we already had.

Chapter Twenty Two

HOLDING STEADFAST

"Where is he? Where did he go?" It was the third time in two days that I had lost sight of Jesus in the crowds, and each time I struggled against panic.

The sense of unease had been growing ever since the night of our arrival when Joseph took Jesus aside after dinner to speak with him. When I walked up to them they both fell silent. They did not have to ask me to leave: I knew the conversation would not begin again until I did.

Mary and Miriam's faces told me I was not alone in my concern. "We should head out in different directions," I suggested. "I'll start with the spice market."

"No, I don't think he would want us to do that," Mary answered. "He told me we should stay together."

"Yes, and he also asked that we stay by him," I protested.

Just then he came back into view, with our old friend Marcus on his arm. "Look who is here," he called out. Coming closer, he must have seen our expressions. "I'm sorry. I didn't mean to run off like that, but he would have been lost in the crowds if I hadn't."

It had been some time since we'd seen our friend, and I quickly forgot the moment of fear as we plied him with questions on the way back to Joseph's. Poor man. We never even asked if he had other plans, or if he *wanted* to join us.

"I worry about you," I told Jesus later that evening.

"I need to tell you something. I am afraid it will not make it easier for you, but I need to tell you anyway." He led me away from the others.

I could scarcely breathe. My thoughts jumped to when he came to say goodbye to me when I had been a girl.

"The city has become dangerous," he began. "and it will get much worse. I wish I did not have to tell you this, that I could spare you and the others what is to come, but I cannot. I do not know why, but these things – as much as I understand them now – must be said. I know you are strong, Veronica."

I shook my head and my hands tried to brush away whatever he was about to tell me.

"Yes, you are. I know you better than you know yourself. You can help me by promising to remember all I have told you since we were children, and to hold the ancient teachings in your heart so when I am gone – you can take them out into the world to offer them wherever they will be received."

"When you are gone? What do you mean? Where are you going?" I whispered.

But he didn't answer. "I do not know if James can be your helpmeet for this quest. But I would not have you go alone. You will know, when the time comes, you will know what to do. Everything is happening so fast now, and I cannot see it all.

"The men will falter; some will fall away while others will rise stronger, filled with wisdom and purpose." His eyes glistened looking out into the distance, and I knew not to interrupt. "You women will build and sustain a web of protection for me as I enter the cave of darkness …"

Protection, my thoughts clung to the word. He'll be alright, then.

"...into the arms of death,"

"Oh God, oh God, no! I wanted to scream, to run away, but I had no voice, no will to move.

"...and from there into eternal life."

He stopped, and his head snapped around with a look of surprise on his face. I do not know if he was surprised to see me sitting there with him, or at his own words. But his final words offered me a small sliver of hope, or at least calm. I did not know what he was asking of me, but I did know I would offer the best of myself, and put my own fears away ... for him.

"Cousin, what is going to happen?" I asked, my voice more even than I expected.

He sighed deeply. "I am not sure. But each side has gotten more fanatical and inflexible. The chasm between them grows deeper and wider."

"What are these sides, and who supports them?"

"They have no name, but on the one hand are the Romans and some of the Pharisees, and on the other my true followers and a few pretenders who hope to profit from stirring up suspicion and unrest. I had purposely kept us away from Jerusalem lately, hoping these divisions would die out. But it has gone too far for that; the boulder has crested the mountain top and begun its descent. Everything in its path will be damaged, and much of it destroyed."

I did not know what to say. All I could think then was I had to be strong for him, *I had to be strong*.

As if reading my thoughts he said, "It is not for me I ask this of you, but for mother and Miriam, and for your own self. My Father has me in hand, and walks with me. Promise you will not interfere; promise me you will stop them if they try to do so." He looked at me imploringly.

"Interfere with *what*?" I did not want to know, but couldn't help the question.

"I am not sure, exactly, but I know they mean me harm, and it is the will of Heaven that I not run from what lies ahead, but bring all the power and dignity of the Brotherhood as far as the fires of hell, if that is where I am led. The light will always triumph over darkness and good over evil – in the end.

"Now please, I know I am laying an intolerable burden upon you, but the Father watches over and guides you as He does me. I am ashamed I could not carry this burden alone, that I have drawn you, and others, in to share it with me."

"I am afraid for you," I said, unable to see his face through my tears. "How do you know that I will be able to stand aside and let ... things happen, that I will not be moved to try to stop them myself?"

I did not say so aloud, but could not believe that the men who love him would betray him when he most needed them. And James, why would he not stand by his brother? Would he abandon me as well?

"You won't, I know you won't. And when I have gone my mother, Miriam and others will need you; you will not let them down."

When he is gone. Dear God, how will I go on when he is gone? My first instinct was to run away, to pretend we'd never spoken. I wanted James to take me back to ... to where? I don't even know if the home we once had still stood. It didn't matter; my life was here, with him, no matter how awful it might become.

"It seems you have forgotten," he said softly, interrupting my thoughts, "forgotten what I once told you. It is not good to lose yourself so completely in another. It does not serve either one. You must shine your own light into the darkness. I have taught you many ways to do this, and you have learned much in Carmel and Alexandria. You are ready to go into the world, my dear cousin, to bring healing where there is sickness, joy to salve the pain, and knowledge to replace ignorance.

"But ...." I had a score of reasons why I was not ready, and even more why he must not leave us. But some men unknown to me came up.

"Joseph said we could find you here. Can we talk?" They eyed me curiously, as I turned to walk away.

"We will talk soon, cousin," he called after me.

I slipped out the gate and into the darkened street. I could not bear the thought of seeing people and having to talk about everyday things. The city was noisy, and so alight with cooking and campfires that the stars were barely visible. But at least no one knew me out there. I walked fast, thoughts and images colliding like bats in my head.

"Oh!" A hand caught my wrist before I landed on the ground. "I'm sorry. I wasn't watching where I was going," I said, not even sure what had just happened.

"Are you alright?" the man asked.

"I think so. Are you?" I didn't wait for his answer, but turned to walk away when a sharp pain shot up my leg causing me to stumble.

"You *are* hurt. Lean on me: I'll walk you back to where you are staying."

I didn't want to lean on a man whom I didn't know, but there seemed to be no other choice – not only could I not walk, I didn't even know where I was.

"Maybe you could send for someone to come for me," I hesitated.

"Alright, but I cannot leave you here on the street alone. It is getting late and soon the fires will be extinguished. Where are you staying?" I told him. "That is some ways from here. Are you sure you want to wait alone?"

He was right, it was getting dark and the few people still out on the street had drunk too much wine. So I agreed to go with him. By the time we neared Joseph's street, I heard someone shouting my name. "Here I am," I called out. James ran round the corner, nearly colliding with us.

"That's what happened to begin with," I said, with a weak laugh.

He looked at the stranger, and then at me. I realized I hadn't even asked the man his name. "I am Dan, he said, with a slight bow as

"Thank you Dan, for bringing her back," he called over his shoulder as he walked me to the house.

"Wait," I said to James. "Dan, if you would, come by here tomorrow so I can thank you properly." He nodded and left.

"Why did you invite him back here? And where were you? What happened?" I ignored the first question and tried to answer the others. "But why were you out there by yourself?" he persisted.

"I don't know," I said truthfully. "I just felt a need to walk."

"By yourself! Why would you do such a thing? I do not need to tell you how dangerous it is for you to be out there by yourself." He all but pushed me into a chair, and I bit my tongue in pain. He was right, of course. It had been foolish. James called Miriam to wrap my ankle and walked away, angry.

I looked up as she attended to me and saw Jesus watching from nearby. He had an anguished look on his face. I thought my heart would break, and tried to smile to ease his pain.

The next dawn brought a soft breeze into the compound. I'd forgotten about my ankle until I tried to get up. Miriam had given me something to sleep so it hadn't kept me awake. Joseph stood in the doorway and when I looked up, came into the room. "So you had a little accident last night, eh?" he asked. "Tell me about it." He led me over to a small table in the room and sat me down. I told him about walking and colliding with the stranger.

"No, I mean *tell me about it*." Tell me why you went out as you did. That is not like you, Veronica."

There was no point in avoiding the truth. Joseph, more than any man I knew other than Jesus could perceive the slightest deception. So I told him about my conversation with Jesus.

"Have you told anyone else?" he asked. I shook my head no. "Well then, let it remain between us. It is good to have someone to share your burden, my child. I will do that with you. Now let us join the others for breakfast."

I went to the kitchen to help and was told emphatically by everyone to go sit down. "Today we will serve you," said mother as she led me to the chair next to James.

He barely looked at me when I sat down, and the pain in my stomach was worse than that in my ankle. I couldn't understand the depth of his anger.

After we'd finished eating one of the servants came and whispered in my ear. "There is a man called Dan at the gate, who wants to see you."

"James, come with me. Dan is here and I don't want to subject him to the scrutiny of this whole group," I said, trying to make light of what had become an awkward episode.

"No, you go. Take Miriam or Sarah with you." I felt my face redden. Miriam was in the kitchen so Sarah helped me up and we walked toward the gate. I wondered if he was trying to shame me, if he thought I had done something wrong rather than merely foolish.

The servant girl had brought Dan a cup of water and provided him a chair under a large shade tree. He smiled when I approached, and I saw he was handsome. I had not actually looked at him the night before. Then I noticed him look at Sarah and his smile grew wider.

"I should not have made you return here this morning, I said."

"I am glad you did," he said, still looking at Sarah. "You had other things on your mind last night. It is good you did not remain alone on the street after your fall."

"Yes, thank you for your help. Dan, this is my friend Sarah." I decided I might as well provide the opening for them to talk, since I sensed her looking at him in the same way. I enjoyed having this distraction and called for two more chairs. We three sat in the shade and talked.

We learned that Dan' father was Roman but his mother was Jewish, so he sat astride two colliding worlds, never fully welcomed into either, he said. I realized after a time that the conversation was really between Sarah and Dan, and excused myself, thanking him once again for helping me. "If you ever need anything, do not hesitate to come here. I have already told my uncle of your kindness."

A heated discussion was taking place around the table when I returned. Martha gestured for me to join her. I walked slowly, with a makeshift cane. My ankle hurt but I could tell it would heal well, hopefully before Passover began. I did not dare miss a thing.

"I carry a dagger under my cloak, in case of trouble," said Paul.

"You are mad," retorted Peter. "If you were discovered, they would imprison you without question, and likely execute you. You know weapons are forbidden within the city walls during the holiday. It has always been so, but the Romans are especially nervous this year. It is rumored they are searching people randomly."

"Now is not the time to have a Roman sitting in our gardens," Paul replied, looking back toward the gate. "Is he still here?" I guessed he referred to Dan, though I couldn't imagine how anyone would know he was half Roman.

Joseph jumped in, "The man did not ask whether Veronica was Jewish or Roman before lending her a hand. Next you will accuse him of tripping her." His face was red with anger.

James glanced at me, and looked quickly away.

"Come, whispered Martha, let us finish cleaning up." I was glad for an excuse to leave. Several of the other women followed us into the kitchen. There was little left to do. I think she just wanted to get me away from the heated discussion. Usually politics and worldly affairs were kept out of our conversations during Passover and the other holidays, but they seemed to impinge on everything those days.

I was on my way to our room to lie down and rest my foot before going out that evening, when I saw Miriam. "Jesus asked me to go into town and supervise preparations for tonight. Maybe you could join me later. We haven't had a chance to talk since we got here. Chaya will be coming in to help me after she finishes up here. You could come with her."

Chaya worked in uncle Joseph's kitchen. She was sister to Dena, a servant in Lazarus' household. It was his sister, Martha who arranged for a private room where a group of us would meet that evening. Joseph had insisted we gather in a neutral setting, since the homes of all prominent Jews were being closely watched.

"Yes, I would like that."

"Good. I'll speak with Chaya on my way out."

Chapter Twenty Three

THE UPPER ROOM

"Auntie, are you up yet? I must leave soon."

It was only when the girl called a second time that I realized she was talking to me. It may have been the first time I'd been called Auntie and it shocked me. Though I was barely thirty, to the young girl I must have seemed already old.

"Yes Chaya, wait for me. I will be ready soon." It took me longer than usual to get dressed. We made our way slowly, and because of my ankle I was unable to help the poor girl with the bundles she carried for the evening meal. I had no idea where we were going; even she was unsure of the way. We stopped to ask directions of a woman carrying a large jar of water on her head, who gestured for us to follow her up a back street where she pointed to the house we sought.

Negotiating the steps was a further challenge. "Oh good, you're here!" exclaimed Miriam. "You can help wash these roots," she said, pulling out a chair for me to sit on. The sisters Martha and Mary were already there with their friend, (another) Sarah, giving instructions to Dena and several other girls who were helping prepare the meal. Chaya dropped her bundles and hugged her sister. Together they ran out the door with empty jars to get more water.

Miriam sat down next to me with a knife and board, chopping the vegetables as they were cleaned. The two older women were busy in the back room and we were alone.

"What is to become of us, Veronica?" Miriam asked, without preamble.

"What do you mean? Of who?"

"Us, all of us. Him. This will not end well, I know it. And there is nothing I can do to turn him aside from what is surely his doom."

I shuddered. He may not have been as direct with her as he was with me the night before, but she knew. I took a deep breath. "If you and I cannot convince him to leave the city or deny who people say he is, then no one can. I have spoken with Mary, and she said she will not ask him to do this – and I cannot."

"Nor I."

"And if Joseph and Nicodemus, with all their influence in the Sanhedrin and in the business community aren't able to mollify the Romans, then there's no hope there either."

Miriam stopped her work and looked at me. "I am not sure if it is the Romans to be most feared or the Pharisees. Salome says some of them have hated him since he was a boy, and were happiest when he went to Egypt those many years ago. They convinced themselves he had died somewhere and were greatly distressed at his return.

"And so they should be!" she said, banging her fist on the table for emphasis. "They are arrogant and greedy for power and riches. *He* is the embodiment of the virtues they speak about, but do not live. People are beginning to see through their deceit and turn to one who actually walks with God."

My friend's eyes were wild. I dried my hands on my apron and took her trembling hands in mine. "Miriam, my sister, this is all true. But to say such things aloud will only fuel their obsession with him. It is not what he wants. He is asking us to stand in silence, to support him without action."

"Why, that's crazy!"

"He asks that we do nothing, at least nothing that anyone can see."

"What do you mean? How do you know this?"

It may be that Jesus loved Miriam more than all others. Or so it had long seemed to me. But I didn't know what he had told her, whether he had told her some of what he'd said to me, or nothing at all.

"All I know is that he asked me not to try to prevent anything from happening. He recalled Alexandria and the pyramids, which I took to mean our training in the resurrection of the body into light and everlasting life." I stopped.

Miriam began to weep, and I saw she understood ... at least as much as any of us could. I thought about those years in Egypt. We had gone through many rituals, learning chants and the movement of body and hands, the control of the breath and more. And while we had attained much, the last and most important powers still lay beyond our grasp. In Egypt I heard stories that my cousin had surpassed his teachers and was honored among them as a great adept. That meant he had mastered the final test, the resurrection of the body.

We had been trained to stand with the candidate in the temple, holding the inner vision true no matter what our eyes saw. We formed a womb in which the new body could take form; a body not made with hands, a body of light ... *a body eternal*. The initiate fashioned the vision and implanted it in us. If he or she faltered for even a moment we carried the vision to the next moment, serving as a bridge until control was regained and the transformation complete.

On a lower level mothers do this all the time for their children, husbands for their wives, friend for friend. We all falter sometimes. In those crucial moments neither the candidate for initiation, nor we have the luxury of holding another in judgment, or being angry or feeling sorry for ourselves ... or for him. We must be as God created us, loving, impartial, standing with and for each other.

Miriam and I continued our chores in silence. After awhile Mary came in and said it was time to ready ourselves for our guests. We returned to Joseph's to bathe and change clothes. In our absence the ritual lamb would be brought in and the men would help the girls to put it onto the spit and hang it in the oven. It was partly because of the size of the oven that Martha had chosen that place.

When we were ready we walked out together into the last rays of the sun: uncle Joseph, Jesus, Miriam, James and myself. Some of the guests had already arrived by the time we got there, and the rest came in shortly after that. Mother and aunt Mary left word they would not be coming, but would see us when we got back.

Mary told me later that she, Salome, the other Mary, Juana and a few of the older women had instead gone to Juana's home. They'd gathered to begin the *holy work*, activating some of the rites that cannot be seen by the uninitiated. (Some of those in the upper room that evening had not been through the required training.) Mary said knowingly being away from her son so close to the end was one of the hardest things she had ever done.

The twelve had come to share the supper, those men called personally by Jesus in the early days of his ministry ... as had Lazarus with his sisters Martha and Mary, our uncle Joseph, Nicodemus and Matthias. Miriam, of course, Anna, Judia, Josie and Edithia were among the women. It was a festive group.

Please God that it not come to pass, I whispered to myself each time the perilous thoughts returned.

"I have never seen the temple so crowded," said Nicodemus. "John and Philip and Nathanial helped Joseph and me with the lamb for tonight's feast. You have these young men to thank; it was they who parted the crowds for us to pass to the inner court for the ritual slaughtering. We priests were busy all day with the blessings and sacrifices. How I hate the stench of burning blood and flesh," he added almost under his breath.

Anna and Edithia were laying the table, brushing aside Miriam's and my offers to help. "You have done enough already," they said. The servant girls had been sent home so they could be with their families; we would do for ourselves that night.

Everyone seemed to be talking at once, as more continued to arrive. "The lamb is nearly done," interrupted Martha. "I'm sorry the seating isn't more comfortable, but there are many of us. Make yourselves ready."

Anna and Edithia had set out basins of water near the entry for the ritual washing of our feet. Edithia held a small vial of spikenard, adding a single drop of the expensive oil to each basin. It was the same oil that Mary had used on Jesus' feet when he visited her and her brother Lazarus just days before. I had heard about it from some of the men who were incensed that she should pour out an entire vial for the ritual cleansing when the money for it might have been used to cover their increasing expenses, or at least given to the poor during Passover.

I think they were more upset that Mary had massaged the oil into his feet and – they said – used her hair to wipe the excess than they were about the cost. Such intimate acts are meant for one's husband alone and not for another man, no matter the circumstances.

Mary herself had come to us afterwards, asking if she had done wrong. "What was Jesus' response?" asked his mother.

"Judas and Simon came in while I knelt at my Lord's feet and began to berate me for my extravagance. I knew my brother worried what others might think, though he said nothing, for he loved us both. Jesus looked up at his friends and said, 'This woman gives honor to the living, saving nothing for the grave. The poor will always be with you; but I am here today and soon gone. Leave us be.' The rebuke in front of a woman was hard for them, and I felt their anger from across the room. But they left without another word."

Now, in the upper room, most set about to wash their own feet. Our group was too large and disparate for social precedent to be useful – such as when a host washes the feet of an aged or wealthy guest. But several vied for the honor of serving Jesus.

While they discussed it among themselves, he rose and went to where Josie sat. Smiling tenderly, he took a basin and knelt in front of her. The girl jumped up, flushed, "No, master, you must not do that! Please sit and though I am not worthy, I will gladly wash your feet."

Peter ran around the table, almost knocking Josie over to get between Jesus and her. "Master, let *me* wash your feet. It is not right that a young girl should do this thing." Peter towered over her. Her face had gone so white, I thought she might faint.

"Sit down Peter." He indicated a place at the far side of the room. "I wish to honor the youngest of us." He gently nudged Josie back onto the bench and silently attended to his job. I heard he had washed the feet of his male disciples before, which was surprising enough since it was custom for a student to attend to his master.

He finished quickly, realizing, I'm sure, that no one would do anything until he was done. He told me later he would have preferred to wash his own feet then, so that the intended respect to us women might be all the more apparent. But as his disciples hovered about him, he gestured to John to attend to him that night. He chose John, he said, because John carried humility and strength in equal parts.

Once all of us had completed the ritual washing, the women refilled the basins and set them near the door for any latecomers that might arrive. Small bowls with fresh water had been set on the tables at intervals that we might wash our hands as needed during the rituals. Conversation slowly returned and by the time we sat down to eat, it could be imagined that nothing out of the ordinary had happened – though none of us would ever forget it.

There were three long tables, facing inward so that everyone might be seen. I had hoped to sit close to Jesus, but the men quickly took control of the benches nearest him. Jesus looked up at us and shrugged his shoulders.

Some of the men clearly resented us women and our access to *their* master, while the others simply indulged us – more a matter of their fondness of us personally, rather than believing we had any right to be a part of their world.

It is fit that men and women have different roles. In my studies and from personal experience I have learned that all religions teach of the Goddess standing to the side of each God. In Alexandria we were trained alongside the men, each according to our nature and interests. The happiest families are those where the woman has the love and respect of her husband, and not just the other way around.

Joseph was the eldest male and Martha sat in for Elizabeth as the eldest woman. They took their places at the far ends of the two smaller tables, representing our father and mother. Miriam and I were at the center of the longest table, directly across from Jesus. James was to his left and John to his right side. The others spread out from there. Some of the men were heard grumbling that we should stick to the old way, with women sitting together in the kitchen while men ate at the big table in the main room. Peter and Paul tried especially hard to ignore us at first, but eventually Paul softened, seeming to enjoy his conversation with Martha's sister Mary, who sat across from him.

As the father of our group, it fell to Joseph to speak about the meaning of Passover. Instead he passed the honor to Nicodemus. His white beard dropped to his chest, and I thought he must have missed Joseph's signal to speak. But then his chin lifted and he looked slowly around the room, as if to memorize our faces.

"Though much time has passed since our people left Egypt, it is good to remember those who came before us demonstrating courage in dangerous times," he began. "It is a lesson each of us must heed this very night.

"That time was a parting of the ways, between the old and what was yet to come – symbolized by Moses parting the sea so our people might return here to Canaan, our ancestral home. This too is a time of departure. No one can see where the unrest of today will lead us. But I do know our lives will never be the same, that each of us will awaken tomorrow to a different world than the one we found this morning."

There were tears in many eyes, including some of the men. But Jesus' eyes were trained above and behind us, as if he wasn't even listening to the old priest. I was tempted to turn, to see what he was looking at, though I knew what he saw was beyond any of us.

"…courage from our ancestors, and draw courage from each other.

Let us help one another and remember we are brothers ... no matter what comes."

His comments were not what one usually hears at this feast of remembrance. Typically a lively discussion followed about our people's history, and what it means to us today. But no one that night wanted to think about what his words foretold.

Miriam cleared her throat and began to sing, dispelling the silence. Her red-rimmed eyes looked determined as she sang about a starry sky overlooking a sleeping city, with angels watching our people, protecting them. While songs were not part of the ritual meal, it helped to lift our spirits.

When the song ended, Joseph picked up a large cup and filled it to the brim with wine from one of the pitchers. Holding the cup in both hands he said a short prayer, touched it to his lips and passed it to Matthias to his right. Matthias closed his eyes and his lips moved in a silent prayer. He too sipped and passed the cup on, and so it went around the room.

Each one dipped their hands into the basins in front of them and patted them dry on strips of cloth dedicated for that purpose. Then Martha picked up the unleavened bread in front of her and broke it. Each of us followed her example. I was hungry, not having eaten since early morning. The bread was dry and it stayed long in my mouth.

After that we filled each other's cups from the many pitchers placed around the tables and waited while Joseph spoke the next prayer. "Oh God of the Hebrews, I ask that you deliver us from those who persecute us, as you have in times past."

I drank deep of the sweet liquid, its warmth filling me. This time I dipped the bread in the wine and touched it to the bitter herbs, meant to remind us of the sacrifices of our ancestors. Chewing slowly, I wondered how long it would be before the sweetness overcame the bitter taste.

The cups were filled again and just as Joseph was about to speak the next blessing, Jesus stood, a loaf in hand. "Break a piece of the bread from your plate and offer it to the one seated next to you." When we did so, he said, "We are of one body, sons of our heavenly Father. In time to come, when you break bread together, think of me and I will be there with you." We took the bread from our neighbor and ate, each one pondering the meaning of his strange words.

Then Jesus held up his cup and said "Symbol of the blood of life, a gift from our divine Mother." James offered his cup to Jesus, and he did sip from it. Using their example we each extended our own cup to the one seated next to us, whether man or woman. "Do this in remembrance of me: for though I am gone from sight, I am always with you, unto the end of time."

He sat down and said, "Now let us share the blessing of the Passover meal." Some of the women went to carve the lamb. Josie brought the first plate to Jesus. On it was a large slab of roasted lamb, along with rice and leeks. He waved her away: "No longer will I eat the flesh of any animal that was slaughtered as offering to God."

I do not think those sitting at the far ends of the tables heard his words, as everyone had begun talking at once. Josie took the plate and gave him another, with fish in place of the lamb. Jesus accepted it from the girl, thanking her with a smile.

After we had eaten our fill, Joseph offered a third prayer for redemption from our oversights and the wrongs we have done. Cups were filled again and the wine drunk along with handfuls of dried fruit. The cool night air drifted up the stairwell. Now and then I felt a draft on my back, though the room was warm.

Enough wine had been drunk to soften even Peter's hostility. I know he and some of the others had expected a quiet gathering with the twelve. But Jesus had said, when inviting us: "This is a time for family to come together … and you are each my mother, my brother and cousin."

The last cup of wine was poured and the final benediction spoken. When Joseph finished, the room erupted again in conversation. In the background of all that noise I became aware of an intense exchange between Jesus and the few men closest to him, and leaned over the table with the excuse of reaching for something, to hear what they were saying.

"One among you will betray me this night," he said. A flurry of protests went up, but he would not be put off. "Go now ... do what you must do." He noticed then that I had heard, and quickly changed the subject. When his followers kept protesting their loyalty, he got up and walked away from them and moved toward the back room. I followed him and stood waiting for his return. As he came back in, he stopped and said, "Do not speak of this with anyone."

I remembered he had said not to interfere, but how could I allow such a thing to happen if I had the means to prevent it? Surely Joseph, at least, should know. But I had promised and resolved to honor his request, no matter the cost. Besides, I did not know of whom he was speaking.

People were getting up from the table and walking around the room. Some few had begun to leave. I tried to discover who among the Apostles had left (so I might identify the traitor), but they were too scattered about and I had to give up.

There would never be another night like that one, lifting me from dread to joy and back again, over and over.

A beehive of images filled my head and when sleep finally came for me, it brought with it disturbing dreams.

Chapter Twenty Four

IN THE GARDEN

"Veronica, come quickly."

I'd been sound asleep and didn't know if the voice had followed me back from the dream worlds, or belonged to where James and I lay.

But it came again, more urgently. "Veronica! You must come … now!"

I looked over to see if James still slept, but he wasn't there. And it came back to me. He and the other men had left the upper room in a tight group around Jesus. Miriam and I started to follow, then realized if Jesus had meant us to go with him, he would have asked us.

I recognized his mother Mary's voice as the one at the window. Though early spring, the cold of winter lingered at that hour. I dressed rapidly. Running out into the still moonlit night, I found Miriam waiting with Mary.

"Why did you not come inside?" I asked, my head clearing. "And why were you outside the gates to begin with?" Both of the women had been staying in Joseph's compound with us.

Not pausing to answer, Mary grabbed our hands, and we went off at a near run. "The sisters and I had just finished our prayer rituals ... when Anna showed up at the door," she said, panting. "She ... stayed to clean up after your dinner, saw the men leaving, and decided to follow them. She saw you turn back ... but went on herself."

Out of breath Mary stopped next to a small brook and looked from one to the other of us, still holding our hands. Her eyes glistened in the silver light. "They have gone to Gethsemane. She left them there at the foot of the mount and ran to tell us."

"Well, that doesn't sound so bad," said Miriam. "Why are we running ... in the middle of the night?"

"They are all there, except Judas." Mary looked at me and asked, "Do you know anything about this, Veronica?"

I began to tremble, remembering what I had heard at the end of dinner. "Why do you ask me, auntie?" The palms of my hands were wet and I tried to pull my hand away from her, but she would not let it loose.

"At the end of our ceremonies, immediately after certain other revelations, your face appeared to me. What do you know?" she asked again, evenly.

"Someone will betray him. If Judas is not there, then it is he who has done so."

"Why did you not come and tell us right away?" she asked, her voice exhausted.

"He said to tell no one. I wasn't even sure I had heard rightly," I said, though I knew I had. Should I have told her, I wondered, ignoring his pleas to not interfere? How could I let anything happen to him that might have been prevented?

A wave of panic began to wash over me, but Mary squeezed my hand and said, "It's alright, child. You have done what he asked, and that is what we all must do now. Come," she said, and we were off again, crossing the brook and moving toward the garden.

Judas ....

Miriam had momentarily fallen back and I grabbed her hand as we continued running. She gripped my hand so tightly I thought my bones would break, and I knew she felt the same heat of anger that surged through me. Judas was always arguing with Jesus and the others, insisting Jesus should take advantage of people's love for him and their hatred of Rome to grab power.

'Now is the time!' he would shout. 'If we do not act now, the opportunity will pass and they will squeeze us harder and harder until we are destroyed as a people. *We are the children of Abraham and not slaves!*' He would go on and on like that until he was silenced.

But why would he betray Jesus, when he placed his hopes on him for throwing off Roman rule? Maybe he'd grown weary of supporting him once he realized my cousin had no interest in political power. I could not help but wonder if he had ever loved him, or cared for his teachings.

We slowed our pace as we neared the mount and circled silently around to the right of the main entrance. Apparently Mary did not intend for us to enter, but to stay outside and watch … and wait. The men were huddled near the gate, cloaks over their heads to keep warm. They too were keeping vigil. Maybe everything was alright then; he was safe. Jesus often went off by himself to pray alone, and I tried to convince myself that's what was happening there.

The three of us found a spot under a nearby tree where we could see the gate and the waiting men, but no one could see us.

"Even though I left, the women are continuing their vigil in Juana's house. And this you should know. Some of our sisters from Carmel have joined us."

"Elois is here?" I asked, hopefully.

"She is on her way, in fact might even have arrived. But as we've all been trained to do, the rest are working with us from a distance."

"But what can we do if he has told us not to interfere?" asked Miriam.

"We are not trying to *change* anything, dear. But we can help all the same. These next days are critical. We must not impose our own desires on what happens. And we must keep our emotions in check. Be prepared to push back the temptation to use your training to deflect the forces of darkness arrayed against our dear brother."

We heard someone approaching, and Mary went silent. I was stunned at her use of the term *brother* for her own son. What must that mean except she no longer views him as her son, but a brother, one of the Brotherhood, son of our heavenly Father? That single word was more shocking to me than any event bringing us out in the middle of the night to hide in the shadows together.

A man walked quickly by, and disappeared around a corner, not even noticing the others who awaited Jesus at the garden gate.

"Let us join hands," said Mary, "and think of our sisters wherever they may be, uniting with them"

A breeze came up, rustling leaves and carrying a faint scent of spring blossoms. Mary named each of the women in a voice so low no one would distinguish it from the sighs of the wind. Our small circle felt suddenly larger as we invited the other women in to join us where we were, so close to the master.

"What can we do, mother?" Miriam asked when she had finished her invocation.

"I have already told you what we must *not* do. All that is asked at the moment is to recall the love God has for us, and hold that in our hearts. As such we are an outpost for divine love in this world."

We dropped hands and settled in for the night. Sleep would not come, but I had found my way to a place of deep calm when we heard footsteps approaching, this time of many feet. They were trying to be quiet, but I heard clanging metal and knew it to be soldiers. Fear shot through my heart, and I was on my feet before I knew it.

"*Sit*," Mary commanded. "Our work now begins in earnest."

I sat obediently, and slipped into the realm of a priestess of Hathor, as I had learned to do in Egypt. No longer aware of our surroundings,

I only learned later from James that they had indeed been soldiers, led by Judas, called Iscariot.

It was said he had betrayed my cousin for a pittance of silver coin. When the soldiers arrested and carried Jesus off, the others berated him for his treachery, a few setting on him with the intent to kill. He cried out, claiming the authorities only wanted to bring him in for questioning. He had seen nothing wrong with augmenting their savings while giving Jesus a public forum for proclaiming his true intentions, demonstrating his divine credentials.

And when he realized what he had done, he begged them to take his life. But John stepped in and said "It is not for us to judge this man. He will be judged on higher authority than ours. The master needs us now and we must go."

He went off at a run, followed by the others. Peter gave Judas one last kick and left him lying on the ground, tormented and alone.

*

When later I had a chance to speak with Jesus, he told me why he had gone to the garden that night. I will let him speak in his own words.

"The storm clouds had already begun to gather the night we met in the upper room. In some ways it was the happiest night of my life, sitting there with so many of the people I love most, celebrating the Passover. It is a joyous occasion in any case. And all I could think of was how blessed I am, and how I loved you all.

"Even Judas. I do not judge him for what he did. I know his heart, and while it is often troubled, he did not mean to do me harm. He played an elaborate game beyond his skill. And he has suffered much already.

"When we made ready to leave the feast I finally had to accept that the time had come to face my accusers. They were not going away; there was nothing I or anyone else could do … at least nothing I could do and remain true to the law of Heaven.

"My accusers were many, you know. Not just the Romans, but our own. Each had their reasons: fear, jealousy, greed – and some just went along, with no convictions of their own.

"But I was not quite ready. Having spent the evening with family and friends, I was vulnerable. I knew I could be tempted to avoid my fate, to leave my ministry and remain with all of you, living an ordinary life, like any man. I could leave Jerusalem and return to the countryside, maybe even quietly teach while staying out of sight until the authorities forgot about me."

He was silent a long while, remembering.

"But that would undo all that I had tried to accomplish in my life, speak against that which I had taught, in effect saying that my life had been a lie. And *that* I could not do. My Father and all the angels of Heaven promised to watch over me in the hours to come, offering the hand of strength and love and forgiveness, if I would but summon the courage to accept it.

"And so I called my brothers and asked them to accompany me to the garden where I would pray for that courage. Just knowing they were nearby helped, though I had to walk through the fires alone.

And knowing you, Miriam, mother and the other women were there gave me enormous strength and buoyed my courage. Even though you were out of sight, I knew the face of each of you and will remember you forever for your love.

"But they faltered, the men faltered. Even James, my own brother, and Peter and John who entered the garden with me – fell asleep! They could not keep watch with me for even a little while during my agony. The wine drunk at the feast had dulled them, and it was late. But still, I would have hoped….

"And those who waited at the bottom of the hill were sleeping so soundly they did not even hear the Roman guards pass by them, they who were left there to protect me."

Jesus disappeared again into his own thoughts. And I wondered at the men who had sworn on their own lives to stand by him, wondered what they were thinking now. But I was not guiltless. Though I did not run I faltered often in those days, forgetting my training and raging inside against the ones who were doing such terrible things to my beloved teacher and friend. I would have destroyed them if I had known how, and taken him away from all who wished him ill.

"You could have, you know."

"What?"

"You could have done so. Especially with the power of your sisters aligned with you, you would have been able to do just what you wanted. Destroy them. Rescue me. You think you did not do so because you are weak. But you are as powerful as I am. You do not need physical strength to claim your power. *You need to know this.* You did not do so because in your heart you are aligned with the will of Heaven, and it was not Heaven's will that I escape from what befell me."

I think I managed a laugh then. "You always know what I am thinking, don't you?"

"I do not have to read your thoughts to know you, Veronica. Your heart and mine are twined, and always will be. One day you will understand.

"But I have to tell you that I wavered in my resolve while in the garden. The moon shone off the olive branches and the night was filled with visions of what lay ahead. You see, at last I understood my fate. It was not the fate ordained for me at birth, but the one that came for me in the end. I had to make the best of it. And I confess I did not like it at all. The man who prayed to his Father on that hill spoke as a child afraid of monsters in the dark. I asked Him to take that cup from me, so I would not have to drink it … because I knew I would die. And I knew that death would not come quickly.

"But I was met with silence. Even the angels' wings stopped beating. My friends lay sleeping, indifferent. I'm sure each one believed I would do as Judas expected: throw off the chains, rise up and grab the scepter of power and proclaim myself King. But this was not what Heaven wanted, not what the world needed.

"It was then I knew that most of what I had tried to teach others had fallen on deaf ears … that much of it had been in vain. I had wanted to show people that they too are children of the one God, that we are brother and sister to each other, that each of us is destined to be born again in light, ascending to Heaven in perfection. And now my Father was asking me to demonstrate this so that all might see.

"I was terrified. And I was a little angry.

"Angry? Why? At whom?" I asked.

"God. It seemed to me then that I had been abandoned. How could He send me into that den of thieves, those murderous adulterers? I had a lot of thoughts like that. I am not proud of them. But having had them, I understand better the fears and judgments of others.

"I prayed long and hard, stripping away every part of me that stood in the way of my mission, ultimately throwing it all into the fires of surrender. An angel of God came to me at that critical moment and spoke my name ... not the name Jesus but the name that was written on my soul at the beginning of time, a name that cannot be uttered with human breath ... and I rose, called the three men to me, saying the hour was at hand.

"Just then the soldiers came into view. And Judas, my brother Judas, approached. He kissed me on the cheek and stepped back. He smelled of sweat and fear and his hands trembled. I knew at that moment he doubted his actions. But it was already too late.

One of the soldiers tossed him a small bag, but he didn't move and it fell to the ground. He just stood there, though they shouted at him to take the money and be gone. He just stood there, anguished. I felt compassion for him. He had chosen a horrible path.

"James ran up to try to intervene and one of the soldiers knocked him to the ground. John just stood there with his mouth open. He is wholly devoted to non-violence and would not have known what action to take against armed men. And Peter, who towered above a number of the guards backed away, in shock.

Shock would be the best way to describe all the men over those days. They just never believed it would come to this. Not one of them in their heart believed I would let the authorities have their way with me, no matter what I had been telling them over the years. And so ...

how could I blame them? They did their best."

Chapter Twenty Five

THE TRIAL

Miriam, Mary and I ran off after the soldiers as they took Jesus away. I kept telling myself, 'do not intervene ….' He was right: what *could* I have done? What could any of us have done? Even if we had banded together, men and women, and our numbers topped a thousand, they would have slaughtered all thousand of us.

He did not seem to resist, walking under his own power. I saw no abuse. We followed him to a small building off the governor's palace where the Prefect, Pontius Pilate lived. The soldiers followed him through the door, which closed behind them. We moved cautiously closer, not seeing any other guards around, and heard the bar slide across the door on the inside. He was locked in.

We retreated into the shadows, where I stayed while Mary and Miriam ran back to uncle Joseph's house. He, of anyone we knew, had the power to resolve the injustice. I do not think I have ever felt more alone in my life as I did crouching there in the dark, and I could only imagine how he must have been feeling on the other side of the gate.

Peter, James and John had reached Joseph's ahead of them. The other eight men had disappeared into the night. No one knew where they had gone, and just then, no one cared. Miriam said that Joseph paced back and forth, muttering about trust, and faith, and friendship.

A servant had been dispatched to wake Nicodemus and bring him back to the house. Joseph wanted to talk with him before confronting the rest of the Sanhedrin. They were both members of that august body, highly respected by most and despised by a few, in part because of their association with Jesus.

It took awhile, but I finally calmed my thoughts enough to pray as I waited outside the governor's palace. I remembered what Mary told us about avoiding the temptation to anger, no matter how righteous it may seem. Anger wouldn't help, but I could lend support by calling upon the forces of Heaven to save him from his captors. I put all of my attention, my will and love into my appeal.

After some time another thought entered my mind: he had not resisted his captors. What if he did not intend to be saved? I do not know where such a thought could have come from, because it made no sense to me. But I changed my prayer because of it, asking instead that Heaven support him in fulfilling his plan, whatever it was.

That was hard. That was very hard. Because it might mean I would not get what I wanted most, to have him back with us, traveling, teaching, healing. I could not imagine that the Father wouldn't want that too!

Later, he would tell me: "There were many Roman guards in the room where I was held. But in an antechamber were some members of the Sanhedrin whom I had seen in the temple. Now and then one of them would peer through the curtains to see how the proceedings were going. It was clear to me the guards were doing the bidding of those men. By their dress they were Pharisees, though later they would be joined by at least two Sadducees.

"The guards held no animosity against me. In fact I don't think most of them even knew who I was. I remembered seeing one of them listening to my talks from the edge of the crowd. After I had been there awhile he whispered that at first he had been sent to spy on me and report back to Pilate's men. But after hearing my words and seeing my works, he became convinced I was at least a good man, and perhaps even the Messiah spoken of by the Jews. He tried to keep the others from mistreating me, risking his own life in the process. I told him that he had no responsibility in what took place there, and that I forgave him should he be forced to act against his conscience. But when some of the others became violent, he wept and left the room. I never saw him again.

"Most were content with taunts, but there was one cruel man who seemed to find pleasure in beating me. I saw his heart. It was not dark as one would expect, but tormented with pain from a childhood with a cruel father. He had lost his own identity, standing there as his father might have done, seeking revenge for something from another time and place.

"It was hard, I admit. Not so much the physical pain, but knowing none of that had to happen. And knowing I had the power to leave and avoid the trauma not just for myself, but for all of you. I would have done most anything to save you from the pain of being there. But I was called to serve a higher purpose than my own desires. If people would not listen to my words, perhaps they would understand if they saw the meaning of those words acted out in the world with their own eyes.

"It took all my strength to surrender my will to the will of Heaven, which meant I could not battle against my captors in any way, not even with words. Prayer provided the key to the inner sanctum where I found love for those who sought to do me harm. Like Judas, those guards were victims in their own way, and were forgiven even as they assailed me.

"At one point the sounds of an argument filtered in through the outer door and I thought I heard Joseph's and Nicodemus' voices, but they were quickly silenced. I think they might have been forced to leave. But others continued to argue, not about whether to free me, but how to present their case with the greatest assurance of winning. I knew they would succeed, that my death was inevitable.

"Silence followed then. I might even have slept awhile. I don't know. They refused to give me water, though my mouth was parched. The guards became increasingly bored, and took it out on me. But you saw enough of that later on.

"It was still dark when they brought me before Pilate. Five members of the Sanhedrin were already present, and more came in once we started the mock trial. At first I couldn't understand why all this was taking place in the middle of the night, or why Pilate would have condescended to participate in something so absurd. But then I realized they wanted to get it out of the way before the Sabbath began, get *me* out of the way – and there was much to do," Jesus said wryly.

His story so intrigued me that I forgot the nature in which he was speaking to me. This was the time in between, after the crucifixion yet before he would leave us, for good. It was the most precious time of all, sacred beyond measure, and bittersweet. I urged him to continue, eager to hear any words from him while I still could.

"They convened a trial, even before the sun had risen. There is nothing in the law that prohibits such a thing, but that is surely because no one had seen need for such a law. Pilate sat in his Prefect's chair, from which he would give a ruling on the case brought before him.

"The accusation against me was two-fold. First I was accused of disturbing the peace and secondly of blasphemy in claiming to be King of the Jews. While there might be some truth to the first, the second was ridiculous. I have never claimed any title, least of all that, nor have I ever sought worldly power. And even the issue of disturbing the peace is not from an intention to cause trouble or even to undermine the power of Rome. My challenge is to how people accept things the way they are, simply because they have always been that way ... along with their tendency to put worldly authority before God's authority.

"We have been taught that the priesthood speaks for God, representing God's authority. It *is* their role, in part, but a role too-often abused. They were the ones who sought to condemn me, though the servants of Rome were eager to placate them. They did not know how the people would react if I were to die, and the thought of an uprising terrified them.

"But there sat Pilate, listening to the accusations from Caiaphas and

Annas. When he asked for evidence, they brought in a string of witnesses who had been carefully rehearsed before hand. They came into the room one by one, saying almost exactly the same thing. After a time I no longer heard them, and only a slap across my mouth brought my attention back to that mockery of justice.

"Pilate had a strange expression on his face. As I looked into his heart I saw that he did not believe a word of what he heard, but that he was himself afraid.

"Afraid of what?" I asked. "Of you?"

"Oh, not me. I think he saw me more truly than did my brothers in the Sanhedrin. The Jewish authorities viewed me as a threat, a competitor for power. He knew that was not true, but also knew that if he did not act, they would go to Rome and he would be called to account if trouble erupted. Of course, the unrest has been growing daily, but for reasons not related to me.

"No, I believe Pilate had actually been thinking about my teachings. For some time he'd been sending out spies (like the guard earlier) who reported on what I actually said, rather than the lies spread by others, along with the testimony of people who had been healed of many maladies. But I was one man and to those who covet power, no man is indispensable.

"He questioned me personally, asking me to say clearly whether or not I was the King of the Jews. I did not answer him. He repeated the question in another way: was I intending to deliver the Jews from Roman authority? Did I challenge the authority of Caesar? Caiaphas interrupted then, practically shouting, 'he says a new kingdom is imminent!'

"'Is that true?' Pilate asked. I still did not answer. Even if Pilate found grounds to dismiss the charges, they would have brought new ones, or simply had me killed outright. Out of frustration he gave a nod and one of the guards struck me for my insolence and when I held my silence, struck me again.

"The Pharisees complained to Pilate that I criticized their interpretation of Jewish law, and said that by criticizing them I was attacking their God which was punishable by death. That was nonsense, he told them, and if they brought up such an argument again, he would throw them all out. He was a wise enough man to know the trouble that would ensue if he got involved with Jewish theology.

"He finally stood, announcing the whole thing was out of his jurisdiction, and sent us over to Herod. But Herod did not want to have public responsibility for my death and walked out of the room where I stood with the Roman guards at my side. When it was obvious he would not return, they brought me back to Pilate who had just broken his fast. I, of course, had been offered nothing to eat or drink that whole time.

"The guards pushed me to my knees in front of the Prefect. I noticed a woman who had not been there before standing against the back wall, and recognized her from some of my public talks. Pilate drew me aside and gestured to her. 'I am conflicted,' he said. 'My wife told me to have nothing to do with this trial. She said she has had dreams about you, and heard you speak and knows you are a just man. But how can I please her *and* please these men if you do not answer for yourself? If you say nothing, I will be obliged to turn you over to them.'

"I wanted to answer him for his sake, and for hers. But I could not. He asked again if I was King of the Jews, and I replied 'Some say I am.' And when he asked me if I counseled people not to pay their taxes I responded, 'I have always said they should give freely to Caesar what belongs to him, and give to God what is God's.' I hoped my words would set his wife's heart at ease, for I saw she was troubled by what she saw before her.

"Pilot groaned and turned to Caiaphas and said, 'You have a tradition to release one prisoner at Passover. There are two men, Jews, who are awaiting execution this day. I will let the people waiting outside choose who shall go free.' He told the guards to bring the men to him. Barabbas arrived first, barely able to stand on his own from the beatings he had suffered. Pilate opened the window onto a balcony and the crowd below roared. They had been gathering since sunrise and were becoming more and more agitated."

"Yes, I know," I said to Jesus. "I was there among them." My cousin smiled at me then, the way he used to when we were children.

"How I wish I could have shielded you from this thing, you and the others." His smile turned to a frown as he continued. "Pilot signaled the guard who pushed the two of us out onto the balcony in front of him and then went out himself."

I wasn't sure why Jesus was going to such detail with the events of that day, unless he wanted to be sure that the story told would be a true accounting when the time came. It was painful for me to hear, but somehow healing too.

"Some in the crowd shouted obscenities. Pilate signaled for quiet and since they knew what was to come, they obeyed.

"'Which of these two men would you have released to you, in honor of your Passover?' he called out. 'This man Barabbas, a thief, or the man Jesus who is called King of the Jews.' Well, you know who they chose," he said in a quiet voice.

"Cousin," I said to him, "you know that Caiaphas' men had been circulating among the crowd all morning, prompting them how to respond to the question they knew would be asked. These were ignorant people who knew nothing of either of you, and were interested only in the bribes being offered: a coin, a crust of bread or cup of wine, or even water was enough for some. Many of us called out your name, and I would have declared there were more for your release than for Barabbas."

"Yes, I know that. It is a barbaric process; someone must lose ... someone must die."

"Pilate came back in and pointing at Barabbas said 'release him.' His face was anguished, and we had to strain to hear him. He turned to Caiaphas and the others and said: 'I can find no fault in him. I wash my hands of this: do with him what you will.' And he left the room. His wife slumped to the floor as the men grabbed hold and dragged me out."

*

We women had been waiting outside since long before dawn. Most of the crowd departed after the one they called Barabbas had been released onto the street. He wandered away, dazed, not sure what to do with his sudden freedom. He had no strength to run and probably nowhere to go. The rabble had gone to the inns or home to their families for a time, but would return later to the mount called Golgotha.

Uncle Joseph and Nicodemus stood with us women and the few men who had returned. I'd seen Peter standing around earlier, but when a man in the crowd asked him if he was with us, he shook his head no. When the man insisted, he said no, no, he had never even spoken with this Jesus. But when he realized there were witnesses to the exchange he turned and quickly walked away. I do not know what had happened to the others. Some I would not see for days.

Chapter Twenty Six

KING OF THE JEWS

The gate groaned open, sagging on its hinges with the weight of ages. The noise startled me into watchfulness. At first I saw only the servants struggling to hold the gate open, staring at the ground. They had been trained not to look at the distinguished personages that passed by.

Then he came into view, and my heart froze. Jesus staggered under his burden. He stopped a moment, wincing in the bright sunlight, until one of the guards gave him a shove. He walked a short ways and stopped again, scanning the area. I thought he might be looking for a familiar face and stepped forward from the shadows. The same guard lunged at me, but I instinctively moved and he stumbled, cursing. Another guard shouted something at him; he cursed again and stepped back into formation.

The mob surged and Jesus stumbled and almost fell, catching himself at the last moment. The guards aggressively moved to push the crowd back. That kind of throng frightened me: too often they took on the worst sort of animal behavior. All it takes is for one man to shout 'kill' and they fall to it in a frenzy. Why, I had often wondered, would it not be the same if someone shouted *help him*? Such a world would transform in an instant.

It was a terrible sight, seeing my beloved cousin stripped down to a loin cloth, wearing a ghastly crown of thorns on his head. It cut into his scalp, and blood trickled down into his eyes. I felt my knees weaken and thought I would faint, but a hand took my arm and strength flowed into me. I looked up into his mother's eyes and saw determination through her pain.

The guards walked ahead, pushing people off to the sidelines, clearing a path for him. But once past, they fell in behind him, forming a single fluid body, echoing his progress at an impossibly slow pace.

He dragged a large cross, fashioned of two trees, the tallest twice his height or more. The trees were freshly cut and heavy with sap. And he was weakened already with hunger and thirst. It was an unusually hot day, with a dry wind whipping up the dust.

Mary fell back to walk with Miriam, directly behind him though not so close as to draw the wrath of the guards, who were as irritable and dangerous as bulls in mating season. I stayed by his side, oblivious of any danger. Our work had begun the previous night at the garden, but by this time had moved into the higher realms where heaven and earth combined in us. It would require all our strength, all our will, and all our training to keep our eye on the light as it moved through the darkness.

The cords in his neck bulged, and sweat poured off him. He glanced up at me now and then, and even managed a smile once. I tried to smile back. My tears instantly dried in the wind, though I wept inside.

His eyes were closed much of the time, and his lips moved. I prayed with him the old prayers, not of protection but of redemption. I said them aloud, though no one heard. Sometimes the deafening noise broke through my numbness. But if I kept my attention focused on the prayers, I could push the noise back. And if I kept my heart allied with his heart, I could forget my own pain, seeking only to alleviate his.

He stumbled and fell. A strange silence washed over the crowd and the guards looked at one another, confused as to what to do. Jesus struggled but couldn't get up. One of the guards moved forward as if to take up the cross himself. His eyes caught mine and I was startled to see Daniel, a man whom I had met only days before during one of Jesus' talks. I did not even know he was a Roman, and surely not that he was a soldier. His questions of my cousin revealed a gentle, probing nature.

The Captain rushed up and shoved him back into formation, muttering something under his breath. He looked into the crowd and indicated a man who I later learned was called Simon, a Jew from Cyrene. Though he had sometimes listened to my cousin speak, he was not dedicated to the teachings and probably would not have wished to take up such a load for him. But it would seem his soul had brought him there for that very purpose, exalting him in service.

Jesus still lay on the ground, shivering from the effort. Without thinking I went to him and with my shawl wiped the sweat and blood from his face, then placed the cloth over his closed eyes and said a quick prayer of healing. The guards were distracted with Simon's efforts to lift the cross and didn't notice that I slipped a slice of orange into his mouth. I had forgotten I even carried the fruit, but my hands did the deed for me.

His eyes opened and his lips formed the words *thank you.* His beloved eyes had always been so full of laughter and joy, even when he spoke of serious things. And now, in the midst of his torment, I found a well of compassion.

Someone's hand yanked me away from him, causing me to fall. I don't remember getting up, but was soon walking again at his side. He too was back on his feet, staggering from exhaustion, even without the weight of the cross. He was a strong man, used to carrying his own load when we traversed the countryside in our travels. But he'd had neither food nor drink; he'd been beaten and was losing blood.

Three times someone tried to rip the shawl from my hands – the one used to wipe his face – but somehow I managed to hold on to it. One man pushed me to the ground, and I thought he would strike me. Madness shone from his eyes. They might have been his followers, hoping for something of him to hold onto … or simple thieves.

But I saw only him, neither his tormenters nor the crowds lining the road that led out of town; not even James who I later learned walked alongside me. Now, as then, I have only the haziest image of cursing men, wailing women, barking dogs, screaming children, of arguments and fights. Yet his face remains clearly etched in my heart.

At last we arrived at the top of the hill. Two crosses had already been raised, and two men hung upon them. The sight startled me. I had not known anyone else would suffer his fate that day, though the Romans had been using the cross more and more to frighten the masses into submission.

The hole had already been dug, and four soldiers stood around the cross that Simon had carried, waiting. When he reached the crest of the hill Jesus looked up at the two men. I saw there not the face of a man himself condemned, but one who looks upon the suffering of another with compassion. Where does he get that strength, I wondered to myself? And I heard his voice in reply, as clearly as if he had spoken aloud: "From our Father. It all comes from our Father. And now He calls me home."

The soldiers grabbed him and thrust him to the ground, tying him to his cross. I could not bear the sight and looked away. Miriam stood next to Mary, weeping. I walked over and put my arms around her. Foreheads touching, I began to feel my fear subside.

The holy women were scattered throughout the crowd, women who had from childhood been trained to serve as midwives, bringing forth a new dispensation of love and compassion. It was not for us to judge whether people were ready, or worthy of such a gift. We were there to stand with our master, knowing others would come after us, carrying the torch into the next age.

Some of the men had returned, though most stayed in the background. It was good to see them. James, John and Peter stood nearby, buoying the three of us.

I am eternally grateful not to have seen the soldiers drive nails into his hands and feet. He made no sound during his ordeal – at least none that carried the distance to where we stood. But I turned around when a collective gasp rose from the crowd. The cross was being lifted, and nailed to the top was a rough sign that read:

Jesus of Nazareth

King of the Jews

"No No No!" screamed Caiaphas, shaking his fist into the air and yelling that they must remove the part that read *King of the Jews*. "He isn't our king! The sign must go! He isn't our king!" He was a man possessed, and because of his position as head Pharisee, the soldiers did not know what to do. And so they lowered the cross until it could be resolved.

Dear God, now they are torturing him as well! For the moment I forgot myself and tried to break away, to run up the hill and smother the old man until he could speak no more. But Miriam grabbed my arm and held me close. I looked at her, ready to argue, but seeing the resolve in her eyes brought me back to the still waters of my training.

It was decided to keep the sign, and the cross was raised again. I swallowed hard and stilled my breath ... and forgot all else.

We stood there together, in the silence. Once I had surrendered, the vigil felt almost effortless. From a distance I watched my pain, and the pain of Jesus – and knew it to be the pain of all men, everywhere, whether Jew or Gentile. I am sure his body agonized, but light pulsated about him, brighter and purer than anything I had ever seen.

People say the day darkened into night, that lightening tore across the sky and thunder struck, so loud it deafened them for a time. But I saw and heard none of it. They say the ground itself shook violently as I had seen happen in a dream so many years before. But I did not feel it. Many ran in terror, convinced the world was coming to an end.

They were right, in a way. The world we had always known, *and* the world the Brotherhood had labored so long to bring to life had both slipped away from us. Yet in that place where I spent the hours of darkness at the foot of the cross, the angels sang and there was a peculiar sense of hope in my heart.

I heard many stories later. I heard one of the men from the cross next to his asked Jesus to intercede with God, that he might be forgiven his sins. Jesus responded that he was forgiven and that he would see him that day in heaven. Another said that Jesus called out to God to save him from the cross. I do not know if that was true, but I could only imagine the small child within me would have given anything to be spared from such horrible pain – and would not have blamed him if he had.

And several people told me that just when they were sure the spirit had left his body, he lifted his head and looked directly down to where his mother stood, crying out in a loud voice, "Mother, behold your son." And then to John, who stood next to her, he said, "Behold your mother." Joseph said it was Jesus asking John to take his place as eldest son, to care for his mother.

I did not know what to think of all that, but God did grant me the grace to hear his last words. How long had he been there, between life and death, darkness and light? I felt a tug during the ecstasy of our vigil and roused myself to hear him say: "It is forgiven."

I fell to my knees then, and wept.

After a time I felt a tap on my shoulder. "Come, we still have work to do." Mary took Miriam's and my hands and led us up the hill, rather than away from it. Several of the other women were also climbing the hill, joining us to form a silent circle around the cross. I was grateful to see mother among them. I know she'd been with the women who supported us from a distance, though I hadn't seen her since the upper room.

My eyes closed for the final vigil, so I was spared the sight of the soldier thrusting his spear into Jesus' side. When blood and water issued from the wound, everyone knew that death had come. (The hill had to be cleared to make way for others who would be crucified that day.)

Jesus told me later that he had withdrawn his breath once all the elements for his transformation were in place. This is a thing known only to the highest adepts, and only a small number throughout time have accomplished it of their own volition. While in Egypt I was also taught the procedure, yet it is one thing to know the rules and another altogether to put them into practice.

Uncle Joseph and Nicodemus, along with James, Peter and John waited for us to finish our work. Joseph had already made arrangements to take the body. We saw him counting out coins to the captain of the soldiers and then turn to the middle aged man who still held the spear that had pierced Jesus' side. My uncle leaned forward and whispered something into the man's ear, then dropped coins into his hand and closed it in his own.

Joseph loved Jesus as much as any of us. He had taken on the role of father after the other Joseph died. He'd looked after Mary and her children ever since, just as he had for my family after father died – until mother remarried.

John approached Mary and asked, "Mother, are you alright?" She nodded. Though she could not have been *alright*, she was certainly the strongest of us. She and mother made sure that those of us who had been trained in the mysteries would stay focused on our part of the ritual until it was completed.

The body was taken off the cross by two soldiers, who also removed the awful crown from his head. They were careful, almost gentle in their treatment of him. Before they walked away Joseph pressed something into their hands as well. He was not paying them for services rendered so much as compensating them in the only way he knew for fulfilling their duty with such dignity.

James took over from there, carrying his brother's body down the hill toward a cart, covered in linens laid atop thick straw. Once there he seemed reluctant to surrender his precious burden -- though the distance was too great for him to carry it all the way back to the family tomb. He finally laid him out on the cart, and covered him with a fresh cloth.

John and Mary, and the rest of us followed the cart through the gate and into the city to Joseph's home. We would prepare the body at his home before transferring it later to the tomb. I wondered absently if Joseph had purchased the sepulcher to use for himself, when his time came, or if he had gotten it specially for Jesus.

We heard singing as we approached. Some of the other women had gone ahead to prepare the way. The men brought the body in, laid it out on a stone bed and left us to our work. As Anna and Beatrice prepared the wrapping, Mary washed the grime and dried blood off, the final act of a mother for her child. Julia stirred the mixture of aloe, myrrh and spices while Edithia began to soak the strips of cloth as they were readied for wrapping.

Miriam stood in the courtyard and sang for us ... and for him. Her lovely voice filled the air, with words of love for God and for man. She called upon the Divine Mother to receive her son, and the Father to bring him home.

The body was made ready for burial, but our work had only begun. This would be the greatest challenge of our lives, the hardest thing we would ever do. To falter, even a little, would doom the ritual to failure. We had only each other for support, and hoped that would be enough.

Chapter Twenty Seven

THE SILENCE AND THE GLORY

Most of the women returned to Anna's house to ready themselves to receive the mourners. Jesus had many admirers, family, friends and students. Countless individuals had benefited from his ministrations over the years, and they would want to pay their respects. By law and tradition we would not gather until the end of Passover, but there were some things that could be done in the meantime.

Junia wondered if people might fear Roman persecution, or recriminations from the Sanhedrin, and stay away.

"He is gone now, said Edithia. "They've had their way with him, just as they did with John." She was especially bitter, having lost her beloved teacher a few years back. She had first been his disciple, but left him to travel with Jesus even before the Romans had him beheaded. "Maybe now they will leave us alone."

Naomi went back and forth between Anna's house and the tomb, where we sat vigil. She brought us news of the city, and food to eat, knowing we might forget to see to our own needs.

Pilate had given orders that stability be maintained at all costs. Passover was a natural container for people's emotions, but no one knew what would happen once it ended. The dramatic events following Jesus' crucifixion unnerved everyone. Many who had derided his followers now wondered if he had indeed been the Messiah, and that God would have his revenge upon those who had him put to death. Everyone pointed fingers of blame at everyone else; even former allies were at each others' throats.

I had little interest in anything beyond the walls around the burial cave. I grieved my cousin deeply, yet was oddly comforted during our watch. I had the companionship of my sisters, of course, but there was something else too, that I did not think to question then.

Pilate's soldiers came to the tomb after the body had been placed on its marble slab, and sealed the entry with an enormous boulder. It took eight men to get the stone moving, but as the earth slanted slightly downward in that place, it quickly gained momentum and slammed into the opening. The seal was so tight I could not imagine it would ever be dislodged.

The only time the soldiers acknowledged our presence was in making sure everyone was out of the tomb before it was sealed. Two guards were posted outside the gate day and night, charged with documenting anyone who came and went. But each time I passed their way, they were sleeping or throwing die, and didn't seem to even notice me. Joseph came twice and sent Thomas over once to check on us. Otherwise we were left to ourselves.

It was just Mary, mother, Miriam and I who kept watch. At least three of us were there at all times. We spoke little, and then not of him. Mostly we remained in prayer and meditation.

The day following the crucifixion was uneventful. It passed as a dream. I won't even say it was a bad dream, since my attention was focused upon the light within, and in that light no harm could come or dark shadows intrude.

*

"Mary, Veronica, Salome, wake up!" Miriam's voice was shaking with excitement. We'd all fallen asleep at the same time, though we had vowed not to.

"What is it?" mother asked, rubbing her eyes.

"Look," Miriam whispered.

I followed her finger and saw, but did not comprehend. The great stone had been moved, leaving a gaping hole into the tomb.

"How? How is that possible?" I stammered.

Mary ran into the tomb, her voice echoing back to us: "He is gone!"

"*I saw him*," said Miriam. "I spoke with him just now, outside the wall. Go quickly and you will find him."

"You saw who?" Mary asked, who like the rest of us struggled to understand that the very thing we'd been working toward had actually happened.

"Jesus. *He is alive*, though he would not allow me to touch him as he is newly risen. Just go!" she finished, shocking us out of our stupor.

We ran to the outer garden. The guards were nowhere to be seen, having left behind their game board. We ran in the direction Miriam indicated and would have collided with him had he not quickly moved out of our way.

Mary trembled visibly with the effort to keep from embracing her son. I felt the same powerful pull. Mother grasped her sister's hand.

"It *is* true. You are here. You have come back to us," I said, barely able to speak.

"Yes, I am with you awhile longer. This body of light is yet unsettled and it will take some time before I can walk among you as before.

"As soon as it becomes known, many will come and demand my time. But first I would speak with you. You have assisted me in the great work, and I shall be forever grateful. You were asked to set aside your belief in death, and you did so. The Holy Spirit came and asked you to let me go … and you did. Most of the men could not, did not do this. But women are accustomed to sacrifice. *You are the womb of the world*: holding and protecting the seed as it grows unseen, then suffering the pains of birth. You already know that anything worthwhile comes with a price; that something you have valued must be surrendered in order that a greater thing can come forth.

"A mother who surrenders her son has offered the greatest sacrifice of all," he added in a tender voice, looking at Mary. "Remain awhile," he said to her.

To the rest of us he said, "Go now and tell the other women. We will gather tonight in the Garden" and he described a place where we had sometimes met before the troubles began.

We ran off down the path, going first to Anna's house, to tell the women the good news. They were astonished, hardly daring to believe what we said was true. Sarah and Junia rushed out the door before we even finished talking. The rest plied us with questions, wanting to know every word he said, over and over again.

"We *must* go now," I said, trying to pull away. "It is not right that we continue in our joyous celebration, while the men still mourn. We must go find Joseph and James and the others, so the men might also know what has happened."

We later heard that while we were talking with the women, Thomas had come upon Jesus on the road. Jesus had already sent his mother away, telling her she would find us at Joseph's. At the same time Joseph had sent Thomas to see how we were doing in our vigil, and if we needed anything. As Thomas told the story, he approached Jesus, wondering who the stranger was standing so near the tomb. The guards were not at their post, which worried him, and he brushed past the man to enter the gate. Seeing the tomb open, he ran inside and discovered it empty.

"I was frantic and ran back out through the gate," Thomas told us. "The sun was in my eyes and I could not see the features of the man standing in front of me. All I could think of was someone had stolen the master's body. I was terrified, and angry. 'Where is he? Where have you taken him?' I shouted. And when the man didn't answer, I cried out again, 'Where is the man Jesus?' And I began to weep."

"Thomas, Thomas, my brother, it is I."

But the words were incomprehensible to the disciple. The man standing there was just a blur through his tears. Thomas said he thought he must be a grave robber, and was about to set upon the apparition, when Jesus spoke again.

"Thomas, it is I, Jesus."

It might have been the calmness of his voice that caused him to stop. "Who? Who are you?" he asked.

"It is I, Thomas, standing here in front of you."

"But it cannot be. I saw him taken down from the cross with my own eyes, and came to see him placed in the tomb here. I have come already to find the stone placed at the tomb's entrance, a stone no man could have moved." He stepped closer to the one he still thought a stranger, and asked in a weary voice. "Where is he? Where is Jesus?"

The man took his hand and Thomas winced, thinking he would be harmed. But the touch was gentle. With his other hand Thomas wiped away his tears and saw before him our Jesus. But still he was not convinced, because the man had died, and tried to pull his hand away.

"Here was where the nail pieced my hand, my brother. The hole remains. Place your finger here that you might believe."

And when he had done so, Thomas fell to Jesus' feet. "Forgive me, I did not believe. Though you told us you would rise again, *I did not believe*. I thought you spoke of rising through the darkness of our world to the feet of the Divine Presence. Oh master, I knew you taught us the resurrection, but I never dared to hope." And he wept

"Stand up, Thomas. It's alright. Even you, who have been with me for so many years, still did not believe the truth. Even some in the Brotherhood who *teach* these things will not believe. It will be your job – you who have seen for yourself – to go out into the world and tell the story of the one who left the tomb.

"But this is only part of the story, and not the most important part. I have told you many times since you've known me that you are capable of doing anything I can do. What you must hear now and believe is you too have it within you to move beyond the grave. Our Father does not give gifts to one son, while withholding them from another."

After that day Thomas would tell the story to any would listen, in his own land and beyond. His enthusiasm and joy brought many people to tears, as death began to lose its sting for them. In the years to come I stood beside him in places far from Jerusalem, among people as different from us as night is to day, and saw hope radiating from faces as he spoke.

Throughout that first day Jesus appeared to the rest of the apostles. And in the days ahead he began to show himself to others beyond the inner circle. At first he seemed almost tentative in his body and I feared he would disappear at any moment. He reminded us to be patient. Resurrection is a three-day process during which the temporal body of flesh is transformed into a new body of pure substance – during which darkness is overcome by light. Even then it takes time for the process to become fixed, while the one reborn gets used to the *feel* and use of his resurrected body.

Beyond that he would say nothing, only that we would know for ourselves one day.

*

"What is bothering you?" I asked my husband several days later. "We have much to be happy about, now he is with us again." He insisted nothing was wrong. But I knew when something weighed upon him. He had seemed troubled for some time, and I hoped he would open up to me without my having to ask.

We sat alone together for the first time in many days. "We have not talked honestly for some time." I took his hand. "Please look at me, James."

He slowly lifted his head to meet my gaze. His eyes were like a stormy sea, revealing a troubled heart. I sighed, glad at least that he had shown himself to me.

"My dear Veronica, I know I have been more like Amos than myself these past months." Amos was a bad-tempered cousin of ours, always causing everyone distress.

I laughed. "Well, it hasn't been that bad. But I confess it hasn't been easy either. You always seem to be angry with me, but I don't know what I have done."

"It isn't you. No, sometimes it is you … but not really." James was not at ease speaking about his feelings. But he was better at it than other men, and most women I knew would have been happy to have such a man for their husband.

"You are so strong that sometimes it scares me." I started to protest, but he waved my words away. "And yes, I have been angry. You do not consult me before making decisions. It is almost as if I am not even here. And when we do talk, more and more it seems we disagree on everything. Not just the little things, but the interpretation of scripture and Jesus' teachings, and the role of women in our community. Everything."

He was right – we often disagreed, but not on everything.

"I wonder how it would have been if we'd had children," he went on. "Would it be different between us? Would it have brought us closer together?

"And now everything has changed, our whole world has changed." He shook his head.

"My dear James, I am sorry I've pained you so. Why didn't you say something before this?

"Would it have mattered? You are the way you are, and I love you. But I am not sure I can live with two streams that seldom meet in the middle."

He looked up at me: "It is not too late for us to have children."

"Now? With all the confusion? Yes, we have our brother with us, but he has already said he will not stay and we will once again be on our own. And you have seen the turmoil in the market and on the streets. Everything we've known is crumbling in front of our eyes. What kind of world is this for children?"

His eyes misted. "I knew that would be your answer. Though you are my wife, you have chosen your own path, and it does not seem to be the same as mine."

The resignation in his voice tore at my heart. I loved him more than anyone in the world, except perhaps Jesus. But I learned to differentiate between these two loves by the time James and I married. Though brothers, they are different in every way – and I'd never regretted marrying James.

I had seen the disappointment he bore that his own brother had come to others upon his resurrection before appearing to him. It was bad enough it was Thomas, Peter and John among the men (and James loved John more than all the others), but for him to have shown himself to the *women* before him was hard to bear. His pain was strong enough to burn through his anger at me, which permitted the open exchange between us then.

"Though no one has spoken of it," he said, "we should be thinking about returning to Galilee. Maybe just getting away from here will help."

"I agree. We need to leave the treachery of this place behind," though I did not believe it would be that easy. "It is dangerous for everyone here, especially him. We do not know how vulnerable he is.

"The space between us has been growing and I do not want to lose sight of you, my husband. There will be time there for just the two of us."

*

I rarely became frightened, but I was then ... frightened of the killing in the streets, of the growing void between James and me, and even knowing that Jesus would leave again, forever, at any time.

The Roman soldiers were acting on orders to kill anyone who disturbed the peace, and they were free to determine for themselves what that meant. Jews, feeling vulnerable, began to strike back, which set the soldiers on edge even more. The violence was rapidly escalating, so we decided to leave the following day before it got totally out of control.

"I have prepared a small pack with provisions for each of you to carry," said Joseph. "Go to the first inn you find in Jericho. You remember, James, the one owned by the Essene Abram? Word has been sent ahead that he is to provide you with whatever you need for the journey. Do not stop until you get there, neither speak to any stranger on the road. I've been told that the unrest extends far from here into the countryside. Leave at sunrise, and move quickly."

"Will you not come with us, uncle?" I asked.

"No. There are other things I must do first. But Elizabeth and the children will leave in two days' time, and join you." They had only recently returned to Jerusalem from Nazareth. "I will be along later. Nicodemus and I will stay and see what can be done in the Sanhedrin. We will try to convince them to work with Pilate to bring an end to this madness."

He did not sound confident, and I worried about him.

"He will be alright, sister." I turned to find Jesus standing behind me. He had taken to calling me sister rather than cousin, or Veronica. We were all one to him now, it seemed. While I missed our old familiarity, I was immensely grateful to have him with us in any form and under any condition. If it were possible, I would not have let him out of my sight. But I had no control over that: he would be there one moment, and gone the next, without warning.

That would be our last night in Jerusalem for some time. A crowd had begun gathering at mid-morning outside Joseph's house. They called out for Jesus, asking him to speak to them, to heal them.

"You are the risen Lord," some shouted, "our Messiah. Do not turn your back upon us," they pleaded.

Finally, after the midday meal he went out to them. A cheer rose up and they crowded in upon him. Our instinct was to push them back, to protect him. He had by then accustomed himself to his new condition and the touch of others had no ill effect upon him, or them. He waved us back, and allowed the people to come close, to fall on their knees, even kissing the hem of his robe or his feet. He reminded me of an indulgent father, looking out over his children with boundless love.

"Master, heal my daughter," a distraught father shouted out. "She has leprosy." And he gestured for the man to bring her to him. She was already becoming disfigured and the crowd shrank back from her. But Jesus took her into his arms and kissed her forehead, then handed her back to her father. The man wept, shaking like a small tree and I wondered if he would drop the girl. Jesus said, "Take her home and bathe her. She will marry and have children, living a long and happy life."

He turned his attention back to the crowd, healing some, speaking quietly to a husband and wife who embraced upon hearing his words. I wondered what he had said to them, and also if he might help James and me overcome our difficulties. After a time when the merely curious left and the crowd quieted down he spoke to them at length, answering their questions and speaking of their own resurrection in time to come.

Chapter Twenty Eight

THREE DAYS

"What happened during those three days in the tomb?" John asked.

Jesus had brushed aside similar questions asked by people who had no training in the sacred sciences. But this was a group of his closest students.

He sat in full light, the sun reflecting from him in shades of rose and gold. We waited silently, content just to be together. His face did not reflect the pain of what he had been through. And since he did not carry the burden of wrongdoing the way the rest of us do, I expected to hear his life review had passed easily.

"I have never known such anguish," he began. "That which still separated me from the rest of humanity died with my human self, and I stepped into the pain of all the people around me.

"It started in the garden, in Gethsemane, increased during the mockery of trial and judgment and intensified while I was nailed to the tree, looking down upon my brothers and sisters who stood below, engulfed in clouds of despair. But that was nothing compared to the three days in the tomb. There I felt the suffering of the people who had been with me in life, and those who had gone before me into the night called death.

"Not all who have given up the body are in pain, only those who have not found their way to forgiveness. Those who haven't forgiven linger in a netherworld, blind to the peace offered them by our loving Father. It is not others who must forgive them; they must forgive themselves. But guilt and shame followed them to the grave because they believed what they were taught by jealous priests and others who draw power from the suffering of others. They are like bats that bite through the skin of fruit to extract its pulp, taking the life force of others as if it belonged to them.

"If people believe they must be punished, they will punish themselves unmercifully. Eventually everyone will understand the futility of this, take up their own cross and return to their heavenly home.

"Only a few men took pleasure in the spectacle of my ordeal. I looked into their hearts first of all, that I might know their suffering as my own, and love them all the more for it. I would ask you to do the same.

"Some of you will be tempted to seek revenge on my behalf. I tell you to put all such thoughts away, and forgive those who sought to harm me, and those who do you harm. They had no power over me, and can never really hurt you. The spirit that dwells within each of you is eternal and unscarred no matter what might be done to the outer shell."

"Did you spend the entire three days in this hell?" asked Matthias.

Jesus looked at him, as if trying to comprehend the question. "Yes, I can see how you might think it was hell," he replied. "But while my Father encouraged me to go to this place of suffering, He did not force me. It was my own decision to do so. How could I know you if I did not know everything about you, the best and the worst of it? How could I know myself if I did not know you: and not just those of you who stand with me now, but everyone, friends and enemies alike?

"They only believe they are my enemy. God knows each one is my brother, and one day will rejoin me in our Father's house. You must remember that often those who treat you the worst are closest to you in spirit. And you must know that everything which happens in this world is with your agreement.

"Yes, I could have escaped the cross. And there were other means available to resolve the fears and concerns of those who tried and convicted me. But they turned their backs on them, and chose the lower road instead. I could have escaped, but they would have hunted me until I was caught in their snare again, and again. The only way out was for me to stand fearlessly in the face of their hatred."

"But this was no way out, master," said Paul. "You walked right into their trap."

"I did so willingly."

"But why? We needed you to put on a crown of gold and not of thorns. You let us down."

Paul's words sounded harsh to my ears, but he had tears in his eyes as he said them, and I knew he loved Jesus as much as any of us.

"I came not to take up worldly power, but to show you your own power. I came to fulfill the law, not destroy it."

"But people don't understand that. Instead they thought you weak, and maybe even afraid," he insisted.

"Maybe so. One day everyone will learn that forgiveness is the source of true power. But it may take many more such crucifixions before people begin to heed the call to love their enemies as themselves. Until then they will suffer.

"While in the tomb I took the weight of mankind's suffering upon my own shoulders, to relieve them of their burden for a little while. In the end, though, it is not mine to carry, but theirs. If any ask me to share it with them – today and always – I will gladly do so, helping them to awaken to God's love so they may surrender their suffering, forever. And then they will join me in our Father's house.

"Will you join me there?" he asked, looking at each of us in turn.

I shivered at his words. Must we all carry our brother's burdens? How could any of us bear such a load? Hearing my thoughts and perhaps those of others, he went on.

"Yes, you are asked to help one another, to stand with them in their time of trial and judgment, just as you did with me. It does not matter if you think of them as your friend or enemy; it does not matter if you *like* them.

"Remember, you are never alone. Call upon me in your days of joy and your days of sorrow. Call upon me in the valleys of fear and doubt, and when you take up the load of your brother I will be there. I will help you, encourage you, love you. I will remind you of your strength, your power, your soul's purpose, and the purity of your heart which you often cannot see for yourself. *This* is what we do for each other.

"In the tomb I descended deeper and deeper into the pit of my brothers' despair. There were moments I feared I may never find my way out of there again. It seemed not like three days but eons of time, for the sun never reaches those dark regions. This hell was created by each one who dwells there.

"But the Father's house is filled with light and open to all who would abide by one simple rule. You must love your brother as yourself, and yourself as God. None are turned away who make this their life's pledge. Everyone stumbles sometimes, but we can instantly make amends for our errors by forgiving ourselves."

"What does this mean, forgiving ourselves?" asked Joanna. "Don't we have to ask for God's forgiveness?"

"God does not judge with the intent to punish us; we call down punishment upon ourselves when we can no longer live with our secret guilt and self-judgment. *God loves*. Love has no judgment.

"I knew the fullness of my brothers' suffering, the dark recesses of despair in every part of my being. I knew it as my own. In my pain I recalled every wrong I had ever done throughout time, the killing during my days as a warrior, the slights against neighbor, wife or child, words spoken in haste or anger."

James called out: "But you have no wife, and have not fought as a warrior."

"Brother, you know as well as any that we have lived forever. Time does not hold us captive, nor do our bodies of flesh.

"I remembered it all," he went on, "and for a moment I was enslaved by my past. Fear took hold of me, and I thought I might never escape the flames of judgment."

I marveled that the man before me had so recently been crucified in the most horrible fashion, been entombed and then *rose from the dead.* I felt shame that despite my years of training I had not really believed it could happen – that someone might take back their body from the grave and live again, live eternally.

"But a shaft of light reached down into the pit," he continued, "a shaft so slender I almost missed it. It penetrated my awareness; I caught hold of it and was instantly free. Light streamed in around me, and I knew the false judgment was over. I had forgiven myself that which I had carried with me throughout time. Surrendering the burden of my sin to the eternal fires, I was freed."

"Master, if you who are blameless could suffer so, what about us? If you, even for a moment, feared eternal punishment, then how can we hope to escape the abyss? Your wisdom exceeds mine, as does your courage. I am not as wise or brave as you."

I recognized the voice behind me. It was Naomi, who had traveled with Miriam and me through Egypt, studying with the great masters about life and the illusion of death. Others nodded agreement, most of whom had not had such training.

His head bowed a moment before he answered. "Some of us take on a greater burden than others. Do not be afraid; you will never be given more than you can bear. Your capacity to serve will grow in time. Only then will your load increase.

"You must call upon those of us who walk ahead of you to aid you in your tasks. We will not do the work for you, but we will walk with you each step along the way, sharing the weight."

"What of the resurrection, master," urged Peter. "How did you do it?"

"Peter, you must know I could not have done what I did without the circle of women around me who had been trained to hold *with* me a true vision of the temple of light. They steadfastly refused to give in to the appearance of death."

"But you *did* die," he insisted. "I saw it. The spear did not lie. And there are many besides myself who will vouch to that."

"Yes, my body gave up the spirit. But that same body had been in the process of transformation for some time before this event, and the process was accelerated unseen in the tomb. Just as I have told you to call on me to aid you in your work, I called upon the greatest of the angels to help me accomplish the task of bringing my body to light, that it might be worthy to hold a spirit exalted in death.

"Part of the process was descending into the darkness and recovering and forgiving that which I had judged. Part was to open my heart to receive the suffering of others not ready to forgive themselves their debts. And the last part was the completion of the physical transformation and the reintegration of spirit and body. This is not unlike the birth of a child, but accomplished in full awareness, and done forever. There is then no more death or need of rebirth.

"The angels formed an inner circle of power whilst I did the great work. The women formed the outer circle. The inner circle exists in spirit and is of the Father. The outer circle exists in the world and is the work of the divine Mother.

"Of this I can say no more."

"And what of the men?" persisted Peter. "What part did we play?"

"You are the body of the Father in the world; the women are the body of the Mother. We will speak later of your work. But what part did *you* play in my resurrection?

"Most of you fled when I was arrested. I do not blame you. Had you stayed, you might have been arrested as well. And if you had fought them, even to protect me, you might have met my fate. It was not your time for that.

"The women did not flee. They were not taken to be a serious threat by the soldiers or authorities, and were left alone. It is good those men do not understand the power of woman, else they would be afraid of them above all else."

He smiled at this, helping ease the tension. We were a grim bunch, listening to the accounting of our brother's suffering. Still, I noticed Peter stiffen at talk of the role of women, and saw the other James (son of Zebedee) turn and walk away.

"But you came back ... all but Judas," he sighed.

Priscilla interrupted: "Is it true, did Judas take his own life?"

"His body is forfeit," he answered, "but his life goes on. I met with him while in the pit, and we talked awhile. He is forgiven for my part, but it will be some time before he comes to that on his own."

I thought I saw a tear in Jesus' eye, and his voice betrayed a great weariness I had not heard before.

"I ask each of you not to judge his act. Things are not always as they seem.

"You came back. Each of you men, in your own way, has gone through your valley of judgment because of this. You have met your fears, and are stronger for it. You needed to do this now, while the women did their work. If you had not, you might have unintentionally interfered with their work, and jeopardized its success. Also, had you not met your shadows now, and strengthened your resolve in the process, the shadow would have returned to haunt you at your time of greatest crisis.

"You, my brothers, are my hands. My sisters are my heart. Each of you has your own kind of wisdom. Power, too, is in both, that of the right hand and the left, joined together as one."

*

His words brought back for me my own experience of those three days. If someone had asked me immediately afterwards, I would have insisted I knew nothing of what Jesus was going through. But since then small fragments of memory have risen, reminding me that though he went through the experience alone, we stood in our vigil as silent witnesses.

It is impossible to describe the pain and the ecstasy. It was both heaven and hell, soaring with angels while fending off the demons that threatened him. There is nothing in our world with which to compare it.

Of the four women who sat outside the door of the tomb, there were always three of us engaged, comprising the inner triad. From the center of the triangle, the place where our hearts were linked, we were connected with the rest of our sisters in Anna's house. Together we composed the temple of light, of which he had spoken.

I confess I cannot say exactly what we were doing or how the work was accomplished – at least not in the way I can tell you how to mix different herbs to heal stomach pains or skin lesions. It was controlled throughout by the divine Mother, and we each did our small part.

Our training began in Carmel when we were young, and continued in Egypt. At first we were taught to create a thought of something simple that we liked. I remember my first thought exercise was of a rabbit I'd seen that day on the way to class. I imagined the rabbit until I could actually feel the touch of its fur and the way its nose twitched when it sensed its surroundings. Next we learned to control the rabbit with our thoughts, making it jump or eat when we wanted it to.

The next step was to imagine something painful, holding that image in the same way I had done with the rabbit. I tried to think of my father's death but I had been too young when he died and did not have a clear image of him to work with. So instead I thought of Jesus' father, Joseph's death. I remembered him well. It brought back the pain of his loss, and memory of the sadness in Mary's eyes.

And then the hardest thing of all was to do the exercise without allowing myself to feel the pain of it. I could remember the pain, but was not to *feel* it. I wasn't pretending the pain didn't exist; it was more like setting it on a table where I could see it clearly and then walk away from it, creating a distance between the pain and me.

And finally, I came to the last exercise where there was no *thing* to put my attention on. I was asked to imagine empty space, like looking into the sky but without the color of it, or clouds or anything. Looking into that empty space, I then called in the light to fill it. This light also had no color or sound or other qualities. There was nothing but light. And once I had accomplished that, my teacher told me I was ready.

"Ready for what?" I asked.

"You will know," he said, "when the time comes."

And that was it. I did know. It took a long time and a lot of practice to learn how to call in the light, and not to be distracted from it by anything or anyone. No one had taught me the final piece. In the knowing it came naturally.

There had been other classes as well where we were taught how to join our thoughts with each other. Some people do this more easily than others. In the garden outside the tomb we women joined our thoughts together, so there was only one thought. This may sound very strange, but I believe there was only *one person* having that thought, because I completely forgot my separate self in it. I was no longer aware of Mary or Miriam or mother or Veronica, but only awareness of the light.

There were moments when that light opened into something I can only call darkness, and within that darkness I knew his experience in the pit. I did not see it, but I knew it. Thanks to the Mother my training held true, and I could hold the darkness within the light when that happened.

From what Jesus had told us, I do not believe he thought about anything outside the abyss he walked through. Nor did it sound like he sent an image of it to us (as he often had done when he was traveling during his younger years) – at least not intentionally. It was like a crack in a clay pot through which the water seeped out, and we women were the ground upon which the water or image settled.

When I ponder now those moments of insight into his world, I shudder. Those images would paralyze me with fear if I did not have the ability to step away from them – as I once did the pain sitting on the table.

I had no sense of the passage of time during the ordeal. It was only when one of the other women touched me gently on the arm that I was drawn back into myself and knew I must rise and attend to my human functions. She (Mary, Miriam or mother) would instantly step into my place in the triad, and I would go out for awhile.

My body grew weary of sitting still for so long at a time, and was stiff for days afterwards. But I do not think it was weariness that caused all of us to fall asleep at the same time on the third day. Something had held us up the whole time, and then withdrew its support when our efforts were no longer needed. Jesus had completed his journey through the netherworlds, reconstituted his body of light and returned to us.

He never said how the stone had been rolled away from the entrance, though I do know he had command of the angels and they must have served him in that way as well as others. But he passed by us unseen. I understand the reason for that too. Even when we first saw him he would allow no human touch, saying he was not fully with us yet. Had we suddenly seen him at arms length, we might have caused him harm. Miriam said he had to shout at her when they met on the road, shocking her out of her headlong rush to embrace him.

I remember the crushing anguish in those first moments when I realized the tomb was empty. I could only imagine that his body had been stolen from us. It was crazy, I know. I absolutely *believed* he would return to us, yet in the confusion still fell victim to my fears.

And then ... there he was, standing perfectly still on the road not far from the gate. I thought my heart would explode with joy.

As soon as my thoughts settled I knew he would not be with us for long. His time was allotted by Heaven to finish training us, and to prepare us for what would come after he'd gone.

*

"Do not be so hard on him," said Jesus. We were together in Simon's home near the lake. It was late afternoon and too hot to be outside. "Pilate has suffered greatly for his role in my death. And even if he hadn't, it is not fitting to place the blame on him."

"And why not? He could have done something to stop it!" Paul nearly shouted.

"How do you know he wasn't fulfilling the mandate of Heaven, as were Judas and others whom you judge? Each of us has a purpose, some large and some small, some joyful, some bitter ... but all are important. And if God does not judge, who are we to do so? I have watched over Pilate and Judas, just as I watch over you."

It did not please some of them that he spoke so lightly of betrayal and judgment. There was still much of the Zealot in some hearts, and a reluctance to let things go. I knew they loved Jesus as much as I or any, but some believed they could choose among his words, which they approved of and which they did not.

"One of those I saw in the three days of darkness was Pilate. Only in a state of self-torment does a soul pass through the valley of shadow while yet alive. He wept when he saw me there. And through him I saw that his good wife, Claudia, was inconsolable.

"'Master,' he said to me, 'while I knew you to be a good and honest man, only now have I seen that you are the one of whom your prophets spoke. I prayed the earth would open and swallow me for my sin, and now my prayers have been answered.'

He fell to my feet. "'Get up, Pilate,' I told him. 'It is done. Go and live your life so that no one else suffers wrongly as I have done. I do not blame you.'"

"How can you say you don't blame him?" insisted Paul. "*He condemned you to death!*"

"He could not take my life from me, except that I willed it. When I saw there was nothing more to be done, I willingly laid my life down, that the truth of life eternal could be demonstrated for all.

"Pilate would not look at me, because he could not face himself. This was not an ill dream of his. He was fully awake in his home as he stood there with me, a shattered man. In time, when he has learned to forgive himself, he will find his way back to wholeness.

"Claudia often came to hear me speak. Many of you have stood next to her in those discourses and even spoken with her, without knowing her identity. She will not easily let him forget the act. And so it will be a hard lesson for her as well, to forgive her husband. Remember the second law: judge not except you be judged in equal measure."

PART IV

Chapter Twenty Nine

WHAT IS DEATH?

"Master, you stand here in front of us, looking like any man. You use the same words and seem to breathe the same air. I have even seen you sit down to eat with your followers. If I hadn't heard about your death and resurrection from so many people, I would not believe it had ever happened. If you *died,* then what do we see before us?"

Others nodded agreement. Samuel was kin to Edithia and often traveled with uncle Joseph, and had been spared the crucifixion.

"Many have asked this question, and many more will ask in time to come. My *body* died. It was tormented, put on a cross and suffered a slow death. But *I* did not die. The eternal does not endure the indignities of the ephemeral. Transitory things will not touch it, cannot affect it, and certainly cannot kill it. Spirit is not harmed; a soul cannot die.

"The body you see before you is different from yours in one important respect. It is not a body of the flesh – as that of any animal – but a body made manifest by spirit. Come here," he said, extending his hand to Samuel. The man hesitated a moment, then reached out to take Jesus' hand. His face flushed at the touch.

"You see, my hand feels like any hand, does it not?" Samuel's brow knotted. "But you will find it warmer than an ordinary hand." Samuel nodded.

Then Jesus reached out to Martha, inviting her to take his other hand. Her eyes grew wide. "You feel the heat of the Holy Spirit."

He let go their hands and they returned to sit among us. "I have told you, unless you are born again, you will not enter the kingdom of Heaven. This body has been restored to life in the fires of forgiveness and the waters of rebirth. You too will one day experience this, each in your own time."

"You spoke of the three days in the tomb," said Miriam. "I understand this is when you entered into the cleansing fires. Does this mean we each must die a worldly death before we can be born anew?"

Jesus looked at her for a moment as if not recognizing the woman who spoke. But then his vacant stare gave way to a look of supreme tenderness. It was in that moment I realized that though he stood among us, he was no longer one of us. The essence of the man had already gone on to be with his Father.

"The fires of transformation cannot harm you when you have learned forgiveness, living according to the commandments handed down to us by Moses. Be kind to one another, give aid to any who need it, whether brother or stranger, friend or foe. Ask for nothing in return. Put no conditions on your love.

"You cannot choose the moment of this second birth, but you can choose the moment you turn your life over to God. You will be tried and tested, but as long as you do not give up you will prevail.

"To enter the fires of renewal before your time would destroy you. But the Holy Spirit knows you better than you know yourself, and will bring you to the fire when you are ready.

"Look at the sun overhead," he pointed, and we all looked to the sky. "You cannot see its warmth or understand how its light comes to you. But its warmth and light are yours just the same. And though unseen by you, the fires of spirit have already been kindled in your heart, consuming everything not like itself. It may take many births and deaths before you are ready to rise from the ashes – but the day *will* come when you will be born into the light."

"When you have passed through the ritual purification of the inner fire you will emerge a perfect likeness of the Source of your being. When you look at each other now," he said gesturing over the small gathering, "you see only a reflection in muddy waters. But I see you pure and perfect, just as you are, the very essence of the heart of the world."

He turned his back on the crowd and walked back toward the house where he'd been staying. When some of us tried to follow, he waved us away with a sweet smile.

Before the cross he would speak to the gathered crowds from morning till night, never appearing fatigued. I thought it strange that now when he walked among us almost as a God on earth, he seemed to tire easily. Once, when no one was around, I asked him about this. He gave me an odd glance and said "It is not easy for me to remain among you." I asked what he meant. "Imagine if you tried to bring one of those clouds down to the ground. Would you be able to keep it here? Unless restrained, it would float back up among its own kind, where it belongs."

We gathered again the following day.

"Tell us, Rabbi, what is death? We have been taught, and our eyes agree, that death is a lasting state. But you have cheated it. And I have heard there were others among the Patriarchs who had also done so."

Devorah had occasionally joined us in the early days when we met out in the desert, but I hadn't seen her again until the previous day when Jesus spoke of his body of light. It was a good question. Though it was talked about in the school at Alexandria, and I had experienced it (in small part) in the *Halls of Amenti* during our initiation there, I was eager to hear his explanation.

"There are different kinds of death. Many in this city are the walking dead." Paul, standing next to me, shuddered visibly. "Their hearts are closed, and they desperately hold on to their worldly goods, refusing to share what little they have, afraid it will be taken from them. And so, while death of the body is a terrifying thing to them, it comes as a liberator.

"Death allows us to lay the body down when it can no longer serve the spirit. If the voice of spirit has been shut out, it loses its motivation or will to keep the body alive. It is better then to lay it down and pass into the higher realms for a time, and after a rest giving the soul another opportunity to return to this world to try again."

"Try what, Rabbi?" Beatrice asked. She and Josie stood next to each, almost inseparable since the crucifixion.

"They come back, with the intention to obey the laws of Moses and to remember their Source. We are born out of our heavenly Father and Mother as children of the light. But if the families of the newborn child have already forgotten, it will be hard for the child to keep his memory alive."

"Do you mean we come back again and again?" A man, whom I had not seen before, standing at the back of the crowd, seemed shocked at the thought. "The Sadducees do not speak of this! This is blasphemy!" The man stomped away without waiting for a response.

Jesus continued. "Yes, life is eternal, both here and beyond the grave. And once we remember our spiritual home, these bodies that are so beset by pain and suffering will be transformed forever."

"And this is what happened to you: the reason you came out of the grave?" It was Esau speaking, uncle Joseph's youngest son.

"Yes, this is what happened to me."

The boy's eyes softened, as if a weight had been lifted from him. Joseph said his son had been having trouble understanding how the man whom he had seen laid out on the stone after the cross could be the same one standing before us.

There were many who had heard of the resurrection, but did not believe it. They whispered it was a trick to embarrass the Pharisees and Sadducees who sent him to Pilate. One story said the guards at the tomb were bribed to say he'd been sealed inside. Others insisted he never died at all. One elaborate story said that we women had given him a mild poison to make it look as if he had died. Why else did Joseph take his body away so quickly after he was taken off the cross, they asked?

And there were some among the Zealots who had begun to exploit the event to sow mistrust wherever they could. Already there had been small uprisings against the Romans, and the number of their supporters was growing daily. They did this in his name, though Jesus in no way agreed with their methods or goals.

It was hard for even his closest followers to fathom how such a thing could happen. I had seen a hundred deaths in my lifetime. Each one was laid to rest and none had returned, save Jesus. (Lazarus had only gone to the door of death.) And here he stood among us, speaking as a man transcendent – but a man all the same.

"And what is to come, Rabbi," I almost whispered, not sure I would want to hear his answer. But I could not help the question: I had to know.

He turned his head and the love that shone from his eyes unnerved me. "I think you know, Veronica," he said in the gentlest of voices. He had not called me by name since ... before it all began.

"You will remember one of the first things I told you women when you saw me outside the tomb." He waited until I acknowledged I remembered. "I am here but a little while ... and the time is now drawing to an end."

"What do you mean, a little while?" asked Julia's daughter, Rachel. She stood near Esau, John and some of the other young people.

"I am only on loan to you from the Father, and must soon return Home. But I will not be lost to you; I will continue to guide you in what is to come."

"How? How will you do that?" she asked.

"When your mother and your father are away from you, you still feel their love, do you not?" She nodded, eyes wide. "And when Michael there thinks of you, even though he is in another town, you know his thoughts. Am I right?" He smiled as he said this, knowing even before they did that the two of them would one day marry. She reddened without looking at Michael, and nodded again.

"I stand here before you, that you might know my love and concern for you. And more," he went on. "If any of you ask for my help, in matters great or small, I will be there to offer a helping hand. I will whisper in your ear the way to go or words to speak when you in turn are helping someone else. You will not see me, but I will be there."

"Why can't you stay?" Michael asked, emboldened by his friends' questions. "You are needed here. It is getting more dangerous all the time, and I think we will all have to take up arms soon in order to survive."

"Fighting is not the way, my son. If you take up arms, the one you call your enemy will have an excuse to cut you down. War does not make you safer. It imperils the soul as well as the body.

"Many of you have listened to my words before, but did not hear me. I told you countless times that if a man strikes you on one cheek, do not return the attack, but give him the other cheek. There may be times to take up arms to protect yourselves, your community. But *doing so will not make you safer.* It simply puts off the time of reckoning to another day, for in the end you must face each other and lay down your arms, and know each other as brothers.'

"The Romans could never be our brothers!" interrupted Andrew. Jesus looked at the man who had been with him from the beginning of his ministry. Andrew had never contradicted him before, or even questioned him.

"They ... *killed you!*" he sputtered.

"Most of the soldiers in Pilate's palace, and those who stood at the foot of the cross are good men. I saw their hearts, and their pain was not so different from yours, my friend. I say they *are* your brothers, as are those who take pleasure in our suffering. Yes, even them. We cannot force them to see this simple fact. All we can do is search our own hearts until we know them as sons of our holy Father.

"Still, you are right," he said sadly, looking back to young Michael. "The peace we had once known in our land is being squandered by a few selfish men greedy for power and wealth, foolish men willing to trade their souls for worldly gain.

"What I have taught you is nothing new. Many have spoken the same words in different lands and at different times. The understanding of righteousness will never be lost, and the Brotherhood will continue unto the end of the world. But you will be scattered to the four winds, for a time.

To survive, you will gather into small groups, each under a wise teacher, one who has made my words his own and patterned his life upon that which I have tried to live. They will guide you by day, and the angels by night. And I will be with them all ... and with you."

"How will we know these teachers?" asked Judah, my young brother.

"Many of these teachers are the women standing among you, including your sister Veronica, and Miriam, Naomi, Sarah and others." There were murmurs in the crowd. Some men still resisted us, though we had received the secret teachings alongside them. Had they known we were privy to certain things even they did not know, they would surely have tried to drive us out long before that

"And the twelve who are my chosen disciples, along with Paul and Barnabas and Judas and others, have much to teach you." (Not Judas Iscariot, whose place had been taken by mother's husband, Matthias.) "Remember to seek out the counsel of your elders – Joseph, Nicodemus, Lazarus, my own mother and her sister Salome, Hannah, Martha and Mary. They have great wisdom among them. And remember to turn to each other; it takes a large crew working side by side to sail a ship through stormy seas. No one can do it alone.

"Help each other, protect each other as best you can. Do not throw the first shot, for if you do, the burden of the whole battle will be yours. The cost of violence is high and long lasting, while the returns from benevolence are pervasive and eternal. The one takes away and the other restores that which was lost."

"You said we would be scattered. Must we leave the land of our birth, our ancestors? Where will we go? What about our families; do we take them with us? I have small children." Jonah asked plaintively.

"I cannot tell you what you must do. When the time comes, go within your heart in search of guidance. Some will stay and many will leave. The time approaches to take what you know into the world and share it with others. There is good news here, even under the gathering cloud. You have seen for yourself that life is eternal and death but a pause in the everlasting journey.

"When you are able to see a brother in a stranger's eyes, and know another's need as your own, you have entered a state of grace. Forgiveness comes from your heart, opening the way for you to be forgiven. Love one another as I have loved you."

"And where will you go, master?" asked Miriam in a faint voice.

"Where I go, you may also go. I will join others who have gone ahead to prepare the way."

People turned to each other, asking if *they* understood his words. While they were talking the late afternoon sky washed white with light ... and when they looked up he had gone.

Since the tomb I had seen him disappear twice like that, and prayed he would return as he had then. I had so many questions yet to ask.

After the crowd dispersed, John (called by some the Beloved), Mary, Miriam, Matthias, my mother and a few others gathered silently to sit in silent vigil. We remained until long after the sun set and while no one said so, our hearts knew he would not return.

Chapter Thirty

LIFE GOES ON

He was gone. I knew without doubt that death does not separate us. Yet he had been my first memory in infancy, even before mother. I could not imagine my life without him in the world with me. For awhile it seemed I did not exist except for the grief that tore at my heart. I am ashamed to say I was angry that others had been allowed to live while he had been taken from me. I did not want anyone near, not James, not mother, nor any of my friends.

I wandered alone through town and along the lake from early to late, until someone would come for me. One evening just after sunset I sat on a rock, staring into the darkening water. My tortured thoughts during those first days had settled into a vague emptiness.

At dusk a wind arose and the waters splashed across the rock, and me. I was only vaguely aware of it, and didn't really notice that it suddenly stopped. My hand brushed at something, trying to make it go away – finally realizing someone had been speaking to me. I had unthinkingly been trying to banish them from my presence.

"Your pain touches me too, Veronica," the voice said.

I jumped up and fell to the ground, tripping over the rocks. "YOU

ARE BACK," I shouted into the night.

"I have never gone anywhere," the voice replied, and I realized Jesus was speaking in my mind, the way he had sometimes done while on his long travels.

"Surrender your pain and stop thinking of yourself. Stop indulging in your personal grief. There is much suffering beyond your little world. People need you. You have been walking in a dream; it is time to awaken."

His rebuke found its mark and I pulled myself up off the ground. "You are not a child and I will not allow you to hide in the folds of your mother's skirts. Come out and stand beside me and the others who have pledged themselves to serve in this time of need."

And then, more gently, "I need you to do your part, Veronica, so my efforts will not have been in vain. The teachings you have received over the years are a trust. You are responsible for safeguarding them, even as you pass them along to others.

"Why do you think I would abandon you now? I am always close to those who love me. You believe death has separated us, that my world is remote and inaccessible. You, of all people, should know better. I am no more distant from you than when I traveled in India or Persia. Indeed, less so since my ability to communicate with you now is so much greater.

"But I need you and the others to take up the work I have left behind. There is no time for self-pity. The moment fast approaches for you to leave this land."

"Leave? Leave the lake? Do you want me to return to Jerusalem?" I had hoped never to return to there. The shadow of that dark hill looms over it.

"You will go there, but first you must pass by Nazareth. You Hebrews will soon be scattered throughout the world, abandoning Jerusalem. Rome has claimed this land for its own, though it too will be vanquished in turn."

I do not know why his words didn't frighten me. Maybe it was because I could not fathom such momentous change – certainly not the abandonment of the temple or the holy city. Or maybe I finally realized he would never leave us, and because of that I would be able to do anything asked of me. I only know I finally found my courage, and purpose returned to me.

"Yes, I will go to Nazareth. What am I to do there? And after that …?"

"Not you alone. I am guiding others to complete their business as best they can, to gather up their families – those who are willing to go with them, and say goodbye to those who are not. It is now the new moon; meet at Joseph's place outside the city by the full."

And then he was gone again. Though I heard his voice, I had not been able to see him. But I was comforted all the same.

I returned home and found James sitting in the shadows in the garden. He rose and came toward me. Things had not been good between us for some time, and we'd barely spoken since Jesus' arrest. He latched the gate behind me and took my hand, leading me back to where he had been sitting. And then he took me into his arms, and I wept for the first time since Jesus had gone from us. I am not sure whether they were tears of relief or even happiness … of a kind. James silently stroked my hair until the tears passed.

There was leftover food on the table, and I realized I was famished. James smiled when I reached for the cheese, and I saw how much I had worried him. "He spoke to me, "I said, in between bites. "I did not see him, but he spoke to me by the lake."

"Yes, I know. He told me," he said, smiling again.

"Then you know we are to leave here and go to Jerusalem?"

"Yes." The smile faded, and he lowered his eyes. "Tell me, Veronica, what did he tell you?"

I repeated the conversation. "We must get everyone together as quickly as we can to make plans. I have no idea how long it will be before we can return here, and there is much to prepare."

"Veronica, we will not be coming back. Did he not tell you that?"

"He said only that we will abandon Jerusalem for a time. I told you he said that." Suddenly I understood. "Oh, *we* will not return, but those who come after us." I wanted to say 'our children will return,' because I thought of them all as my own, but knew James felt differently.

"*We will leave here forever*. There is more, my dear, that he did not tell you." James' face was lost in shadows. "We will be going in different directions. We will be scattered as we were at the destruction of Solomon's temple – except instead of being taken to Babylon, we will go out two by two into the world, bringing the good news of his resurrection and the promise of life eternal.

"But one thing I do not understand," he said turning back to me. "Beyond our borders are few cities where Jews are congregated in sufficient numbers to merit our going to them."

"We will increase their numbers, making their communities stronger," I offered.

"But think about it. We are Essenes. We do not find acceptance, let alone respect from other Jews here where they know us. I am not sure we will be welcomed by strangers. *They* are not refugees, after all. Many of them are in positions of power. They owe their power to Rome, and it is Rome we are hoping to escape."

"Well, let us not think about that now. You look tired. We need to sleep." In fact the exhaustion I had been keeping at bay suddenly closed in on me, and I barely made it to our room before collapsing into a deep sleep.

The next morning I lay awake with my eyes closed, thinking of the night before. I felt enormous relief at the burden that had been lifted with Jesus' visitation. But another had taken its place. I knew that the moment my feet touched the floor, I would connect with an inescapable current that was sweeping all of us somewhere we'd never been, and did not really want to go. The river of change would take me in directions that would have seemed inconceivable at the time.

I remembered the fear I heard in James' voice the night before: I had been so entrapped in my own anguish that I'd been unable to see what he must have endured since the crucifixion. He was, after all Jesus' own brother, and the closest to him in age. Though he grew up without his older brother around, over the last years they had become close.

James was already up and I heard others outside preparing the morning meal. I rose and pulled a warm robe over my head and went into the outer room. Though it was spring, the first rays of the sun brought no warmth.

"Come, eat, Veronica," said Miriam, putting her arm around me. "You have gotten too thin." She pulled me over to the table and sat me down. "I will serve you this morning," she said in a voice that did not invite argument.

We ate in silence, talking only after the plates were removed.

"Where are the servants?" I asked.

"I sent them home to be with their families today so we could talk freely."

There were voices at the gate. "I've invited everyone to join us this morning," said Simon, Miriam's brother. "The decisions we make this day will affect everyone for a long time to come."

As we waited for the others to arrive, Miriam and I talked off to the side. "I do not think he came to all of us individually, but yes, he did speak to me," she said. I shared with her what he had told me. "Yes," she nodded, "that's most of it, but ...." She put her hands on my shoulders and looked me in the eye: "You and I will not be traveling together."

"But that makes no sense!" I protested. "We have always been together; all our travels have been together since we were girls. You stood with me at my first woman's ceremony and are sister of my heart. James and I would have you with us always!"

"Things are not always as we would want them, my friend. In fact it has become the exception for it to be so. I trust he has a reason for this."

"He told you then? He said we must part ways, and you did not ask him why?"

Miriam looked at me carefully. "No, I did not ask him. I knew from what he did say that it is not for us to question at this time, but to do what lies before us. I know in my heart that if we balk now, we will only make things more difficult. You have always been strong, and I have admired you for that."

"I have hardly been so since he left us. And poor James. I have neglected him, hardly even thought of him. It was already hard between us before ... this."

"I had noticed that, and wondered why. His attention goes elsewhere. You say you've neglected him, but I had thought him cold and detached for some time now and wondered how you could bear it. But I cannot imagine he would turn away from what Jesus is asking of us. I wish I could go with you; you need a friend now. As do I."

"Good, I think everyone is here now," said Simon when we returned with cups for the water, and bowls of ripe olives and dried figs. I was glad to see Naomi and my cousin Anat among all the men. Everyone looked at Miriam and me, and I realized they waited for one of us to speak.

I cleared my throat. "I am not sure I know more than any of you, but this is what he told me." And I repeated Jesus' words at the lake the night before. "I know he spoke with Miriam and James, and maybe more of you. I hope you will all say what I have missed."

"He told me that we would be breaking into small groups, making it easier to travel, and to pass unnoticed when need be," added Miriam.

My heart beat hard at the implication of her words. The intent behind Jesus' request was only then beginning to penetrate my awareness. We would be fleeing for our lives. And what of those who remain behind, I wondered – the elderly or infirm, and those too impoverished to make any kind of journey, let alone have the capacity to start anew in a place where they are completely unknown? We had a tradition of taking in strangers here, but could we expect that in these new lands?

"We cannot take much with us," James was saying. "There is no time to sell property or dispose of everything as we would like. But we should gather up what we cannot take and distribute it among the poor, to keep it out of the hands of the Romans who are sure to sweep in and confiscate everything we leave behind. Take only small valuables that can be exchanged for food or other necessities along the way, and a few clothes or family keepsakes.

"He said we need to be in Jerusalem by the full moon, if possible, so we have some time for this, and to say our goodbyes to those we leave behind."

We had non-Jewish friends and I hoped they would not be punished for their friendship with us. "Don't worry," one of them told me when I came to say goodbye to her. "It would not occur to the Romans that we had been friends. They restrict their friendships to their own kind and assume everyone else does the same."

"Simon," said Miriam, "I would like to keep our gate open for any of our friends to gather here each evening, if that is alright with you. We must know where to find each other in the days ahead."

"Yes, of course." Simon would never deny his sister anything. I was amazed at how calm Miriam appeared, though she later told me she constantly felt ill from nerves during those difficult days.

We set about saying goodbye to friends, some of whom we had known since childhood. James and I set out for Nazareth a few days later. Though I was sure mother and Mary would already know to meet us at Joseph's, I wanted to say goodbye to my childhood home and to travel with them to Jerusalem.

Miriam came with us, as did our old friend Marcus. It was a long day's walk and we arrived as it was getting dark. I was glad to have Marcus there, one of few men I knew who carried a sword and was prepared to use it. There were increasing numbers of bandits on the road in those days, but we arrived without incident.

"Mother," I called out into the darkness. "Mother, are you there? I did not want to walk in and startle her if they had gone to bed early. But there was no answer. We let ourselves in the gate. I found an oil lamp just inside and lit it from the dying embers of an earlier fire. Soon the place was fully lit. "She must be at Mary's," I ventured. James insisted on going after her alone, and left Marcus to stay with us.

"Oh Veronica," mother sighed when they got back. "You have come! And Miriam," she said, pulling us both into an embrace. Matthias had come with her, but they'd left the children at Mary's. "No sense in waking them," he said. After a quick embrace he and James went off to talk alone, and we three women sat down to catch up.

I had only heard and not seen Jesus when he came to tell me we would be leaving our homes and go out into the world. But I learned he had appeared to Mary and a few others around the same time.

"A transfigured body differs from ours." Mary explained. "You were taught in Egypt about the conversion of light for dark substance. And you have seen the miraculous as well," her voice quavered. "He ascended *with* his body instead of laying it in the ground as the rest of us must do. You remember being told about a holy oil that enables one to do this, but you must know this oil is not something to be bought in the marketplace. It is produced *inside* one who has prepared himself. *This* is the anointing by the Holy Spirit."

"I am not sure what this means, *Holy Spirit*, even though he has spoken of it now and then," said Miriam. "Nor do I understand how someone produces oil inside himself."

"The Holy Spirit is that part of you that never dies," answered mother. "It is the portion of the Eternal that lives within you, the breath and hand of God."

"None of this can be described, even to one who has lived and studied in the mystery schools as you have done," added Mary, "but something you must discover for yourself. All of our training leads us in the direction of that knowing, but that's all it can do. In time you will see."

Matthias and James had gone into the town to let people know that we, at least, would be leaving for Jerusalem in a few days' time. It was a long journey and we needed to get started if we hoped to be there by the full moon. And since nothing of import is begun at the full moon, I knew we would remain there until the next new moon, giving everyone time to catch up with us. But I also knew the time would not pass idly by.

I could not comprehend that I would never again see the place of my birth or walk the roads so often traveled during the first thirty years of my life. I had forgotten how much I loved the house where James and I lived, the home built by his brothers as our wedding gift. And now I was back, I was loathe to leave it again, trying to convince myself we could find a way to stay amid the coming storm.

But I knew better, of course. He would not have counseled us to leave unless it was the only way. Some families decided to stay behind, and would not be dissuaded from their decision. We gave many of our possessions to them. And we buried a few items of value that could be used for barter, should anyone need it, along with some non-perishable foods in nearby caves.

Saying goodbye was hard, though we tried to make light of it, speaking of seeing everyone again when the storm clouds passed. But we all knew better. Farewells were tearful, and I wondered how many of them would survive.

We took several carts filled with the remainder of our possessions with us to Jerusalem, disguising them with squashes and other produce piled on top of the valuables. It would have been simpler to leave it all behind, but there were more people living in poverty in Jerusalem than in Nazareth. We hoped in this way to prevent at least some of their suffering.

I would take little when the time came: silver and gold coins, a few pieces of jewelry given me on my wedding day, and the shawl that mother had embroidered for that occasion. I also carried two dresses: the one from my first woman's ceremony and my wedding dress. Those I would leave at Joseph's in hopes of recovering them one day. Everything else I would give away.

I also carried the shawl I wore on the day my beloved cousin carried his cross, the shawl I used to wipe away the blood and sweat from his face …. This I had wrapped carefully in a piece of newly spun white linen and tied about my waist along with the other valuables. One other thing: I kept a small carved doll he had made for me when I was a child, hardly bigger than my thumb, and a folded portrait he had made of me on parchment one happy night when he, James, Miriam and I sat talking until dawn.

Chapter Thirty One

TELLING STORIES

The road to Jerusalem was filled with people, coming and going. It was less than two moons since we last arrived at those gates. *Nothing in our world remained as it had been before.*

Once again my husband barely seemed to notice me, spending all his time talking with the men about what was to come. They spoke as if the women had no say in the decisions being made, never once asking our opinions.

"I am glad sometimes that I never married," said Miriam. "I would not be as silent as you in such matters. As it is, their decisions have little bearing on me. I am free to go on with my life according to my own will."

People used to ask Jesus why he did not marry. This was no small matter to our people, as both men and women could only become full members of our community through marriage ties and in fulfilling their responsibility to bear children. When he replied at all, he said it would not have been fair to wife or child. But I sometimes wondered if Miriam might have thought it preferable to what fell to her.

He always encouraged the rest of us to marry though, and he took great pleasure in being around those of us who did. He especially loved children; indeed I do not know anyone who loved them more. I sometimes thought I saw a wistful look on his face when he watched them at play. But that might have been my own feelings reflected in his eyes.

"James no longer asks for my opinions as he once did. Some of the others do not think well of us women, and their attitudes seem to have rubbed off on him. He is not the man I married."

"No, but then you are not the woman he married either, Veronica. You are stronger now, and sure of yourself. Not that you were ever without opinions," she laughed. Miriam grabbed my arm and we dropped to the back of the procession to find our own pace.

"Remember when we were in Carmel and Judy was talking to our group about working with the spirit of water?" she asked. "This was long before we went to Egypt and I think the first class we'd had on the subject. What was the girl's name? Wasn't it Alana?"

"Alana, yes. She had been teasing me since we got there about some boy, and I had had enough of her foolishness. I think there were six of us gathered around the caldron of water, and Judy called on me first. I was supposed to try to get the water to move a little using only the power of my will, but I was so upset with her it just seemed to rise up out of the pot and splashed all over her. I was as shocked as anyone! Thank goodness it had not begun to heat yet."

It felt good to laugh. Joy was hard to find in those days, and walking through our remembrances of happier times was healing for both of us. Hearing our laughter, mother and Mary dropped back to join us and were soon regaling us with stories of their own younger years.

"Do you know that Mary almost stayed in Egypt after Jesus was born?" asked mother. We shook our heads no. "Sister, why don't you tell the story?"

Mary giggled. "I think Joseph wondered then, if he hadn't before, how on earth he was going to tame this girl he called his wife. I was very young, you know, and the time immediately after the birth was frightening. We barely managed to escape to Egypt, and just about the time I started to feel at home there, a messenger came and told us it was time to return to Judea. We had been sheltered with a Hellenistic family near the school in Alexandria and had made good friends among them. I did not want to go back, even though Herod had died and the danger passed."

A frown brushed over my aunt's brow, and she laughed again. "I told Demitra about my concerns and she brought me to Aisha, one of her Egyptian friends. Aisha offered to hide Jesus and me in hopes that Joseph might eventually come to his senses and agree to stay on in Egypt."

I was astonished. "You would have stayed there, and I might never have come to know you, or my cousin!" I could not even conceive of such a thing.

"Well, life certainly would have been different. But, Jesus had been sleeping under the watchful eye of Rhea, his nurse, and I had to go back for him. By then I had regained my senses and didn't follow through on the drastic plan. I cannot say I was enthusiastic about returning here, but I would never have done that to Joseph, who by then I had grown to love."

"But you can see something of your aunt's hidden side in this," laughed mother.

"Well auntie, what can you tell me about your sister that I don't already know?" I asked, pointing at mother.

"Salome was the mischievous one in our family."

"Well, I agree I wasn't as serious as you, but …. "

"Do you know she sometimes sneaked out of the school in Carmel when we were in training there?"

"Yes, but you came with me!" said mother.

"But only to keep an eye on you so you wouldn't get into trouble. Most of the time we were gone only a short while, wandering out along the cliffs on sunny days, gathering flowers or talking with the shepherd boys."

"I had always imagined you two models of perfect conduct and piety, reproaching myself for falling short of your example," I said, laughing. "And now I see I set my sights too high."

"Well, one day Salome decided to climb down the cliff to the water's edge. It was an unusually hot day and she was determined to go swimming. Since I couldn't get her to change her mind, I followed her down. After wading in the cold water, she decided she'd had enough and started back up. But while it had been easy scrambling down the steep cliff, the rocks started coming loose when we attempted the climb. When one large boulder nearly landed on my head, we decided it was just too dangerous and gave up.

"Judy sent a search party out after us when we didn't show up for afternoon class. After a time we could hear our names being called, but the sound of the waves overpowered our voices when we tried to reply. They never heard us, and it began to look as if we would have to spend the night on the little sliver of land between the cliff and the sea."

"That didn't scare me so much as the thought of father's temper when he heard about it," interrupted mother. "He did not anger easily, but it was a sight to behold when he did."

"What happened then?" I asked, eager to hear the rest of the story.

"As I said, it was a hot day and we were becoming thirsty, and hungry. We tried to drink from the sea. There was a strong taste to it, unlike the water from our wells, but it was better than nothing. The sun was shining full upon us as it neared the water. I started to look around for a place to shelter for the night when I spied a small boat not far out. Salome had fallen asleep, and I shook her awake to help me call out to the fishermen.

"We were already hoarse, but they eventually heard us and came ashore. You should have seen their faces when they realized we were two young girls. They argued whether they should take us or leave us there. After all, it was not seemly for two grown men to take two girls whom they did not know into their boat unsupervised. But thanks to God they did.

"They paddled up the coast and set us upon the first pier they found, quickly pushing off before they could be seen. We were soon surrounded by a group of strangers, astonished to see us standing out there alone. Apparently none of them had even seen the boat, so it seemed to them we had just appeared out of nowhere. Fortunately one of the men knew Judy at the school and put us into a cart and had us back there by nightfall.

"You can imagine they were not happy with us. We were confined to our room for a whole moon, and kept under strict watch after that for a very long time." Mary looked at her sister lovingly. "Though there was an adventurous streak in her, your mother loved learning and deeply regretted anything that would cause her to miss classes."

"Far worse was your being subject to the same punishment, since you went only to protect me," said mother.

"To tell the truth, I am glad you brought me along," Mary said. "I would have missed much otherwise."

"Now you, Miriam, we have yet to hear of your misadventures," she added.

Those who did not know her well would think Miriam shy, because unlike most people she did not speak unless she had something to say. But with her friends she was free and open. She had been my closest friend since I was ten, or thereabouts, and she a bit older ... and she had stood with me at my first woman's rites.

"I don't believe I can top that story," she said, laughing. "But you know my brother Eli, and how strict he was with me after our parents died. How I envy you attending school at such a young age, learning to read and studying the sacred texts. Eli believed, as too many do, that women should not be allowed to read from the Torah, nor should they discuss religious doctrine.

"Samuel was just the opposite. He was the one who taught me to read in the first place, though he had to do it in secret. And he listened to me when I had questions and though he was not as learned a man as his brother, he would attempt to answer them just as he would had I been a boy. But one day Eli came home and heard us in the back room. He stood outside listening, and then stormed through the door and grabbed me. Pulling me outside he struck me with the back of his hand, forbidding me to ever do that again."

"Oh Miriam, I am so sorry," said Mary, putting her hand on the younger woman's shoulder.

"Oh, but I got him back," smiled Miriam. "Eli is not such a bad man, but the creation of a world that places women beneath men. *They* are the ones who suffer most. Anyway, that night I got up after he was asleep and went outside where he had carefully folded his nets into a pile. I spent the entire night unraveling the nets, winding the twine into neat balls, as they had been before they were ever knotted."

"You didn't," whispered mother.

Miriam ignored her. "I heard him rise early the next morning as he usually does. He went out to get the nets to take to the lake. At first he was silent but then I heard the sounds of things being thrown about, and finally a curse broke the air. He called out Samuel's name, and then my own, but I pretended to sleep. Samuel went out and I could hear the two of them arguing.

"He never did ask me about it, nor did Samuel. But I think Samuel knew. For awhile he just grinned when he looked at me. We were also more careful after that in our lessons, meeting far up the lake, or even at one of the caves. And by the time I went to stay in Nazareth, I was nearly as good a reader as you, Veronica," she ended her story proudly.

Sharing our stories did much to lift the heavy burden we'd been carrying, and by the time we arrived at the city gates we were all in good humor.

Chapter Thirty Two

A BROTHER FROM PERSIA

People referred to it as *the cross*. It would forever be a dividing point for us, whether we had been present or not. If someone used the words 'before' or 'after' we all knew what they meant, even if they did not specify before or after what. And whether or not people accepted the teachings of Jesus and his many disciples, everyone's lives were changed by that single event. This may seem odd, given there were virtually hundreds of crucifixions around that time, but none other impacted so dramatically our relationship with the Romans, ultimately resulting in the loss of our homeland.

We came to Jerusalem in small groups, as we did not wish to draw the attention of Roman authorities. It would have served no purpose to raise their fears, since most of us would soon leave the area anyway. Most of us had no intention of challenging them. Nor did we have the heart to confront our Jewish brethren who had not intervened to prevent the crucifixion. Ours was not to judge.

To my surprise there were many there whom I had not seen in years. I would have liked to sit down with them, to share stories of our families, our lives, and what they knew of current events. It was no accident they had come to the holy city. Some manner of network had brought them the news, drawing us all together.

I tried to be discrete when we happened upon each other in the street, but when I saw Helen and Reuben from Alexandria, I ran up to embrace my old friends. Helen's eyes were troubled, looking nervously over my shoulder. It was then I noticed that Reuben had slipped away. She grabbed my hand and pulled me off onto a quiet street. "Oh, I have missed you, and the others," she said. "Are you staying at Joseph's? In town or outside the walls?"

"Outside. You must come tonight. Bring Reuben. Why did he leave so suddenly?"

"We were told to walk in two's; alone we would have no protection, but more than that might attract attention. Yes, we will come after dark. Reuben and I will arrive separately."

"Have you married?" I couldn't help asking. They had always seemed a perfect fit to me.

"Yes, yes we have," she smiled for the first time. "Last spring, just before Passover."

"Good, I am pleased for you. Miriam will be there, and the rest."

James had not wanted me to go out alone either, but he was engaged in discussions with the men and had I waited for him, would never have gotten my errands done. I hurried back into the market, bought the few things I needed and headed toward the gate. And there I saw him.

He had a large build, though wasn't especially tall. His robe was coarse, with a hood pulled over his head. The rope at his waist looked to be made of silk, inconsistent with a peasant's robe. But it was the object he wore around his neck that drew my attention. It was a small gold Ferohar, the symbol of Ahura Mazda in living form. It appears to be a winged man or a winged bird-man, depending on how one looks at it. Ahura Mazda is the name used by Zoroastrians for their Father God, and this symbol might be likened to God walking among man, the way Jesus walked among us after his resurrection.

I was unable to move as he walked toward me, his eyes trained on mine. "Veronica, come with me," he whispered, and turned and walked back off the main road. I did not think to question his request though I did not know him, following him into an alleyway and through a door that had a small winged disk painted over its lintel. He quickly drew me through a darkened room and out into a sunlit courtyard.

"Thank you for coming with me," he said.

"Who are you?" I had not thought till that moment that such actions are often the end of people, especially in those dangerous times. But Jesus' friend Pursa had been Zoroastrian, as were others whom I had met over the years. They had all been his advocates.

"I am Babak, cousin to your old friend Pursa. He is a leader to our people and has many obligations, no longer traveling. But some of our brothers continue to live and move among you, keeping him and others informed of what goes on here."

"I am sorry," he said, putting his hand on mine. "We loved him too."

Tears sprang to my eyes.

"Let us sit." A servant brought us cups of water and dates to nibble on. He thanked the girl warmly for her service and I liked him immediately.

"I know you must get back soon, so forgive me for overlooking social pleasantries. I knew your cousin when he lived among us many years ago, and I grew to think of him as a part of my family. It broke my heart that some of my brothers turned against him then. Yet, in some ways I could understand that – but his own people turning against him......" He looked away, swallowing hard.

"I have heard he came to Pursa after the cross. That I could not believe until I heard he appeared before many of you too. Is this true?"

"Yes, he was with us for forty days after he left the tomb, spending some of each day with us, continuing his teaching." I went on to tell Babak how there was little difference to the eye between that time and before…. How, in the beginning we were not allowed any physical contact with him, but as the days wore on he would occasionally touch one of us on the hand or shoulder, just as Babak himself had done with me.

"And now he is gone?" he asked.

"Yes, he had told us from the beginning he would not be able to stay long, that he was on loan from the Father and would soon leave us to go to Him. But before he left he told us to gather here, in Jerusalem. He said we must leave here at the new moon, but should get here as soon as we could." Babak nodded thoughtfully.

"But tell me," I asked, "I would like to know more about him appearing to Pursa. How is it possible for him to be here, and there?"

"Can that be stranger than him appearing to you, from out of the grave?" he countered.

"Well, you're right," I said. "He told us the grave cannot hold one who walks in a body of light."

"Just so. Nor can distance restrain one who travels with the sun. The man Jesus is no longer your cousin, but a companion of Ahura Mazda, who dwells in the sun. *He is your Israel, the son of God as written in the Torah, the son of the sun.* Wherever the sun shines, there he is. Though this is the destiny of all who walk a righteous path, he is the first I have known for myself to have achieved this."

Babak seemed in awe at his own words.

"But, such talk must wait for another time. I have business here. I have spoken with your Joseph, and he has asked our help. The Romans will not grieve your departure, considering all of his followers to be troublemakers. And some in the Sanhedrin will also be relieved. But they will try to prevent you from taking treasures of any description that they will say belong to Israel. And believe me, their greed will allow them to designate anything of value as such. So he has asked us to gather those things you wish to take away from this land and then return them to their owners once you arrive at your destinations. There are too many eyes on your uncle for him to be a part of this, but you, Veronica, a woman, are not watched. Will you help?"

I wondered how he knew my name. And as if he heard my thoughts, he said, "I know all about you, that I can depend on you. For our part, we will provide assistance along the way when it is needed."

"Thank you. But I do not know how I can be of help to you."

Babak told me that Matthew had begun drawing up a list of accounts to which each of us could contribute what we wished. He said that members of the Brotherhood would serve as bankers and guardians of our treasures, returning them to us at a later time when we were ready to take possession of them.

"There is much to be done by the new moon. The women of each family will gather their family's wealth and pass it to you, or to another you designate to help you. Matthew will tell you where these things should be taken, and to whom you will give them. He will set up the meetings, but cannot risk carrying the items himself. A code for each collection will be given for the family to remember, necessary to redeem the items when the time comes. Matthew will explain more in the days ahead.

"And Veronica, one last thing before we part...." He smiled and said, "Pursa asked me to tell you he awaits the day you visit him in his own home."

"What do you mean? I would not go so far as that, would I?" But even as I asked the question, I knew the answer.

"Yes, you will travel there, and further. You will walk many of the same paths your cousin took. Have you not already gone to Egypt and to Britannia? You will see."

"He went to Britannia? I did not know that."

"He has now," he smiled. "You must leave immediately, or you will be missed." He handed me my purchases and showed me back out onto the main street, then turned and walked away, calling back over his shoulder, "I will see you again."

I ran back to Joseph's, and dropped the packages in the kitchen where the women were gathered to prepare the evening meal. I noticed James and the others still huddled together under an ancient oak tree deep in conversation. No one noticed me come in. I was glad to see Joseph wasn't among them and went to his private rooms and knocked on the door. When no one answered, I called to him: "Joseph, are you in there. I must talk with you. It's Veronica."

The door opened and I went in. Closing the door behind me, he walked over to a group of chairs and gestured for me to sit down across from him. Without him asking, a girl appeared with a pot of steaming tea and cups, and went out without a word.

"I am glad to see you, child. It is long since we've had opportunity to sit alone together. I wish it were a happier time, though just seeing you here lifts my spirits."

We sipped the tea together in silence.

"You have seen Babak," he said after a time.

"Yes, how could you know?"

He laughed. "Very little escapes my notice."

"Yes, I'm glad. We need you now, uncle, more than ever."

"My dear, you know that we are each born for something special, unique to us alone. It takes most of us a whole lifetime to begin discovering what it is. This thing, however important, might not be obvious to anyone else. In fact, it might not appear to be important at all – while being the very thing to make the difference between failure and success.

"This business network that I have so carefully built over my lifetime is the perfect cover for helping many of you escape to a new life. I am wealthy. I will help in any way I can, adding to the storehouse you are helping Matthew accumulate."

"Uncle, does Matthew know he is to work with me? Though he has not been one of the strongest voices to speak out against us women, neither has he defended us. And now you are asking us to work together."

"I have already talked with him. It will not be easy for either of you, but you are more alike than you know. And you were both devoted to him."

Joseph explained the system he had set up, and my role in it. "Matthew knows many well-placed people, Roman and Jewish, and they continue to trust him despite his having been one of the disciples. I do not think Miriam is the right person to help you in this project, but Naomi might be good. And because she is my daughter she will be able to get things done that other women could not."

I did not like hearing that Matthew would be entrusting our things to people not associated with the Brotherhood – who might not even know of its existence. And some of them Romans as well! But uncle assured me they could be trusted, and in fact their ignorance of the Brotherhood served to protect it. Besides, he asked me, what choice did we have? The alternative would be to leave everything behind, leaving us without means to start our new life. He was right, of course.

When we'd finished discussing the plan, I changed the subject. "Uncle, did you know that Jesus visited Pursa in the days after the cross?"

"Yes, Babak told me. I have had word from our brothers in Egypt that he appeared to them as well, on more than one occasion. And I would imagine he saw others in the Brotherhood, especially those whom he knew in earlier days from his travels in India, Tibet and elsewhere."

"I am glad, as I know many loved him. And do you know …."

"Yes, I know that you too are about to begin your travels, following many of the same paths your cousin took. I have known that a long while."

"But I worry. James does not like to travel. Wouldn't we be of more service here? We cannot let the seeds planted in our homeland stagnate, or worse…die. Don't we have a responsibility to carry what he started? James is a strong teacher, and I love to teach. And there will be much need of healing …."

Joseph put up his hand to silence me. "Let it unfold on its own, daughter. I can see some things, but not all, and have many questions myself. We just need to let it happen, knowing he has not abandoned us. I know his hand is upon all that we do, as long as we trust in the message he brought."

I wasn't concerned only with James, but with mother and Mary and Miriam and all the rest. The men would fend for themselves, as men do. But many of them did not hide the fact they thought us a burden.

"Go now. We will talk again."

Chapter Thirty Three

SEEKING DIRECTION

That evening I tried to tell James about my meeting with Babak, but he interrupted, saying he did not have time to hear about my encounters on the street just then. The men had been arguing about some decisions that needed to be made. It had not occurred to him, it seemed, that something of consequence might take place apart from the twelve.

I took my leave and went to join mother and Mary. The two sisters moved apart that I might sit between them on the bench. We had already discussed my meeting with the Persian while preparing dinner, but I wanted to tell them about my talk with Joseph.

"Take care, my dear, that you do not get involved with carrying anything of value on your own person," said mother. "There are many thieves about, and I do not always trust one or two that sit among us as friends. I will not name them, but you know who they are."

"It would surprise me if they coveted wealth," added Mary, "but they hunger after the power that comes of authority and will not like that Joseph has handed such power over to you. But I do understand why Joseph did this. There are aspects of the plan that only a woman could carry off under the nose of the Romans, and you might be the best person to do it. I wish it were otherwise."

"Mother, there is something that concerns me even more. For some time now James has been closing me out of his life – as you commented on once – spending more and more of his time with the other men. He does not trouble himself to listen to my thoughts and brushes away my opinions on things as though I were a servant girl and not his wife. I see Matthias sitting with them as often, and have wondered if you suffer the same treatment."

"It is true my husband spends more time with the other men since they drew lots to put him in Iscariot's place. But I have encouraged him to do so. His calming influence was much needed. We are lucky we aren't privy to their discussions: there has been too much hysteria since Jesus left us.

"But," and she looked me in the eye, "he comes home to me when he can, the same man I married, kind and thoughtful." She paused, "I am so sorry, daughter. I'd hoped things had improved between you."

"He lost his brother," said Mary quietly. "This is a hard time for him too. The men are maneuvering for position in the void left behind. They argue how to interpret his words to them. Some insist Jesus wanted Peter to take the lead; and it looks to me that he might be lining up men to side with him against James. This must hurt."

"The change between us did not start at the cross, but long before. There is more to it than that."

"I think you are right," offered Mary. "Peter has not hid his feelings about the proper role of women in spiritual matters. He has always argued that the law prohibits women from reading the sacred texts, and especially hates that we have presumed to interpret Jesus' words to others.

"But most galling was our access to him, and the fact we might have been privy to certain teachings that he and the other men did not enjoy. Some of the others share his feelings, and it may be James has allied himself with them – whether by intent or simply to protect his standing among them. This would require him to distance himself from you, because of your unique relationship with Jesus. He does not mean to hurt you, Veronica."

"But Mary, how are *you*?" I asked, wanting to change the subject. "Everyone's attention is pinned on their own pain, but you have endured more than all the rest of us. How does a mother see her son suffer so, and still go on?"

I got up and brought back a bowl of nuts for us to nibble on.

"I am alright. *Really*. Of course I sometimes lay awake at night thinking about how it might have been, if people had only listened, really listened to what he said. *It didn't have to happen*. But God has blessed me at every step of the way, and continues to do so now.

"He was never really my own, though I treasured every moment I had with him. None of us belongs to another. One day we will all be separated too, by distance or death. And life will go on, beautiful in its own way."

"Thank you for saying this, aunt. It helps me to remember that the James I married still lives, though he is hidden from me just now. Everything about my life, our lives is changing, and we cannot control the direction of that change.

"Maybe you can help me understand something. The first night back in the city, I had a dream. I had dreaded returning here, not wanting to stir up the nightmare. But our last day on the road, when we were laughing and telling our stories brought much healing to me."

"Yes, to me as well," said Mary, squeezing my hand. "Tell us about the dream."

"A large group of us had gathered here, at Joseph's, though his place was very much larger than even this great place. There were many people I had not seen in some time and others I did not know at all. Some were from other places, with all manner of dress and color of skin. Many of the strangers sat around the edge of the compound, just inside the wall, and I knew there was another circle of men and women outside the wall.

"The rest were clustered in small groups here and there, all talking amongst themselves. I walked from group to group but as soon as I approached any of them, they fell silent, even if no one looked up at me. James was in one of the groups and I thought I would be welcomed there at least, but the same thing happened when I approached him. Finally – and this is the strangest thing of all – Thomas left James' group and walked over and put his arm around my shoulders. This he has never done, I can assure you, and even in my dream, his action surprised me.

"I could see both of you and some of the other women some distance away and I wanted to go over to join you, but Thomas still held me, talking about things I could not understand. That is, his words made no sense to me. But instead of feeling uneasy, I was relieved because I knew he was giving me a message from Jesus. I think the reason I could not understand his words is because Thomas does not yet know himself about this conversation. Does that make sense to you?"

Mother nodded, and Mary looked out into the distance. I wondered if she had been listening at all, but then she turned and said, "Yes, he is guiding us. Though I have not *seen* him since he ascended to the Father, I sometimes have felt his thoughts in my heart, and I know what he is saying to me, asking me to do. This dream is not a dream at all, but a message from him about what is to come."

While we knew our gathering at Joseph's signaled the dispersion of his followers, no one knew what form it would take. We had been waiting for guidance, and it was this that added to our unease.

"The Brotherhood has drawn close to us from many areas of the world. This is the group encircling us inside the wall. Most do not interact with us directly, preferring to remain at a distance and watch – at least for now. They are able to better support us that way, holding inner spiritual power, reserving the ability to act quickly if need be. Those who stand outside the walls are doing their work in the spiritual realm, from their own homelands." Mary was speaking of my dream.

"This they have always done, and no more so than during recent events. Those lining the inside of the wall will engage with us as we go out into the world, sometimes accompanying us in our travels. We have met a few of them already, but most will come into our lives for the first time in the near future. They are working with us to assure that his sacrifice was not in vain, that the lessons he gave us can be salvaged and in turn offered to people in other lands who are ready to hear.

"We will go out from here in small groups. You, it seems, are called to go with Thomas."

"Thomas? Why Thomas? Why not you or James, or the other women?" A feeling of despair began to fill me.

Mother grabbed my wrist. "Veronica, listen to me!" Her voice was quiet, but urgent. "We are each being given a mission, some of which we won't understand …just as this does not make sense to you. But the dream is clear. You must see that."

I saw the sorrow in mother's eyes, and knew she spoke the truth.

"And what of you?" I asked. "Do either of you know your own path?"

"John will take me with him, away from this land," said Mary. "We go first to Patmos. After that I do not know. He will determine who else goes with us."

"Mother? At least you two should be together!"

"No, dear. Matthias and I will remain here for a time. We have come to Jerusalem to see you off, and then I will return to Nazareth with John and Judah. Matthias will come and see us when he can."

"How do you know this? Did you have your own dreams? Will you be safe here? And what about Elizabeth?" I tried hard to keep the panic I felt out of my voice. My brothers John and Judah were still young – especially Judah – and I was glad they would not be traveling far.

"We will be as safe there as anywhere, for now at least. I am not sure if what I had was a dream or a vision, but when I told it to Matthias last night, he agreed it was the right path for us. As for Elizabeth, she is old enough; maybe she could go with you."

"Oh yes! … if she would come." It felt as if the ground beneath my feet had disappeared. The possibility of Elizabeth coming with me brought a glimmer of light to the abyss. "And James?" I wondered aloud.

"You will have to ask him for yourself," said Mother. "Each one receives the call for himself. But let me offer some advice: say nothing to him just yet about Thomas, nor say anything to Thomas. Let him approach you as he is guided. I sense this will happen very soon."

"Mary, what of *your* children? Will they go with you and John?"

"They are no longer dependent upon me, not even Ruth and Andrew. But I would have them with me if I could. Joseph has offered to divert one of his ships to Patmos and will accompany us that far. But I haven't told any of the children yet. I worry they might be resentful about being passed over in favor of John – especially James – as it is the eldest child's responsibility to care for his own mother. But I am sure their brother has other things in mind for them."

We walked back into the main courtyard. People were walking about and talking casually. It wouldn't have been hard to imagine just then that we were gathered for a wedding or some other happy occasion.

James stood with Martha and Jude, talking. The sun cast its last golden rays over the garden, and I stopped to enjoy the beauty of the moment. Some of the women were busy in the back preparing the evening meal. I started out to go join them, but went instead to stand beside James. For a moment he looked as if he didn't even recognize me, but then he smiled and my heart warmed.

"Veronica, we haven't seen you all afternoon," said Martha. "We were talking about the confusion in the city."

"Confusion?"

"Jude has spent the last two days walking around, talking with people. I'll let him describe it."

"Many people knew me as his brother, and felt safe confiding in me. It is hard to know who to trust these days," he added. "I was asked over and over again how is it, if he was the Messiah, that he could be killed? This is a difficult question to answer, as I am not schooled in theology, nor was I privy to the years of teaching you were exposed to. So I am hopeful you might guide me in how to answer such questions in the future."

"What did you say?" prompted Martha.

"When I told one man I did not know, he became angry and shouted how we had all been deceived. And while I am not sure the reason he died, I know with certainty that he could never have deceived us. Never. And so when the next one asked me, I said it must have been the Father's will that he die. But then this man wanted to know why a Father would allow His son to be killed. But I didn't really believe my own answer ... that God willed this for my brother, and so did not know how to respond."

I put my arm around Jude. "Cousin, you were with us after his resurrection and you heard him tell us that this was not in God's plan, but man's. It was men who wished him dead and conspired to bring it about. Even Judas had expected him to confront his captors and free himself. But Judas and others had not listened to what he had been telling us all along: he did not seek an earthly kingdom and had no interest in worldly power. If he had destroyed his captors and fled, he would have made himself a liar. And so he decided to use the circumstances in front of him to demonstrate the truth of the resurrection, and life eternal. His death was not a contradiction to his life or his teachings, but their fulfillment."

"But many feel they were abandoned by him. There is grief and anger in their loss," Jude said, sadly.

James put his hands on his younger brother's shoulders, looking him in the eyes. "I confess I too have had moments of anger, at those who did this thing, Jew and Gentile ... and even at him."

"How could you ....?" I began, then stopped myself.

He did not look up at me. "There are moments I felt betrayed by our brother. I have given my life to stand by him and support him in his mission, and then he threw it all away." James was shaking, and I reached for his hand. He started to pull away, but then relaxed and allowed me in.

"Those moments pass quickly and I know it to be my grief deceiving me. As Veronica said, he sacrificed his body to *fulfill* his mission, not abandon it. Nor did he abandon us, since he is with us even now, and always will be, helping us with the difficult decisions." James looked up at me when he said that, and I wondered if he *knew*.

"Do you not feel him, here?" he asked, touching Jude's heart. The young man nodded. "And do you not sense his presence among us now as we talk?"

"Yes. But what do I tell these people? There will be more questions." His eyes teared up again: "And what is to become of us?"

"Tell them just what we have been saying here," Martha answered. "He has charged us with a mission to take his teachings into the world, and share them with others. It is up to us how we do this."

"And he *is* guiding us, cousin," I went on. "You must pray and expect to receive an answer as to your personal part in this. And remember his courage when you look to find your own."

"You asked what will become of us," said James. "The truth is I do not yet know. But the Holy Spirit has come among us, and we will be guided. This you can trust."

Chapter Thirty Four

RESOLUTION

The twelve frequently disagreed about the interpretation and intent of some of his teachings, and more so about what we were to do, now he was gone. I wish I could say we women were more in accord than the men, but we were not.

Some loved argument for its own sake, others were sincerely convinced they knew what was best for everyone else and did not hesitate to say so, while the majority of us were often unsure of ourselves. But even in our uncertainty we had to stand firm or else the first two groups would have taken over every decision that needed to be made.

I am quite sure that not a single day of my life had gone by, from my very first memories, when I did not think of Jesus. It didn't matter whether he was near or far away. There were few days after his return when I did not at least have a glimpse of him, and countless days in which we talked or I was privy to his inner teachings. And now I often felt lost, wondering what he would want me – or any of us – to do.

I missed him.

During those first days in Jerusalem, people naturally gravitated to different groups, mostly under one or another of the twelve. None of the women sought control, not even Mary, though a few of them might have made good leaders. But ours was a male-dominated world and this was not the time to try to change that. There were halfhearted attempts by some to marginalize us, but rather than fight with them we would step back in those moments, effectively neutralizing their efforts.

Most people congregated around James, John, or Paul. Many assumed that since James was his brother, he would know best what had been in his heart and mind, and what he would want for us now. People were drawn to John simply because he was the best of men, beloved by all, and especially by Jesus. And Paul … what can I say about Paul? Everyone had intense opinions of him, some one way and some another. In a like manner, Paul felt strongly about everyone else, mostly believing none were worthy of being called a disciple of Jesus. He might have been well-intentioned, but could be merciless in his treatment of people because of this.

In the early days of Jesus' ministry Paul did all he could to expose him as a fraud. He did not believe such a mild-mannered man could lead the great nation of Israel, misunderstanding his intentions from the start. Eventually Paul came to understand that Jesus had never sought worldly power.

In the end he looked on Jesus as the Messiah, and the rest of us as unworthy to be in the presence of the Anointed One. He considered the twelve ignorant peasants (not necessarily true), and found ways to show his disdain. And though he professed to love women, he did not think of us as equals. Still … Paul could be charming, and there were many women willing to overlook his arrogance.

Once, when I complained of him to Jesus, he told me "He is not so different from you and me, Veronica. He yearns to know love, and seeks respect. We all tend to forget, only when we discover our common Source can we realize love. And then, coming from love we automatically respect others, men and women. This in turn elicits their respect. Despite his lapses, Paul is a good man. One day great things will come from him." Jesus told me I would stand next to Paul one day, both on land and sea. I believed what he said was true, but it was not a happy thought, and I changed the subject.

In spite of himself, James seemed always to be in competition with Paul. I think Paul brought that out of people; he seemed to take pleasure in it. But I could see it made James uncomfortable. He would become quiet and moody after spending time with him. They disagreed on almost everything now Jesus was gone, especially whether and how the teachings should be brought to the Gentiles. But that is a subject for another time. The two of them, and John, were dedicated to carrying on the work of our teacher and friend, and would find their own footing as to how they would accomplish that.

I often thought about how different the twelve were, and wondered why he had brought those particular men together. Some of them had already known each other; a few were brothers. Only Thomas, Matthew and my James had any real education. Neither Matthias (mother's husband) nor Paul was among the original twelve, nor of course were the older men – uncle Joseph and Nicodemus, Lazarus and others.

They were an unlikely lot, but Jesus had told me they were a perfect fit, like words to a rhyme. Apart they seemed unrelated and imperfect, but together they made a whole. And twelve is a sacred number, signifying the balance and harmony of heaven and earth. They are like all men, said Jesus, imperfect on the outside yet with the stamp of the Creator printed indelibly on their hearts. They were his family, he said, and I would do well to think of them as my brothers.

Recent events had taken all of us from the safety of our walled compounds and dropped us into the marketplace of murderers and thieves. Even if we had wanted them, traditional roles were no longer available to us, men or women.

As the men gathered to discuss their plans, I made myself available to serve them. And each evening I returned to the other women and told them what I had heard. As the days passed and the new moon approached, almost everyone had arrived (except a few coming in from outlying areas).

Thomas was among the first to state his intentions. "I will follow the master's path, and travel to Persia and the Brahmanic lands." When some asked why he would go so far when there is such great need closer to Palestine? "I have been called," he said quietly.

I was fond of Thomas, and I know James liked him too. He was quiet and I had always thought him shy. But now I was getting to know him better I realized he simply did not squander words like some, speaking only when he had something to say. And that was often laced with humor. He seemed opposite to Paul in almost every way.

After Thomas spoke his decision, Paul stood and said he would journey to Antioch, and from there go to the Greek lands. Barnabas said he would accompany him. His decision surprised me. Paul would prove to be one of our ablest apostles, but even for the men he was a difficult partner.

Simon stood and said he would like to go with Thomas, as did a number of others, including some of the women. The other Judas announced he had been asked by uncle Joseph to lead a trade mission to Armenia. He would at the same time bring the teachings of Jesus to the people there. And then Joseph stood to say he would provide cover to any who desired it, clothing their apostolic work in the guise of a trading company. His offer to do so likely saved the lives of many hundreds undertaking dangerous journeys.

Matthias then stood. "I am torn, my brothers, between staying and leaving. If only for the sake of my family I would choose to leave this land which seems to be slipping into anarchy and destruction."

Even as he spoke we heard shouting and threats outside the walls. Metal struck metal, followed by screams. We all fell silent and knew the agony of the wails in our own hearts. Many eyes around that table were filled with tears, as the heaviness of the road ahead began to weigh down upon us.

Matthias' voice quavered when he continued. "But some must stay. Our work here is not finished. I do not seek to challenge any authority. I will fight no one, Roman or Jew. Though I tried to convince her to go, my beloved Salome will stay behind with me, along with our two youngest. Elizabeth will go with Veronica."

I froze. Did this mean he knew where I was going? And what of James? I desperately wanted to know the answers to all my questions; at the same time I dreaded hearing them.

And so it went around the courtyard. This one would stay, that one go, some to neighboring lands and others far into unknown territory. Peter would stay.

And then it happened. James stood; he glanced at me and then away. Suddenly I knew what he would say. "My work is here, for now. I will stay."

No one asked the women what they would do, and I for one was not ready to put what I knew into words. As soon as the group broke up and people began to talk among themselves, I went up to James. "I will stay here with you. Elizabeth and I will stay."

He looked at me a long while, and I thought my legs would give out under me. But then he took me in his arms and whispered, "No, you must go, Veronica."

"But why?" I asked through sudden tears. "It makes no sense. I am your wife. Why would we part? Why now?"

James took my hand and led me to our room where we could talk. "He came to me, Veronica. Just like he has long done with you, he came to me."

"Who? Who came?" At the moment I had no idea what he was talking about.

"Jesus came. All he said was 'It is now your time, my brother. Take up the shepherd's staff and lead our people. Your place is in Jerusalem."

"But he didn't say I must go, did he?" I asked. "He only asked you to stay. Well then, I will stay here with you." James would say nothing else, and I thought the matter was settled. We would both remain in Jerusalem.

Similar conversations took place all around us that night, as people began to understand this was a parting of the water and that – just as happened with Moses – some would remain on one side of the river and the rest would cross over into the unknown, paving the way for a new life for all our people.

It had grown quiet in the courtyard by the time I fell asleep. And in that sleep Jesus came to me, and said, "He is right, you know. James is needed here, but your path lies elsewhere."

The dream went on forever, it seemed, as he led me on long journeys, overland and across vast bodies of water. The journey seemed interminable, but each time I grew exhausted and thought I could do no more, a great light came upon me and I felt renewed, ready to face the world again. Sometime I walked alone and other times with people unknown to me. Now and then I traveled with old friends, and some I had not thought of as friends but who became dear to me in our shared struggles. And my family? Some I never saw again, while a few came and went through my life until I was too old to continue my travels.

Even then I spoke to the crowds whenever they gathered, telling them about Jesus, the man who was crucified and with the grace of God returned to life. I shared many of the great teachings I had been given during the course of my long life, by the women in Carmel, and the brothers in Alexandria, Jesus in Judea and later, the masters of Persia and India.

I awoke the next morning, three days before the new moon and turned to James. "Now I know," I said.

It would be awhile, but I would see him again. There were others, too, that I would see again, yet I would be saying goodbye to most of them for the last time.

Chapter Thirty Five

THE HOLY SPIRIT

The time had come. We would gather that evening in a private home just outside the Essene Gate, not far from Joseph's place on the road to Ein Karem. Someone had proposed we meet in the upper room where we shared our last meal with Jesus. I do not know if the memories of that night would have eased the pain I felt if we'd gone there, or worsened it. But there would be many times our number from that night, and we would need more space to accommodate them all.

Lucius and his wife Gaia were taking a great risk in inviting us to their home, and did so out of love for Joseph and Nicodemus, and for Jesus. Though they never publicly proclaimed themselves his followers, they had often listened to his talks from the edge of the crowd. And unknown to all of us (save Joseph) they now and then provided material support to his work. Lucius had sworn allegiance to the Emperor Tiberius, as do all highly placed Romans working afield, and depending upon the whims of Pilate, might have been branded a traitor and executed for his good intentions. On the other hand, our meeting at his home provided us more cover than if we had met openly at Joseph's, who was being closely watched at that time.

We had spent maybe half our days in the city out among the people as we waited for everyone to arrive, offering healing wherever needed, and speaking of Jesus and the message he brought. All the teaching had grown out of the simple imperative to love one another as we love God. Such a thing is easy, he said, when we understand that everyone is our brother, our sister, and that we are all children of the one Father in heaven.

The other days we spent cloistered among ourselves, knowing our time together was short, preparing as best we could for the troubled times ahead.

On one particular day close to the new moon Peter stood near the temple steps, speaking to the growing assembly. It was still early, and we had already filled the square. The soldiers were becoming uneasy at the size of the crowd and began to herd us like animals down the street and away from the temple. They didn't care where we went, as long as it was out of their jurisdiction.

Peter called out for us to reassemble just outside the gate on the first mount on the road to Bethany. By the time I got there, a multitude had already gathered, and Peter had resumed his talk. I didn't feel like pushing my way through the crowd to get close enough to hear him speak. Now and then a phrase or two reached Miriam and me where we stood under the shade of an ancient tree.

"I saw him with my own eyes, on many occasions," Peter said, speaking of Jesus after his resurrection. ... "... no death; there is only life," he went on. The crowd roared with excitement when he reached a crescendo in his talk.

It was a mixed congregation comprised of people from many lands, a commonplace in Jerusalem. Most appeared to be Jews, some well-to-do, while others were poor peasants or even beggars from the marketplace. The latter were not there seeking alms, but listening to Peter's words like everyone else.

Jesus had several times referred to Peter as a rock, a steadying influence among us. That day, he stood upon the hill like a pinnacle of strength and conviction in a time of great uncertainty – and it seemed to me he was aptly named.

Some of the crowd shouted encouragement to him, and his voice rose to meet theirs. I had never seen anything like it, except a few times when Jesus spoke on the hills around Galilee. The excitement grew, and a chill ran up my spine.

As he sometimes did when speaking to a crowd, Peter's right hand rose to emphasize a point he was making. On that day his hand punched the air, and a clap of thunder roared down the hill, though we stood under a clear sky. The blast made me stumble and in its wake I saw that some lay stunned on the ground.

I looked up nervously, afraid how the Roman soldiers would react. But they appeared unfazed, as if they hadn't heard or felt the blast. But before I could question why, they were pulled out of their stupor by the chaos spreading across the hill. Many were shouting or running, terrified.

"Do you hear that?" asked Miriam, grabbing my arm. "What is going on?"

I had been so concerned at the soldiers' reaction, I hadn't noticed what was happening. There was a riot of tongues being spoken all around us.

"Miriam, *I can understand them, all of them*! I know what they are saying! Do you?

"And look ...." I pointed.

Just above each person's head in that vast assembly flickered a tiny flame, as if separated out from a hearth somewhere to float above them. I felt it upon my own forehead, like hot oil that did not burn. It seemed to penetrate my skin, drenching me from the inside out ... until I pulsated with its power. When I think back on it, it's a wonder I wasn't frightened out of my wits. But at the time I felt the breath of the Holy Spirit moving among us, and felt no fear.

Once my initial surprise wore off, I looked up to see the soldiers slowly pressing in on the crowd. *They* looked frightened. I looked up, suddenly frantic to get Peter's attention before the crowd became aware of the Romans. I did not want to imagine what might happen if they panicked. Peter was looking into the sky as if entranced, when a violent seizure took hold of him for a brief moment. And when it had passed he drew himself up and shouted to the crowd: "Behold, the spirit of the Lord!"

The crowd fell silent. The soldiers stopped their forward movement, and everyone waited to see what would come next. The tongues of light continued flickering over the crowd.

"Behold, the spirit of the Lord has come upon us," Peter repeated.

I heard, and I understood him. But I do not know how, because the words he spoke were alien to my hearing.

And then he spoke again. "He has given us a sign that in our coming together we are one with *Him*. No matter our differences, we recognize each other as sons of the one God … setting down our swords, putting aside our quarrels, standing together with one heart."

As he spoke, his words shifted from one tongue to another. No matter whose words he drew upon, from which nation, everyone understood him as if he were speaking to them alone. And when people turned to talk to their neighbor, the same miracle was repeated. The Holy Spirit had come to remove our ignorance from us.

Even the soldiers stood back, spears now turned up or set upon the ground, so no one would misunderstand their intent.

And Peter spoke again, this time of Jesus, who came to show us the way to live in peace. As his final gift to us, he demonstrated the lie of death, rising from the tomb, offering himself as a bridge into eternal life.

On that day it is said that thousands of people came forth to declare themselves followers of the teachings of Jesus, as proclaimed to them by Peter. Many begged to be baptized, though there was no river nearby. But Peter told them they had been purified with fire, which is the baptism of spirit.

I hardly remember returning to Lucius' house after that, though word had gone ahead of us and everyone was talking when we arrived about Peter's sermon and the miracle that followed. I was overwhelmed by the commotion inside the gate and was about to escape into the house when a loud bell brought a halt to the clamor.

"We welcome you with all our hearts to our home," said Lucius, standing on a step so he could be seen by all. "You honor us by celebrating Shavuot with us. Though we are not Jewish, in Rome we have a similar festival, giving thanks for the first fruits of spring. It is also the day we open the first vat of wine from the previous year. And so – since we all know that the many Gods of others are no more than fingers on the hand of the one God – let us join in that celebration of thanksgiving by opening this new wine."

All talk of Peter and the multitude was set aside for the moment, and we toasted our hosts and sipped the fruity wine. Servants began setting the tables in a great circle around the courtyard.

One of the sad tasks of preparing for the journeys ahead lay in releasing our servants and workers from duty. Several from Nazareth and Galilee had traveled with us to Jerusalem in hopes of finding other employment. It lifted my heart to see that some of them had been brought into Gaia's household, as I knew she would be honest and fair with them. (The same could not always be said of others.)

The courtyard was filled with flowers, yellow camphor, white and purple water lilies and red poppies. They grew in pots which had been moved into the center so they could be seen by everyone when we sat to table. Laughter began to fill the air, lifting our spirits.

I prayed to God that day would last forever. It was a foolish prayer, I know, but I could not help myself. There would not be time to talk to everyone, and so I stayed close to those whom I loved most as I did not know when or if I would see them again in this life. And while I wanted to understand what had happened out on the Mount of Olives that afternoon, I was at that moment more interested in the small talk that binds friends together.

Something I will always cherish from that day was the shift that took place between James and me. Now that our fates had been decided, the heaviness between us lifted, leaving a bittersweet joy in its place. His hand moved often to rest on my wrist or shoulder as he spoke, a touch I had not felt for a long time. I vowed not to spoil it by asking, either of him or myself – why not before now?

And mother ... I would miss her most of all. I loved Matthias and was glad she had found such a noble and loving husband. She would be well cared for, as long as the troubles did not find her. I knew in my heart – though none had said so – that that I would see Mary again. But I did not know about mother.

I had known Miriam since childhood, and outside my family she was my closest friend. Fate had joined us in nearly every important event, from my first rites to our travels to Britannia and Egypt. We worked together fluidly as teachers and healers, and had always assumed we would mentor the younger women who were then coming into their own power. The thought of them traversing the world of womanhood without such guidance made me shudder.

I know Miriam had been a comfort to Jesus, and (from what she told me) he confided in her in ways he did not with anyone else. Only once did she express regret they hadn't married. 'He said he cannot,' she told me. I knew she'd have been willing to pay any price for that to happen. And the one time I asked him about it, he said only it would not have been fair to her.

We spoke briefly of our futures on that last day. Miriam said she would be returning to Capernaum, to her brothers' home – though it wouldn't be long before she too would venture out into the world. "Will we see each other again, sister?" I wondered aloud.

"I think so," she said, embracing me. "But it may be awhile. You have a long journey ahead of you, and it is impossible to know when you will be back."

She was right. Something greater than us was directing our actions, and I would try my best to surrender to it. Thomas was a decent man and I knew I would be in good hands with him on our travels. And knowing my sister Elizabeth would be with me brought a measure of peace to my heart.

We had been so busy over the last years traveling with Jesus and teaching our own groups of students that I had grown distant from many of the younger children. In ordinary times a woman my age would have been intimately involved in their lives, as their aunt. But those were not ordinary times. I hardly knew my own brothers, John and Judah, let alone Mary's children, or the others.

At dusk we were called to eat. Mother and James sat on either side of me. It was a balmy night, foreshadowing a long, hot summer, and I wondered what the weather would be like on the road to the east. Already it seemed my thoughts were going ahead of me, and I felt strangely at peace with the prospect of traveling into the unknown.

Joseph stood and everyone fell silent. He was our patriarch, at once stern and protective, loved by all. He had risked his standing in the Sanhedrin to petition Pilate to give Jesus' body to him after the crucifixion. Unknown to most, he had often championed Jesus within that group, keeping the wolves at bay as long as he could, when so many of them lobbied to have him arrested.

"Again I offer our thanks to Lucius and Gaia. We will never forget your kindness. Your home is an oasis to us, and it fills me with hope for the future knowing there are Romans such as you.

"I want to remind you why we are here," he said, looking out over the gathering. "Our friend, our Rabbi and many believe, our Messiah told us he would go ahead and prepare a place for us at our Father's table. He said many times that wherever we are gathered in the Holy Name, he would be there with us."

Joseph paused to allow his words to penetrate, then went on. "Jesus told us that the light which lives in him -- that which lifted him up -- *is the way, the truth and life eternal.* Each of us must find this light within ourselves. We are blessed to have already seen God – for God shone forth through him.

"This light will see us through the dark days to come, when we are once again scattered over the face of the earth. The Brotherhood exists everywhere, among all people. Our brother Jesus was among the greatest of them. He lives now in our hearts, helping us to teach and heal, lifting others up, even as he did."

Joseph's eyes closed and a sudden wind began to whirl dust and debris about us. Some rose to cover the food that it not be spoiled, and others reached to cover their faces, but all stopped in their tracks when they saw what the wind carried. Like the thunder rushing down over the multitudes that afternoon, the wind delivered beads of fire to each one's brow. A brilliant shimmering light settled down over us and I recalled Jesus telling us that the *Comforter* would come after he had gone.

James took my hand and said something to me – not in Aramaic or Latin or Greek – but a language I had not heard before. "What is happening here?" And then, "What are these strange words that I speak?"

I replied in the same tongue: "I do not know their origin, but my heart knows their meaning."

Joseph's voice rose above the others and everyone stopped talking at once. "This is a gift of the Holy Spirit, a symbol of God's blessing, which will go with us into the world. We need not fear whether we are ready to witness to the spiritual life, whether we are qualified or capable of speaking to strangers. God is with us, even to the ends of the earth."

He sat down then and buried his face in his arms on the table in front of him. A clamor arose, only this time people spoke in their own voices and tongues. Some talked about the miracle of fire. A few stood and announced they were ready to go, while others insisted they could never leave their homes. It was a place of confusion, a mixture of doubt and certainty. I myself flowed from one to the other, my emotions as turbulent as the wind had been a short time before.

"Dearest," said James, squeezing my hand, "forgive me for failing you. I have been distracted and fearful, jealous and angry." There was anguish in his eyes. "Until now I did not believe this moment would come. Forgive me," he repeated.

"You are forgiven. I wish I had known how to reach you." He took me into his arms, and I felt his fear. These would not be easy times for him, and I would be more hindrance than help, if I insisted on staying. Jesus was right. My work was elsewhere.

After a time I noticed mother had left her seat next to me and told James I needed to find her, talk to her. "You and I have this evening," I said, and tried to smile. He nodded.

She and Mary stood together, and I realized they too were saying goodbye. For a moment I felt unutterably sad that they should be parted. Walking over I put an arm around each sister and the sadness lifted, a flood of ineffable joy taking its place.

Jesus had always told us we had the capacity to do everything he was able to do. It is all right here, inside of us.

* * * * *

AFTERWORDS

The first book in this series, "Veronica: The Lost Years of Jesus" weaves two threads together into a single narrative. It chronicles Jesus' youth, his training among the Essenes, and travels through many lands in preparation for his work. Along the way he comes face to face with personal doubts and fears, and in that we recognize our own challenges. The book also brings to light the story of Veronica – his cousin – and the other women who were an integral part of his life and ministry. The unraveling of these stories – placing Jesus on an unreachable pedestal and removing the women from his life – has been one of the great tragedies of human history, and bringing them back together will aid in the healing of our world.

In this second book we followed Jesus through his public ministry and untimely end. We learned that the circle of women comprised the circle of power, enabling him to fulfill his mission as it evolved. We saw that his life did not end with the death of his body, and that he continued to interact with those closest to him for forty days after that death. And in the end he enabled each of his followers to awaken the inner spirit, so they might continue the work he began.

Jesus would have us know that his story has purpose and meaning only through us, then as now. What have we done, and what do we intend to do to spread the good news in a world as troubled as the one he knew then? Not the good news of his personal life, but the essence of his message. What are we doing to help humanity realize we are all One, to see that how we treat others is how we will be treated, and that sharing is the only way forward?

Jacelyn is currently working on the third volume of the trilogy. This last book will trace the lives of a small number of disciples during the Jewish diaspora that began after Pentecost and intensified when Rome invaded Jerusalem in 70 CE. The followers of Jesus spread out into the world bringing his teachings to any who would listen. Veronica travels to India with Thomas, later spending time with Paul and Jesus' mother Mary in what is now Turkey, with Miriam [Mary Magdalene] in France, and the family of Joseph of Arimathea in Britannia. This book will be available early 2011.

Visit Jacelyn at www.jacelyneckman.com

Books by Jacelyn Eckman

Veronica: The Lost Years of Jesus

Veronica: Eyewitness to the Ministry of Jesus

Veronica: Taking the Message into the World

> Veronica, cousin of Jesus of Nazareth, shares her memories of the time: the studies, travels and eventual ministry of Jesus and the parallel role of the women in his life, without whom his mission would never have come to fruition.

The Spiraling Dance of Creation: The Seasons of our Lives

> Combining the Chinese Taoist and Native American traditions, Jacelyn offers meditations and practices to help the reader become intimate with life's cycles to empower themselves personally and spiritually.

Children of the Light

Children of the Stone

Children of Prophecy

> A trilogy that begins with the final destruction of Atlantis, and follows a small group of survivors as they recover, rebuild and finally reseed human culture. The series ends in modern times as we face the same challenges that brought ruin to that once great land.

The Travel Tree

> An adventure tale involving Sheila, a girl of eleven, who discovers a gateway to other lands and times in a hollow tree near her home.

The Crystal Web

> Jacelyn hitchhikes through Latin America and across the U.S. and Canada, encountering strange and wonderful beings and experiences that cannot be explained by ordinary means. It's a grand adventure tale with profound esoteric insights.